Divisions and Solid

Is class analysis obsolete? What are the links between class and gender? How do labour market divisions affect social identities and solidarities? In *Divisions and Solidarities* Alison MacEwen Scott stresses the crucial importance of class and gender in analysing the situation of the urban poor in Latin America. She provides a major critique of conventional labour market and class theory, using case study material from Peru to develop a new approach which will be of great interest to social scientists in general.

The author argues that theories of class and gender have placed too much emphasis on divisions between social categories and have underestimated the shared interests and solidarities which crosscut these divisions. Despite great diversity in employment, there are common class identities and sentiments amongst formal and informal sector workers, and men and women. This is because of the role played by family and gender in articulating survival strategies in employment and consumption. Thus within the 'labouring class' there are both divisions and solidarities which are mediated by the family. Paradoxically, while the family is the source of gender inequality, it is also a base for class solidarity.

Dr Scott considers that class analysis can be defended, but that it must be reformulated to take account of the links between production and consumption, structure and subjectivity, and the role of family and gender at all these levels.

With its new approach to class analysis, *Divisions and Solidarities* will have a wide appeal across many disciplines. It will be of special interest to teachers and students of anthropology, sociology, economics, politics, geography, development and gender studies.

Alison MacEwen Scott is Senior Lecturer in Sociology at the University of Essex.

Divisions and Solidarities

Gender, class and employment in Latin America

Alison MacEwen Scott

London and New York

First published 1994
by Routledge
11 New Fetter Lane, London, EC4P 4EE

Simultaneously published in the USA and Canada
by Routledge
29 West 35th Street, New York, NY 10001

Typeset in Times by Michael Mepham, Frome, Somerset
Printed and bound in Great Britain by
Mackays of Chatham PLC, Chatham, Kent

British Library Cataloguing in Publication Data
A catalogue record for this book is available from the British Library

Library of Congress Cataloging in Publication Data
A catalog record for this book has been requested

ISBN   0-415-01849-8 (hbk)
ISBN   0-415-01850-1 (pbk)

Cover image from Turismo del Dolor photographs, published
by the World Student Christian Federation (Latin America).

For Chris, Ben and Nick

Contents

Figures and tables

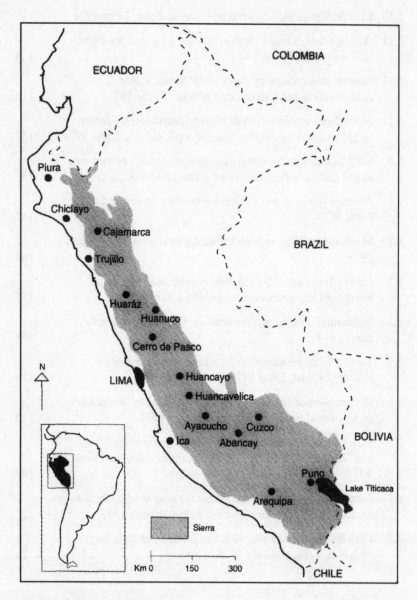

Peru: Lima and main urban centres

Preface

Up to the 1970s Peru was a poor Third World country with good prospects. Despite the existence of a large peasantry engaged in near-subsistence pursuits, it had sustained a process of rapid industrialization and export expansion for thirty years and looked set to develop further. It was a country with extreme economic inequality and deep social and ethnic divisions, a country with a history of authoritarian government and suppressed populism. At that time social and economic reform was high on the agenda, and there was apparently sufficient growth in the economy to be able to afford it. A reformist military government, under the leadership of General Velasco, had taken power in 1968, pledged to liberation from foreign domination and the displacement of the local oligarchy. It was a period of economic and political energy, full of confidence and optimism.

Within five years, the economy was heading for the deepest recession in its history, reformism had given way to reaction and hope to despondency. Since the mid-1970s, the country has lurched from crisis to crisis, repeatedly forced to take measures that exacerbated inequality and poverty. Established political parties gradually lost their credibility while a Maoist guerilla movement, *Sendero Luminoso* (Shining Path), progressively extended its control over the countryside and some urban areas amidst appalling depredation of human life. It is a terrible, sad story.

During the last two years, however, a glimmer of hope has appeared. Inflation has dropped and foreign investment in Peru is increasing. There is the prospect of growth taking off again although it is too early to say what the long-term prospects are. Terrorism seems to be on the wane and the tourists are returning to Peru. Once more there is a mood of cautious optimism.

When I visited Peru in 1993, after a long period away, it was the continuities that struck me, rather than the changes. Undoubtedly there has been a dramatic fall in living standards, and people have been traumatized by terrorism; however, the broad structure of poverty and inequality is remarkably similar. There is still a large informal sector, though not as large as some would have it. A stroll round the city centre suggests that there is still great diversity within it, and there are the same signs of differentiation and mobility in the shanty towns. The institutions of the poor, which enabled them to respond quickly to the opportunities of the growth period, have been important in helping them to adjust to economic crises. Family and community are still as important as they were twenty years ago. Despite the promise of change, the poor are as alienated from politics as before, and there is still the fear that the government's inability to do anything about poverty will provoke them to revolt. The policy debates are still the same – the concern with stimulating growth in the informal sector, with organizing squatters in the shanty towns, and with building a more representative political system.

One thing has changed though – gender has become visible. During the early 1970s, women's issues barely figured in academic or policy debates. However, in recent years an active feminist movement has grown and diversified, and there is an abundance of aid agencies working with women. There has been a sharp rise in the involvement of women in grass-roots organizations, especially soup kitchens – over 7,000 in Lima at the last count. The conditions of women, their consciousness and actions, now have a high political profile.

I believe that it is necessary to study the interaction between continuity and change in a country like Peru. Social science tends to work with timeless models that are applied to very different circumstances without regard to context. There is a tendency to stress short-term conjunctural issues without looking at long-run continuities. Moreover, social science memories are short, so there is substantial replication of research effort and a certain tendency to rediscover the wheel. The work on the informal sector is a case in point. The model itself has changed very little over the years – although there are some differences of emphasis – yet the contexts to which it has been applied could not be more different. The informal sector is assumed to be the same whether the economy is expanding or contracting.

In Peru there is a long tradition of work on this problem, but it has no historical memory. The research of the 1980s (Carbonetto *et al.* 1985, 1988, De Soto 1986) made no reference to the work that was done in the 1960s and 1970s (Gianella 1967, Lewis 1973, Vega-Centeno 1973, Webb 1977, Reichmuth 1978). Findings that were hailed as recent discoveries then were largely consistent with earlier studies, suggesting that the extent of change produced by economic crisis may have been exaggerated. We need more longitudinal analyses of labour market structure in Latin America. This is just beginning in Peru at present, and it is hoped that this study will provide a useful benchmark for a comparative analysis of growth and recession over the 1972–92 period.

Other social science theories have been less constant. We have seen the shift from modernization theory, through dependency theory to neo-liberalism; a change of emphasis from structure to culture and subjectivity, and from class to gender and race. The polemical nature of academic and political debate prevents a measured evaluation of theories and policies. Just as it was heretical to talk of 'trickle down' during the 1970s, it has become unfashionable to mention 'class' and 'interests' at the present time. Neo-liberal critics of structural reform are rewriting the history of the Velasco period. Yet whatever the fads and fashions of intellectuals and policy-makers, the facts of inequality, poverty and political violence are inescapable in a country like Peru. Moreover, it is clear that none of the academic models on offer 'got it right' and none of the policies has yet been successful. Therefore there is a real need to combine careful analysis with the benefits of hindsight.

This book presents an analysis of class and gender inequalities in Peru during the early 1970s. This was a particularly interesting period because of the extent of growth, the prospect of reform and the attempt to incorporate the poor into the political forum. However, I have taken issue with the theories that were prevalent at that time regarding the extent of marginality, the nature of labour market divisions and their effect on consciousness and political action. In my view, class analysis placed too much emphasis on labour market divisions, and not enough was given to broader solidarities created by mobility, consumption patterns and kinship. This book shows that gender was an important dimension of inequality in the 1970s, as now, and was strongly linked to class. Indeed, class cannot be understood without reference to gender and the family, and the incorporation of gender into class analysis forces a reformulation of class itself.

This research was initially funded by two grants from the Social Science Research Council (now the Economic and Social Research Council). Some of the analysis was financed by a Social Science Fellowship from the Nuffield Foundation, and by the Fuller Fund of the Department of Sociology at Essex University. I am grateful to these institutions for their support. Unfortunately, I have not been able to include race/ethnicity in the analysis here. This is a major source of inequality in Peru, and is strongly linked to class and gender. Ideally, I should have liked to add a third strand to the analysis, but the task of unpacking *two* systems of inequality was complex enough, and constraints of time and space inevitably limited the scope of the current project. However, this should not imply that I consider race to be unimportant or class and gender to be separable from it.

Thanks must go to all those in Peru who facilitated my fieldwork between 1972 and 1974, and who provided me with a stream of material thereafter. I am indebted to the Ministry of Labour, particularly the Technical Office of

Labour Force Surveys (OTEMO), who gave me access to the raw data of their 1973 and 1974 surveys. I should especially like to thank Flor Suárez in that office. The Pontifícia Universidad Católica kindly provided an office for a fieldwork base. I would like to record my gratitude to my two main research assistants, Raul Santana and Hermías Montes, who worked with me for about eighteen months. Themselves from humble backgrounds in the *sierra*, they brought great insight to the project and I learned much from them. Olinda Bendezú, Benin Rengifo and Miguel Zamudio also helped with the interviewing.

A period at the World Bank in 1980 was particularly stimulating and forced me to rethink the specific contribution of sociology and anthropology to the analysis of employment issues. Mark Leiserson, Dipak Mazumdar, Richard Sabot and Praveen Kumar played an important part in sharpening up my ideas. I should also like to thank Dennis Anderson, Joan Nelson and Elsa Chaney for their intellectual support and personal friendship over subsequent years. My greatest debt, however, is to Richard Webb and Caroline Moser, with whom I have shared an enthusiasm for this subject over many years. They have been a constant source of stimulus and encouragement throughout this project.

At the University of Essex, Phil Holden, Randy Banks, Phil Scott, Graham Heath and John Simister helped with computer programming. I am indebted to a number of colleagues in the Department of Sociology for their professional advice, intellectual stimulus and friendly pressure over the years, particularly Leonore Davidoff, David Lockwood, Judith Okely, Maggie French and two Visiting Fellows, Sonya Rose and Margaret Levi. In the final stages of completing this book, Jacquie and Peter Horswill and Judith Okely provided me with places to work without interruption, for which I shall be eternally grateful. Tom Brass and David Booth kindly read the entire manuscript at the eleventh hour and convinced me it was ready to go to press.

I am grateful to the World Student Christian Federation (FUMEC) for permission to use one of their photographs from the Turismo del Dolor series, published in Peru during the 1970s, for the cover of this book. This image powerfully conveys the intertwining of class, gender and family, which is the focus of the book.

Finally, I must thank my own dear family; my late mother and father who always took an interest in the book but could never quite understand why it was taking so long, and my husband Chris and sons Ben and Nick, who have shared its joys and frustrations without complaint. Their encouragement has been worth more than words can express.

Colchester
January 1994

1 Introduction

This book has two objectives, one theoretical and one substantive. The first concerns the development of a theoretical framework for integrating class and gender as linked systems of inequality. An important aspect of this project is the systematic analysis of employment divisions, their relationship with the family and the impact of both on consciousness and action. The second objective is to develop this theoretical framework through a substantive analysis of the labouring class in Peru during the period of import-substituting industrialization (the 1960s and 1970s). This was a key period in the development of urban class formation in Latin America, and one on which many class theories were based and subsequently rejected. The analysis presented here involves a reinterpretation of what actually happened then as well as a rethinking of the concepts through which the period is studied.

The project to integrate class and gender theoretically is fraught with difficulty. One major problem is the lack of consensus about the nature of class. Sociological writings on this matter have been riddled with debate and dissent. There are many disagreements about the appropriate conceptual and methodological tools for its analysis. In comparison with class, the debate about gender is yet in its infancy, although many of the same problems are already developing.

In order for class and gender to be integrated theoretically, the concept of class has to be reformulated. Traditionally, class analysis has been too narrowly focused on work-based categories. This has given it a static and individualist emphasis that is inappropriate for societies experiencing rapid social change. The formalistic, abstract emphasis of some Marxist theories, in particular, has left little room for subjective experiences of inequality and the influence of other systems of oppression besides class. However, in contrast with some authors who have made similar criticisms, I do not think that the solution is to abandon the concept of class altogether. Rather it should be modified, so that links can be made between individual experiences and macro-social structures and between class and other systems of inequality. This means extending the concept of class beyond the workplace.

The theoretical framework I have adopted in this study assumes that class and gender are *systems of inequality* which entail a relationship between the structure of inequality, the subjective experiences and consciousness associated with that structure, and political action. Both systems involve a division of labour, a distribution of resources and power, and a legitimating ideology. Both systems include men and women – it is important to include women in the analysis of class and men in that of gender. The situation of each group can only be understood within the context of the whole. It assumes that these systems are interlinked; therefore we cannot understand gender without looking at class, and vice versa. Moreover, the linkages between these two systems affect the structure of each one: for example, gender shapes the labour market and class shapes the family. The interrelationship between gender and class can create a coincidence of interest between men and women in some situations, and differences of interest in others.

Specification of the linkages between class and gender is still relatively undeveloped. There have been many descriptive studies of the situation of women in particular classes, and of the effect of specific class processes, such as proletarianization, on women. But aside from the fact that men have to be included in the analysis if it is *gender* we are looking at, these descriptive studies do not address the question of whether gender is an *explanatory variable* in the formation of class itself and whether class has a similar role in the construction of gender. It is at this theoretical level that the interaction between the two systems must be examined. We need to know, for example, how gender is incorporated into the occupational division of labour, in what ways it contributes to the construction of power and privilege and how it affects class ideology. On the other hand, we also need to understand how gender is constituted by class – by wealth and power or by poverty and dependence on welfare – and whether relations between men and women are influenced in some way by relations between classes.

This framework will be contentious in some quarters. Whereas initially, class theorists rejected the claim that gender could have any relevance for them (see critiques by Acker 1973, Garnsey 1978, Stanworth 1984), more recently the problem has been a shift away from systemic approaches in general and the demise of the concept of class itself (e.g. Laclau and Mouffe 1985, Hindess 1987, Holton 1989, Pahl 1989). In Latin America, class analysis has increasingly been challenged as a useful framework for studying inequality and political action. It has been replaced by two quite separate bodies of theory, labour markets and social movements. Much of the recent work on gender has focused exclusively on women, more interested in their specific subjectivity than in the dynamics of gender oppression as a system.

Research on women in poverty virtually ignores class, unless it is equated with paid work. The broader relationship between poverty, employment, consciousness and action has been lost from focus. 'Gender' has become synonymous with women; men are shadowy figures, the invisible oppressors and patriarchs. The idea that women and men could *share* a common interest – that of class – borders on heresy. Ironically, this pattern is the reverse of the earlier tendency to equate class with men.

The project to integrate class and gender requires an adaptation of the central concepts to the specific historical context being studied. In my view, one of the reasons for the demise of class was the rigidity with which it was applied to different empirical situations. This was particularly the case with the Marxist formulation, which was influential in Latin America when class analysis was at the height of fashion. Relations of production and labour market positions may have been important for the system of capital accumulation but they were not the major sources of identity and solidarity at that time. Mobility, kinship and the struggle for better living conditions were just as important and needed to be brought into the analysis of class.

Gender theories have also relied heavily on frameworks developed in the West which assume a nuclearized family structure which only has an indirect effect on the labour market. In Latin America, kinship systems are much more diverse and have been linked to the economy in more complex ways. Gender inequality is framed by the extended family as much as by the nuclear household, and is reinforced by direct control over productive resources, rather than via the labour market. The analysis of class and gender therefore has to pay attention to the institutional framework within which these systems are embedded.

CLASS AND GENDER DURING THE GROWTH PERIOD IN LATIN AMERICA (1950s–1970s)

Like many Latin American countries, import-substituting industrialization in Peru produced rapid growth, high rates of internal migration and urbanization and increasing income inequality. Debates about the effect of these processes on class formation were at the top of the political and academic agenda at that time, fuelled by the hope – or fear – that urban workers would propel revolutionary change in their society. Class was the favoured concept for analysing the urban poor because of its explicit connection between economic structure and political action, although there was considerable disagreement about the correct theoretical formula to apply. Concerns about gender were largely absent then; the debate about class was still framed in terms of a masculine discourse about men's work, men's trades unions and men in political parties. Women's roles in the labour market and in neighbourhood-based social movements were largely ignored.

The major theoretical problem for class analysis during these years was differentiation. The growth process had produced a diversity of forms of production in the urban economy, ranging from factory production and modern public service bureaucracies to small artisanal workshops, street pedlars and personal servants. Most of the manual workers in these different forms of production were poor although they were not all wage earners and some had higher incomes than others. How were these different situations to be theorized in class terms? Were they separate classes, differentiated according to their degree of dependence on wage labour, or fractions within a more amorphous category of 'marginal mass' or 'urban poor'?

At the time, structural Marxism was the dominant influence in class analysis, giving prime emphasis to the process of production as the main criteria for class location (e.g. Dos Santos 1970, Nun 1969). This approach in turn was influenced by two bodies of theory which attempted to explain the reasons for economic diversity: dependency theory and informal sector theory. Dependency theory was concerned with the specific nature of capitalist development in Latin America. It held that the industrialization process there was stunted by its dependence on foreign capital and technology; this limited the process of proletarianization of the workforce and perpetuated so-called 'marginal' forms of employment living on the periphery of capitalist production (for a review of these theories see Kay 1989).

Economists, focusing on the structure of urban labour markets, had come up with a similar interpretation, i.e. that the extent of 'formal' sector growth was limited by capital-intensity of production, and that the residual workforce was having to find a living in the 'informal' sector, in self-employment or other small-scale forms of production (see Bromley 1978, Moser 1978). Although there has been much debate between Marxists and economists over the concept of the informal sector, they have much in common, as I shall show in the next chapter.

Differentiation amongst manual workers was largely analysed in terms of relations of production and labour market segmentation. The distinction between wage labour and self-employment or capitalism and petty commodity production was the basis for a separation between a capitalist proletariat and a class variously described as a 'marginal mass', a 'lumpen-proletariat' or a 'petit bourgeoisie'. Their different locations within the sphere of production were assumed to correspond to specific objective class interests and forms of consciousness and action. Hence they constituted separate classes within the overall structure of inequality (e.g. Portes 1985).

During the 1980s, structural Marxism was criticized for its functionalist and economistic style of analysis (Cutler *et al.* 1977, 1978, Hindess 1987,

Booth 1985), and dependency theory was attacked for underestimating the extent of growth within dependent development (Cardoso 1972, Warren 1973). Informal sector theory was also subjected to a number of critiques, amongst them excessive dualism and insufficient attention to internal diversity and intersectoral mobility (Bromley 1978, Moser 1978, Nelson 1979). Nevertheless it has remained the major paradigm for the analysis of class and employment in Latin America and research on women has largely worked within it.

There was increasing dissatisfaction with this form of class analysis. The view from below, from anthropological work in shanty towns, suggested that subjective attitudes were at odds with structurally defined positions or merely considered them unimportant. 'Actors' models' of inequality were more concerned with consumption-based issues and social mobility than with conditions of exploitation at work (e.g. Lloyd 1979, 1982). Evidence on movement between different forms of production or labour market segments contradicted the picture of stable class cleavages amongst manual workers (Nelson 1979, Lloyd 1982). Finally, consumption issues, particularly housing, were a more significant basis for political mobilization than the workplace (Castells 1983, Slater 1985). Attention increasingly concentrated on social movements based on residence, nationality and gender (Castells 1983, Slater 1985, Schuurman and Maerssen 1988). Since such movements could not be explained by production relations, there was a shift of focus to subjectivity and discourse which stressed more diverse and volatile social identities (Touraine 1981, Castells 1983, Laclau and Mouffe 1985).

Recent years have seen the burgeoning of theoretical and empirical work on gender, with a huge increase in the 'women in development' literature. This has revealed the importance of women's work in the urban economy and their role in political movements based on the neighbourhood (see Young and Moser 1981, Moser 1987, Brydon and Chant 1989, Jelin 1990). However, it was difficult to accommodate this new information into existing class analysis. Because of its exclusive focus on production relations, the vast majority of women who were not in paid work had no class position at all. Within the sphere of production, the informal sector model did not help with the analysis of gender, for much of the inequality between men and women was *within* the formal and informal sectors, not between them (Scott 1991).

Most women were concentrated in the informal sector, which excluded them from traditional forms of class action, such as unions. Yet they were extremely active in residence-based actions, when necessary confronting the police and the army to defend their rights to land; but such actions had no place in a Marxist theory of class. Since Marxist class theory is based on *individual* positions within the class structure, there was no theoretical role for the *family* as a source of class identity for women or men. Yet many of the struggles for consumption goods, such as land and housing, were carried out by both men and women in the name of family and class. Therefore, if class was to be able to incorporate gender into its framework of analysis, the exclusive focus on individual production relationships would have to be questioned; if not, class would clearly have little relevance for women.

CLASS, GENDER AND THE FAMILY

In Lima, the division between men and women within the sphere of production was dramatic. On all possible measurable dimensions – income, skill, types of enterprise, types of work and mobility opportunities – they were poles apart. The extent of the gender division amongst manual workers far surpassed all other employment distinctions in terms of segregation and inequality. Whereas male workers could expect to move in and out of different employment situations over their lifetimes, and thus experienced labour market disadvantage as temporary, women faced a much more restricted set of options and were confined to them for most of their lives.

How could one speak about a class with common interests and experiences when the men and women of that class were in such very different positions? In most class schema, such a division would merit the identification of separate class categories or at the very least class 'fractions'. Yet men and women were married to each other and in many respects identified with the same class interests despite their very different work experiences. As already mentioned, they would struggle together to defend the living standards of their families and the future prospects of their children, and the forms of consciousness and struggle involved were expressed in *class* terms. How could one explain this apparent contradiction of identities and interests?

All these questions required an analysis of the family, both as the source of differences between men and women as workers and as a basis for personal identity and communal action. Yet the theoretical tools for such an analysis were still very underdeveloped. Much of the old-style theory of the family had been swept away by feminist critique, but little had been put in its place. Was the family a consensual unit or the site of a 'class' conflict between men and women? Or could it be both? The more I examined the structure of the labouring class family in Lima, the more contradictory it appeared, for it combined internal inequality and often considerable violence with a strong ideology of unity and solidarity. Was there a parallel here between the family and class? Were there circumstances in which internal class divisions could be subsumed under a wider framework of communality?

Such questions would take us well away from structural Marxist theories of class, which gave primacy to individual production relationships; they would lead to a much wider consideration of the role of family, community and culture in the formation of class identities and consciousness. The more I considered this possibility, the more sense it seemed to make in the Peruvian context. But this required a fundamental re-examination of class theory because questions were now being posed about the appropriate units of class analysis and the whole relationship between economic and non-economic aspects of class. In essence this involved a rejection of structuralist theories of class that relied solely on individual production relationships.

MODIFYING THE CONCEPT OF CLASS

In my view, it is impossible to comprehend a society such as Peru's without some concept of class. Unquestionably, poverty is rooted in the social organization of production and power relations between the major economic classes. However, class is more than this; it also refers to the *quality* of relations between classes, the experiences of oppression and derogation that shape class identities, and the solidarities that arise on the basis of these experiences. Class is about how economic divisions acquire social and political meanings and produce social and political effects; and about the way in which the life chances of whole families and communities are affected by economic inequality.

Weberian theory facilitates a broader approach than Marxism, but it does not provide all the answers. For example, it pays more attention to the process of group formation within structural positions, and the influence of social interaction within these groups on class identities and consciousness. It pays particular attention to mobility: its effects on individual attitudes and expectations, and on the stability of classes over time. It is more prepared to examine the nature of inequalities created by the market and the uses to which market advantage is put in terms of life style and status.

I believe that the analysis of economic relations within the sphere of production needs to remain at the core of class theory, but that a series of more diffuse concepts need to be developed to encompass broader structures such as class institutions, class cultures, class communities etc., which arise on the basis of economic relations. Clearly, these different conceptions of class cannot be subsumed under a single concept. Therefore, following Giddens (1973), I suggest that we use the terms *economic class* and *social class* to refer to the narrow and broad usages respectively.

Economic class, then, refers to production-based categories such as property and labour relations, control over resources, market capacities and life chances. Social class refers to the distribution of material resources, the organization of consumption, the construction of social status via social networks and symbolic processes, and the institutions that give effectivity to these processes. A crucial point here is that these institutions may modify the formation of class identities and affect political action. Therefore consciousness and action cannot be derived in any deterministic way from economic positions.

The concept of social class creates a theoretical space for the analysis of the family, which mediates between the individual production roles created within the economy and the broader-based institutions of social class. Through their role within the family and in the system of gender inequality, women thus play a part in the formation of social class, if not in economic class.

THE CONCEPT OF A 'LABOURING CLASS'

The term 'labouring class' (*clase trabajadora*) is derived from the discourses used by manual workers in Lima to describe themselves as a social group. Work was the focal point for their social identities; it was a broad category that included formal and informal sector workers such as factory workers, street pedlars, taxi-drivers and domestic servants. 'Labouring' connoted jobs that involved physical effort, hard work, low status, low incomes and economic hardship, poverty and *sufrimiento* (suffering). It described both the type of work people did and the type of people who depended on it, as in 'working people'. It thus had narrow and broad meanings which correspond to our definitions of economic and social class, mentioned above.

Analytically, 'labouring class' jobs were differentiated in terms of relations of production, skill and levels of earnings. However, there were also similarities which provided a structural underpinning to the subjective term: (a) labouring jobs depended on the use of manual labour; (b) whether they were self-employed or wage workers, 'labourers' experienced little power in the product and labour markets; (c) the physical conditions of work were similar; (d) they were in a similar position in the distribution of resources vis-à-vis other classes; and (e) they had low social status (social derogation).

As an economic class, the term 'labouring class' thus referred to a common degree of subordination to capital, common vulnerability in the market for labour or the products of labour, and a common position in the societal distribution of economic power and resources. As a social class, they had common patterns of consumption, social status, family and community institutions and elements of a common class culture derived from their migrant and ethnic background. Most of the analysis in this book will be of the labouring class as an economic class; however, when we come to consider class consciousness, political action and the family, the analysis will shift to a focus on social class.

Some readers may think that the characteristics of this 'labouring class' are too heterogeneous for the category to be valid. The point is, however, to analyse these phenomena as we find them, not how we would like them to be; to give full weight to the categories that people themselves use, and not impose our own on the basis of concepts derived from a different historical experience. My aim has been to search for the material underpinnings of this 'labouring class' identity, and to explore the role of gender in it, rather than to rule it out of court as 'false consciousness'.

OUTLINE OF THIS BOOK

In this book I argue that class fragmentation amongst the urban poor has been exaggerated because of the importance given to economic diversity. In particular, the formal/informal sector division has been overemphasized. I shall show that this was only one of a number of employment divisions, gender and skill being at least if not more important. However, these divisions did not lead to the formation of stable groups or class fractions, associated with particular segments of the labour market. They were crosscut by movement between segments in the course of people's working lives and by occupational diversity within the labouring class household. These were central elements in forging a common, potentially radical, class consciousness. 'Labouring class' identity was neither apathetic nor deferential as some have said, but had elements of a populist radicalism exhibited in strong lateral solidarity and antagonism to the rich. This radicalism failed to be expressed in political action, not because of internal economic divisions, but because of alienation from political institutions.

There were profound gender divisions within the labouring class, both in the family and in the labour market, but little evidence of a gender-specific or feminist consciousness. The stress was rather on family and class. Women's consciousness and action, which has been interpreted in terms of gender needs or interests was in fact an expression of the convergence of class and gender interests. I argue that the family played a crucial role in mediating these interests because of its capacity to mobilize resources in the labour market as well as the community, through the organization of the domestic economy and the ideology of kinship solidarity. Ironically, the common interest in the reproduction of the family protected men's and women's class position while at the same time perpetuating gender inequality. In sum, differences of gender were subsumed under communalities of class, and this was so because both family and class were centrally concerned with the struggle for physical and economic survival.

The next chapter provides a review of the 1970s' theories about the nature of class divisions, which are extensively criticized in subsequent chapters. The main focus here is the debate about the informal sector and the way it has been used as a device for analysing class and gender. Chapter 3 considers the nature of the growth process in Peru, with specific reference to the formal/informal sector division. The main point here is that although growth produced a widening gap between the rich and the poor, the absolute incomes of the poor were rising. Moreover, the process of occupational mobility meant that some manual workers could realistically aspire to a substantial improvement in class position, if not for themselves, certainly for their children. As a group, women benefited from this process, although there were marked differences between manual and non-manual women.

Chapter 4 analyses the structure of the labouring-class family in Lima. It was a strong institution, both in its nuclear and extended forms, and was an important source of material and ideological support for its members. There was pronounced gender inequality within the family in terms of power and the division of labour, with low rates of labour force participation amongst wives. Yet despite this, there was a strong ideology of solidarity between men and women, expressed in their joint commitment to collective consumption projects such as housing and education for children.

Chapter 5 presents a detailed analysis of divisions within the manual labour market with special reference to the informal sector and gender. It shows that differentiation did not take the form of a single dichotomous division between formal and informal sectors, but consisted of several overlapping axes of segmentation based on enterprise size, skill and gender. However, gender was more consistently associated with patterns of advantage and disadvantage in the labour market than any other variable, men being in the better jobs and women in the worse ones. Men and women were highly segregated in terms of their experiences of work and women's work was strongly associated with the domestic domain. Thus employment was differentiated not only by productivity or enterprise-related factors such as skill, entrepreneurship, scale of production etc., but by family roles and gender ideology.

Chapter 6 shows that there was extensive movement across these divisions in the course of people's working lives. The proletarian 'core' of people who had been in wage work continuously over their lifetime was extremely small – only 10 per cent – and the majority of manual workers had had *some* experience of wage work during their working lives. Similarly, a large proportion of those currently in wage labour had experienced self-employment.

Chapter 7 describes the trajectories or 'career' patterns which carried people across these labour market divisions. There were two types of career: first, an upward movement through skill and income levels within both formal and informal sectors, and second, lateral mobility between unskilled jobs, largely within the informal sector. There was a marked difference between the mobility profiles of men and women, with women having less upward mobility than men.

Chapter 8 analyses the reciprocal relationship between the labour market and the family. It shows that family and kinship were deeply embedded in the labour market and played an important part in reproducing gender inequality there, particularly in the informal sector which was largely structured by kinship. It also looks at the contribution made by women's work to household income and the effect of labour market diversity on the occupational composition of the household. We see that differentiation and mobility were mirrored in the family, with an enormous diversity of employment experience.

Chapter 9 analyses consciousness and political action within the labouring class. It shows that there was a common class identity amongst those working in very different employment situations, and that this was an effect of their varied work histories and occupational diversity within the household. Perceptions of class inequalities, class self-identification and attitudes towards other classes were common to wage workers and the self-employed, factory workers and street traders and women and men. Moreover, the data show little evidence of conservatism, apathy or clientelism. Rather there was a latent radicalism, manifested in a profound distrust and antipathy towards the rich. It was latent because it was manifested in attitudes and sentiments rather than organization and action.

I argue that years of repression and reliance on vertical class alliances had alienated workers from the political system. The fact that self-employed workers did occasionally mobilize to defend their interests, showed solidarity with unionized factory workers, and expressed themselves in the class language of the latter, shows that there was no *inherent* opposition of interest or consciousness between formal and informal workers. The fact that neighbourhood-based movements allied with unions in broad-based mobilizations is further evidence that these different forms of action were not expressions of structural cleavages within the labouring class, but merely different bases for action. However, there were other constraints on action derived from the wider political system, which would require another study to elaborate properly.

In summary, this study shows that while the growth process did produce widespread differentiation and mobility within the labouring class, it did not result in a lack of class consciousness nor was it responsible for the lack of class action. Forms of solidarity created by *social* class straddled divisions within *economic* class, creating common identities and informal collective action. The role of gender in these processes of class formation was paradoxically to segment and at the same time to unify workers via the family. Thus the contradiction between division and solidarity within the family was replicated at the level of class.

METHODOLOGY

Details of the methodology used in this book are provided in the Appendix. However, it may be useful to draw the reader's attention to three specific features which distinguish it from other studies on this topic.

First, this book presents a holistic analysis of the labouring class, based on a representative sample of manual workers. Other studies have suffered from inadequate coverage of the class as a whole – either because they have focused on particular occupational groups or residential communities or because they have relied on aggregate data in which manual and non-manual employment are mixed up (e.g. self-employed professionals are included with informal workers, and bureaucrats and office workers with formal sector workers).

Representative sampling is crucial for the analysis of internal differentiation so that all the relevant groups can be detected and their relative proportions properly measured. This has not been carried out in many studies. For example, much has been made of subcontracting as a process within the informal sector, but no-one has measured precisely how prevalent it is. Anthropologists have talked about the process of upward mobility within the labouring class, and movement between formal and informal employment, but the extent of this process has rarely been measured (an important exception is Balan *et al.* [1973]).

In this study, a sample of 2,377 manual employees was selected from an existing household survey conducted by the Ministry of Labour in 1973. This provided coverage of many workers who would normally have been excluded, such as domestic servants living with wealthy families. The representative nature of this manual sample permitted a systematic comparison of the different internal segments and measurement of the rates of mobility between them.

A second feature of the methodology is that it combines qualitative and quantitative techniques of analysis. The manual sample acted as a proxy universe for the selection of 200 case studies, who were re-interviewed during 1974. These case studies provided in-depth investigation of life and work histories and attitudes towards and perceptions of class.

Finally, this study attempts to bridge macro- and micro-levels of analysis by locating manual workers within the wider framework of the national class and gender systems. Class and gender are essentially relational: the structure of one group is conditioned by interaction with others. These interactions develop over time and are influenced by institutions and cultures which also develop historically. Tracing these interactions requires an eclectic methodology, drawing on a wide variety of anthropological, historical and even literary sources.

2   Class, gender and the informal sector

This chapter reviews the problem of economic heterogeneity created by the period of industrial growth after the Second World War in Latin America. It outlines the way Marxism and informal sector theory analysed this phenomenon, and some of the difficulties with these approaches. It then discusses how these theories were incorporated into the debates about class and gender.

ECONOMIC GROWTH AND DIFFERENTIATION AMONGST THE LABOURING CLASS

In most Latin American countries, the 1950s and 1960s saw rapid industrial growth based on import substitution coupled with high rates of internal migration and urban growth. Compared to the industrial revolution in Europe, these countries experienced rates of change that were two or three times higher (Turnham 1971). This applied to population growth, internal migration, urbanization and industrial output. For example, in Peru, annual industrial growth averaged 6 per cent and urban growth 5 per cent between 1940 and 1972. The population of Lima trebled between 1940 and 1961 and doubled between 1961 and 1972. However, growth was also more erratic: gold-rush style booms were punctuated by periodic crises produced by balance of payments problems, external debt and political instability.

Rapid economic change produced great diversity in forms of production as modern enterprises sprang up alongside artisanal workshops, department stores in the midst of street markets, and huge skyscrapers beside crowded shanty towns. Many of the new enterprises were financed by foreign capital and had modern technologies; they relied on a labour force with scarce industrial skills and often paid high wages for them. They occupied a monopolistic position in the local market which produced large profits. On the other hand the volatility and unevenness of growth created a space for small enterprises as well as cheap personal services. Although the dynamic for growth was the industrialization process, manufacturing represented only a small part of the expanding urban labour market. A high proportion of employment was based on petty trade and services. In Lima, about two-thirds of the labour force were manual workers engaged in a wide variety of work situations with relatively low earnings.

Growth was increasing the unequal distribution of income. In Lima in 1973, 4 per cent of the labour force were earning over ten times the minimum wage while around 70 per cent were earning less than two minimum wages (Ministry of Labour 1974). The top 5 per cent of households earned 22 per cent of household income, while the bottom 50 per cent earned only 18 per cent Ministry of Labour 1973: 69). However, high incomes were not just going to the propertied classes, but to all those associated with the growing sectors of the economy, e.g. white collar employees and factory workers.

The large numbers of low-income groups placed great pressure on urban housing and services, which was reflected in the mushrooming of shanty towns in and around the cities. Urban growth and industrialization had swollen the numbers at the bottom of the labour market and concentrated them into physically segregated communities. A quarter of Lima's population were living in shanty towns around this time, and more were in inner-city slums (Collier 1976a: 144).

The visibility of urban poverty in the form of swarming street traders and sprawling shanty towns brought the political behaviour of the urban poor to the forefront of public attention during this time. Politically, most Latin American countries had only recently emerged from military dictatorship and were moving tentatively towards populist democracies based on fragile interclass alliances. The combination of an interventionist state with a popu-list ideology, near-universal suffrage,[1] and a highly politicized media, all raised the profile of urban workers in Latin America. Their large numbers and pressing needs made them an important political actor courted by all political parties.

Urban workers were involved in politics at three levels: in unions, in community organizations and in political parties. Experiences varied be-tween countries, but on the whole, research showed that despite bursts of militancy and radical action, their participation in political organizations was sporadic and inconsistent and they were as likely to support reformist or conservative parties as radical ones. Workers' organizations were prone to internal sectarian conflict, and particularly susceptible to patronage and clientelism. There was no clear-cut correlation between poverty, proletarian-ization and radicalism.

Most attempts to explain this paradox concentrated on internal differen-tiation amongst urban workers. There were three aspects to this. First, the diversity in forms of production made for very different types of employment within manual work, e.g. wage labour, self-employment, subcontracted wage work, outwork, domestic service, and family labour. Second, there were marked differences in the levels and stability of earnings, and third, there were great variations in the standards of housing and service provision within low-income neighbourhoods. These forms of differentiation were generally thought to produce internal divisions and organizational weakness which impeded the development of collective consciousness and action. However, the theoretical basis for this interpretation was very unclear.

MARXIST AND ECONOMISTS' ANALYSES OF DIFFERENTIATION

Both Marxists and conventional economists put forward theories to explain why the process of industrialization produced so much inequality and diversity in Latin America. There has been a long-standing polemic between both bodies of theory, with major differences between them in terms of theoretical and policy objectives. However, they shared a number of common assumptions about how the problem was to be characterized and explained. There has also been some cross-fertilization of ideas over the years, so the two approaches have developed along similar routes.

During the 1960s, both Marxist and economists' theories framed the problem in terms of an oversupply of labour due to migration and an inability of the new industries to absorb this labour because of capital-intensive production techniques. Both characterized the residual workforce as a 'labour surplus'[2] that performed little useful function within the urban economy. Neither paid much attention to how people actually survived within this situation. During the early 1970s, both bodies of theory came to recognize that this residual sector had an internal economic logic of its own which required analysis. Both accepted that it was linked into the economy in a number of ways and that it was necessary to examine and explain these linkages, both recognized that there was internal diversity within the two sectors; but both remained inherently dualistic.

The main difference between them was that Marxists were concerned with the implications of economic differentiation for the process of capital accumulation (defined in terms of the production and appropriation of surplus value), while economists were concerned with the relationship between growth and income distribution. Thus while Marxists focused on the internal relations of production within formal and informal enterprises and the way in which these relations contributed to the process of surplus appropriation, economists were analysing the effect of enterprise structure on labour market efficiency.

Why should any of this be of relevance for the analysis of class and gender? In brief, Marxism considers classes to be fundamentally linked to the process of capital accumulation, hence relations of production within different sectors of the economy and the linkages between them are important indicators of class location. This in turn is associated with class interests and political action.

In Weberian theory, class is associated with advantage and disadvantage in the market and its effect on life chances and status. Hence formal and informal sector differences in earnings, stability of employment, working conditions, access to unions and fringe benefits are relevant. In contrast to the Marxist approach, which focuses on the sphere of production for the analysis of class, the Weberian approach is primarily associated with the sphere of consumption. Although both Weber and Marx were more subtle in their own analyses, the divorce between production and consumption has bedevilled class analysis in Latin America, as elsewhere.

As far as gender is concerned, the high concentration of women in the informal sector was seen as an indication of the way capitalist development marginalized women from the growth process and converted them into a secondary labour force. This was thought to undermine their personal and economic autonomy and weakened their consciousness and capacity for political action. Later on in this chapter I shall consider these theories in more detail, but for now let us see how economic differentiation itself was explained by informal sector and Marxist theories.

THE INFORMAL SECTOR MODEL

During the 1960s, economists' analysis of urban poverty had focused on the high rates of rural–urban migration and the limited absorption of labour in the manufacturing sector. This was said to produce an 'urban labour surplus' which manifested itself as 'underemployment'. Failing to find jobs in manufacturing, this group was forced to eke out a living in urban subsistence activities such as street trading and personal services. The situation was described in terms of 'over-urbanization', 'tertiarization' and 'urbanization without industrialization' (see Gugler 1982).

At this stage, the question was why the industrialization process was so exclusionary rather than how the underemployed survived. The main focus was on the characteristics of factory production – its imported technology, capital intensity, barriers to entry, presence of unions etc. (Singer 1970, Jolly *et al.* 1973, Edwards 1974). The low absorption of labour was seen as a problem of internal rigidities which failed to diffuse growth and technological progress throughout the economy.

The 'informal sector' model arose in the early 1970s because of the inadequacy of the term 'underemployment' and the need to understand the economic basis of survival amongst the underemployed. The model developed rapidly within international agencies as an explanation of income inequality with policies for stimulating labour-intensive growth.[3] With it, the focus shifted decisively towards the small-scale end of the economy. Originally, the informal sector was defined in terms of any type of income-generating activity that took place outside the wage labour market, e.g. self-employment, clandestine, unregistered or illegal activities such as theft, prostitution and drug trafficking (e.g. Hart 1973).[4]

Later, it was associated with enterprise structure rather than self-employment, the usual research definition being enterprises with less than five workers. This enabled unpaid family workers, wage workers in small workshops and domestic servants to be included in the informal sector. The linking of labour market divisions to enterprise structure made it possible to show why small enterprises were unable to accumulate capital, but at the same time could absorb labour. The model drew heavily on earlier notions of exclusion (from the formal sector) and labour surplus (in the informal sector), but with a more detailed elaboration of the characteristics of formal and informal enterprises.

There are now many versions of this theory but it remains a two-sector model with the following main assumptions. The 'formal' sector is associated with large-scale enterprises based on wage or salaried labour, where the dominant technology is foreign and capital-intensive, the skill level of the workforce is high, there are barriers to entry in the form of educational credentials, unions play a role in wage bargaining, and the state confers special privileges in terms of protective legislation. Wages and salaries are assumed to be high here because of the scarcity of industrial skills, the high productivity of workers and because of union and state intervention in the labour market. Job stability is also high because labour legislation and unions give workers greater security of employment, because firms develop internal labour markets, or because workers prefer formal sector jobs.

In contrast, the informal sector is characterized by small-scale enterprises where workers are mainly self-employed, unpaid family helpers, apprentices or servants. The technological level of such enterprises is simple or non-existent, and the labour input is high relative to other inputs. There are no barriers to entry in the form of access to capital, markets, or technological and educational skills, and there is a high level of competition between producers. In the face of an expanding supply of labour due to migration, there is assumed to be internal involution within the sector, with a downward pressure on incomes and instability of employment.

Over time, the emphasis on different aspects of this model has varied. Initially the main focus was on technological discontinuities between large and small enterprises and differences in the ease of access to employment in the two sectors. This position has been particularly associated with the work of the ILO (e.g. Sethuraman 1976, 1981), especially its regional office in Latin America, PREALC (Souza and Tokman 1976, PREALC 1978).

Later theories stressed institutional intervention in the market – unionization of the formal sector workforce, differences in the application of labour laws and social security benefits, and bureaucratic controls over the establishment of formal businesses. It was argued that these factors encouraged potential formal sector firms to remain within the informal economy and large enterprises to subcontract to them. This viewpoint has been much publicized by De Soto (1986), who believes that market forces should be freed from state and union intervention.

Informal sector theory has been extensively criticized on empirical, methodological and theoretical grounds.[5] Theoretical criticism has come from both neo-classical and Marxist economics; the former arguing that the extent of 'labour market imperfection' (i.e. segmentation, institutional intervention) was exaggerated (Gregory 1986, Sabot and Berry 1980) and the latter that the functions of the informal sector for the economic system as a whole were ignored (Portes and Walton 1981).

However, the main problems were empirical. The informal sector model proved to be factually incorrect on a number of counts (see reviews by Nelson 1979, Kannappan 1985). Research showed that markets in the informal sector were not always competitive and that barriers to entry did exist in the form of apprenticeships, custom markets,[6] local trade monopolies etc. (e.g. Bromley 1982). Evidence that workers moved between the two sectors in both directions destroyed two of the core assumptions of the model – barriers to entry into the formal sector and preferences of workers for formal sector employment. Various studies showed that the effect of institutional factors was exaggerated.[7] Others showed that earnings differentials could not be attributed solely to enterprise characteristics, such as scale, capital and technology, but that individual characteristics such as experience, age, and gender also needed to be considered (e.g. Mazumdar 1976, 1981, Morley 1982). Finally, the extent of the 'urban labour surplus' may have been exaggerated since tertiarization turned out to be due to the expansion of state bureaucracies and financial services as much as to petty trade and personal services (Scott 1986a).

MARXISM, DEPENDENCY THEORY AND FORMS OF PRODUCTION

From the late 1960s onwards, the main theoretical paradigm for the analysis of class, and Latin American development generally, was Marxist. This approach analysed the problem of poverty and inequality in terms of capitalist accumulation and argued that it had to be understood within the international framework of capitalist imperialism. In Latin America, it was held that the accumulation process differed from the 'normal' path of capitalist development because accumulation was dependent on imperialist countries, via export markets and direct foreign investment. As a result, foreign firms implanted an inappropriate technology into the dependent economy, being more capital-intensive than would have been appropriate given the local scarcity of capital and abundance of labour. Profits (surplus value) were drained out of Latin America rather than re-invested there, producing a number of internal discontinuities such as lack of agricultural or local industrial development. Forms of production that would 'normally' have been eliminated in the process of capitalist development, such as the peasantry and urban petty commodity production, survived and even expanded as a result of the growth process. There are many versions of this theory and excellent reviews can be found in Booth 1985 and Kay 1989.

The concept of petty commodity production (PCP) was used extensively to analyse urban poverty (for reviews see Moser 1977, Scott 1986d). In essence this refers to the production of commodities without a separation between capital and labour. Petty producers have independent access to means of production, use their own labour or that of their families, and have a capacity for 'self-exploitation' which enables them to provide cheap wage goods at below their value and thus to compete in the capitalist market (e.g. Smith 1986, Cook 1984). Some researchers pointed to an intermediate category between capitalist and petty commodity production, which consisted of 'semi-autonomous' producers or 'disguised' wage workers, engaged in outwork or subcontracting arrangements with capitalist firms. Both these cases were said to have a specific function within the capitalist system, which explained their persistence within the growth process and identified their particular class location.

The analysis of these activities centred on the question of how non-capitalist forms of production were incorporated into the process of capitalist development without being destroyed, as was posited by classical Marxism. This led to an extended discussion about the internal structure of PCP: whether or not self-exploitation was taking place, in what ways it was subordinated to capital and under what conditions surplus labour could be extracted from it (see Scott 1986d). Two possibilities were considered: (a) a surplus was extracted from these forms of production through the market (because of unequal terms of trade) or through subcontracting, and (b) PCP provided a 'subsidy' for capital because its cheap goods and services lowered the cost of labour within capitalist firms. This latter argument was further developed by world systems theorists who argued that since low industrial wages in the Third World were also serving as a 'subsidy' to First World capitalism, the transfer of surplus was not merely national but international (De Janvry and Garramon 1977, Portes and Walton 1981).

The PCP approach brought into relief the full diversity and complexity of informal production, not analysed by economists who were mainly interested in factor prices. It was possible to distinguish between independent artisans producing directly for the market, quasi-dependent artisans who were reliant on merchants for some of their inputs and sales, outworkers who were employed by industrial and commercial firms but worked for wages in their own homes, and small workshops that were subcontracted to larger firms (Scott 1979). These various situations implied a process whereby labour and capital were gradually being separated *within* small enterprises, and where producers were gradually losing their autonomy and becoming subordinated to capital.

Marxist theories had a number of deficiencies which limited their potential as an alternative theory of economic differentiation. One problem was a mechanical and formalist method of analysis which relied excessively on the abstract categories of value theory. PCP was analysed in terms of formulae which were virtually inapplicable to empirical reality, especially to petty commerce and services. Perhaps for this reason, some Marxists adopted the informal sector terminology to refer to non-capitalist forms of production (e.g. Portes and Walton 1981, Smith 1986). There has been substantial criticism of theories of surplus extraction through unequal exchange and some doubt cast on the validity of the 'subsidy thesis'. Too much emphasis has been placed on the role of informal production as a central dynamic of capitalist accumulation, which must in the last instance depend on relations within *capitalist* production (Schmitz 1982).[8]

One major problem was the reliance on functionalist explanations in the analysis of relations between PCP and the wider economic system. The assertion that PCP or informal production performed positive functions for dependent capitalism (e.g. as a source of cheap goods and services for the proletariat), was considered sufficient to explain why it persisted. Aside from the fact that these 'causes' were asserted without empirical substantiation and indeed were often empirically unverifiable, a simplistic functionalist analysis, pitched at the level of the overall system (international as well as national) actually obscured the complex ways in which petty commodity producers were linked into the urban economy.

It is difficult to establish whether the goods and services produced in the informal sector are consumed by formal sector workers because data are not classified in these terms. However, evidence from Lima suggests that informal sector producers were not necessarily confined to low-income markets and that the practice of subcontracting was confined to only a few branches of industry (see next chapter). Therefore there is still much to be explained about informal production.

One major problem with the Marxist theories is that they failed to account for the existence of some high earnings within the informal sector, comparable with factory workers. The focus on exploitation, surplus appropriation and subordination to capital left little room for a picture of informal sector growth and rising real incomes. The fact is that many informal sector workers, such as self-employed bus drivers and highly skilled artisans, managed to find niches within the urban economy where they had a competitive advantage vis-à-vis capitalist employers. It is difficult to explain this within the standard Marxist framework.

RELEVANCE OF THE INFORMAL SECTOR MODEL FOR CLASS ANALYSIS

As mentioned, Marxism was the major influence on class analysis in Latin America during the 1970s. In this approach, classes are identified according to their function within the accumulation process. Production relations play a fundamental role in the identification of class categories, and these are assumed to correspond to objective class interests, class consciousness and political action. The problem in the Latin American context was how to analyse class relations within non-capitalist forms of production, and what kinds of consciousness and action to predict from these relations.

Early writers dealt with these problems through the concept of 'marginality', arguing that a 'marginal class' emerged on the basis of marginal forms of production (Quijano 1974).[9] However, the empirical bases for these ideas were vague. The petty commodity production debate introduced more rigour into the analysis of production relations within small-scale production and helped to identify the links between non-capitalist producers and other classes, thereby indicating the likely nature of their class interests. Later versions incorporated aspects of informal sector theory that had to do with markets rather than production relations, such as earnings differentials, institutional protection and contracts of employment.

The Marxist approach to class analysis was highly structuralist and was centred exclusively on employment as the basis for analysis. It had difficulty in predicting consciousness and action from within its own theoretical schema, and was forced to ignore political activity that took place in residential areas around issues of consumption. It did not consider occupational mobility to be relevant to class, and paid no attention to status.

One of the most systematic Marxist analyses of Latin American class structure is provided by Portes (Portes and Walton 1981, Portes 1985), who transposes the categories of the informal sector model directly on to his class framework. I want to consider Portes' work in some detail because it provides a good illustration of the kind of class analysis that has been dominant in Latin America, and of the difficulties it has encountered in explaining consciousness and action.

PORTES' FRAMEWORK OF CLASS ANALYSIS

Portes writes from a world systems perspective which locates class relations in the process of capital accumulation at the national and international level. The argument is that high levels of surplus value need to be extracted from peripheral economies in order to compensate for the falling rate of profit in the core economies; this cannot be obtained by direct exploitation of wage labour within capitalist sectors of the periphery for economic and political reasons, therefore it has to be obtained indirectly by targeting areas of labour with low subsistence costs. This is facilitated by the cheap goods and services produced by the peasantry and the urban informal sector, which in turn is explained by their internal relations of production (self-exploitation). Informal sector output thus represents a 'subsidy' to capitalist accumulation by facilitating a lower wage level than would otherwise be possible.

In the 1985 publication Portes puts forward five classes:

(i) the dominant class: domestic and foreign capitalists and managers, top civil servants,
(ii) the bureaucratic–technical class: salaried professionals and technicians in public and private employment,
(iii) the formal proletariat: clerical and manual wage labour,
(iv) the informal petty bourgeoisie: mainly the self-employed,
(v) the informal proletariat: casual wage workers, unpaid family helpers and those intermittently involved in subsistence activities.

This classification is a modification of the one put forward in 1981, in which the last two categories were put together in one 'informal sector' (Portes and Walton 1981: 103).

This class schema relies on three main definitional criteria: control over the means of production, control over labour power and mode of remuneration. The first two classes are distinguished by greater or lesser control of the means of production, and salary levels correspond to this function. The formal proletariat is defined by its lack of control over means of production and labour power and its access to unions and social security. Institutional protection of employment justifies including white collar employees and factory workers in the same category here. The informal proletariat is distinguished from this class by the fact that wages are unprotected and casual and are supplemented by subsistence activities. It mainly consists of casual wage earners, unpaid family helpers and domestic servants. Unlike the formal and informal proletariat, the informal petty bourgeoisie has control over means of production and labour power, and the mode of remuneration is therefore profit; however, the profits are small and irregular compared with those of the dominant classes.

Each class is identified by its function for capital accumulation. These functions are associated with a specific set of production relations which are manifested in the criteria mentioned above. However, market factors do come into the analysis and most of them are taken from informal sector theory. This produces some curious results: manual workers are located in three different classes, while manual and clerical workers in the formal sector are in the same class. Therefore workers who are separated by formal and informal divisions are seen as separate *classes* rather than segments or fractions within a common labouring class.

Portes' classes are the occupants of structural positions rather than specific individuals or social groups:

> The distinction between manual workers in the formal and informal sectors refers to the separation between types of labour and not physical individuals.... The attributes of formal and informal employment and the interrelationships between them must therefore be understood as characteristics of economic structure and not of physically separate groups.
>
> (Portes and Walton 1981: 105)

These class positions and functions are synonymous with class interests and correspond to determinate forms of consciousness and action:

> Cleavages between the classes described above are important because they define configurations of material interests that determine the long-term political orientations of large social aggregates.
>
> (Portes 1985: 35)

However, it is unclear how these material interests translate into political action. Portes stresses union action as the major political expression of the formal proletariat, but is unclear about the actions of the informal petty bourgeoisie and proletariat. We are merely told that it is difficult for them to mobilize politically around the workplace because of its fragmented nature. Significantly, he switches to mobilization around consumption issues in their case (Portes 1985: 31–2).

Portes' derivation of class positions and class interests from production relations is highly formalistic. He pays little attention to the nature of the labour process in experiential terms. We know that the formal proletariat have no control over the use of their own labour, but we have little idea of how they *experience* control by others, e.g. the forms of authority in the workplace, the types of supervision, the intensity of work, or workplace relationships with co-workers. Labour process theory has shown that within modern industrial establishments, forms of control over labour vary greatly (Edwards 1979). This is likely to be the case within the informal sector too. There is a world of difference between the work situation of a skilled artisan and a domestic servant, just as there is between a large engineering plant and a clothing sweatshop. These different experiences of the labour process may have a crucial influence on workers' consciousness and political action.

Interestingly, when Portes comes to a consideration of political action, the analysis shifts away from production relations to issues of consumption. Mobilization is focused around the 'means of collective reproduction', i.e. access to housing, transport and urban services. These are residentially rather than occupationally based and revolve around neighbourhood and community rather than factories or other workplaces. Portes mentions that these movements are heterogeneous, thus members of his different classes participate in them together.

This raises two theoretical problems: first, what is the role of class categories in this analysis, if the major political mobilizations are not in fact based on those class interests? Second, how are these mobilizations themselves to be theorized outside the class schema? Significantly, when Portes talks of these consumption-based mobilizations, his language shifts away from the rigorous discourse of class divisions to the more broadly based categories of 'popular classes' and 'popular struggle' (Portes 1985: 32).

Portes' study demonstrates the difficulties encountered by a structuralist production-based class analysis, particularly for the development of consciousness and action. Let us now see how other writers looked at these issues.

CONSCIOUSNESS AND ACTION

How were other analyses of economic differentiation linked to the consciousness and action of urban workers? One common thesis was that the small size of the factory proletariat in comparison with the more numerous petty producers, their relatively higher income levels and better access to fringe benefits created a labour elite that was more concerned with the protection of sectional privileges than with solidary action on behalf of more disadvantaged workers (e.g. Landsberger 1967). This position was vigorously criticized by Humphrey (1982) who argued that the apparently high incomes of such workers belied particularly intense forms of labour exploitation and that – in the case of Brazil – they were at the vanguard of the struggle against military dictatorship.

Orthodox Marxists would say that self-employed workers had petty bourgeois interests that led them to identify with the system rather than against it. Others have argued that such workers were in an ambiguous position since, even though they retained some control over their means of production, they were subordinated to capital through the market. This ambiguity produced a contradictory consciousness that was part proletarian and part petit-bourgeois (Gerry and Birkbeck 1981). A common contention was that wage workers in small workshops or in private homes lacked class identity and organization due to the dispersed and small-scale nature of their workplaces and their lack of access to unions. It was also argued that the personalistic style of their workplace relationships (structured by patron–client relations or kinship) impeded an awareness of class. In such situations, despite appalling poverty and exploitation, workers developed fatalistic and acquiescent attitudes towards inequality and a passive political disposition. Alternatively, it was said that such working conditions did not inhibit class conflict as much as make it less predictable. Feelings of resentment and antagonism could suddenly erupt into the 'uncontrolled violence of the mob, prone to the influence of demagoguery'. This interpretation was influential in explaining the rise of populism in postwar Latin America (Germani 1964).[10]

Despite the stress on internal differentiation as a source of division and organizational weakness within the labouring class, there was no consensus about the *forms* of consciousness and action that were produced by this differentiation. In particular, there was little investigation of the nature of consciousness and action amongst informal sector workers (De Soto's work is an exception, but it is not framed within a class perspective). Although economic structures were generally held to be the most important causes of differentiation, on the whole they played a negative role in predicting class action. The *lack* of large-scale employment based on wage labour relations meant that the workplace was *not* a significant site for political struggles by urban workers. On the contrary, it was argued that community and neighbourhood were more important for collective action because collective consumption goods (common squatters' rights, urban services etc.) were more of a basis for common interests than employment (Castells 1983, Portes 1985). However, as indicated earlier, these arguments were not accommodated within a *class* analysis.

Research on political action amongst urban workers maintained that it was weak, deferential and clientelistic. There was a low level of participation in formal political organizations and within those that did exist, there was a susceptibility to manipulation by reformist or even reactionary political parties (for a comprehensive review see Nelson 1979). Much of this literature focused on internal divisions amongst workers, rather than wider political institutions. The vulnerability of workers' organizations to manipulation by wider political agents was seen as an effect of their economic weakness, rather than the political system itself (Castells 1983). Only a few (e.g. Jelin 1976) pointed to the importance of the political conjuncture in shaping class consciousness, stressing the limits placed on possible forms of action by the political system.[11] In this book I shall argue that manual workers did have a common class consciousness in Lima, despite internal differentiation, but it was accompanied by a political alienation that was a product of the political system not the economy.

THE EFFECT OF OCCUPATIONAL MOBILITY

During the 1970s, many writers took issue with the pessimistic portrayal of marginalization and exclusion that was being perpetrated by the Marxist dependency model – and with its static economistic style of analysis. Micro-level studies consistently pointed out that in the shanty towns all the talk was of progress, of building for the future, of sacrificing themselves for their children, of investing in education and hoping for a better life to come. Life was organized around hard work, collaboration with friends and relatives, and building links with influential patrons (Mangin 1967, 1970, Leeds 1969, 1973a, 1974, MacEwen 1974, Perlman 1976, Roberts 1978, Nelson 1979, Lloyd 1979, 1980, 1982).

Migration was thought to have an independent effect on class attitudes, diluting the effect of workplace relations: 'Even when they stay in the factory for a long time, rural migrants are subjectively oriented outside the factory and do not identify with their working class condition' (Lopes 1964: 51, quoted by Jelin 1976). Germani (1964) argued that since migrants were less integrated into the system they were more prone to anarchic behaviour and more influenced by demagoguery (see discussion in Humphrey 1982). On the other hand, writers such as Perlman argued that migration produced an integrative rather than conflict orientation within the labouring class. It created a sense of relative advantage vis-à-vis those in the place of origin which stimulated bourgeois ambitions and offset the sense of deprivation produced by poverty (Perlman 1976, Lloyd 1980, 1982). The fact that migration was followed up by occupational mobility and residential stabilization created status divisions within the community that destroyed broad-based solidarity.

Aspirations for the future are always voiced in terms of individual or familial upward mobility rather than in terms of class solidarity. They are more concerned about the status differences amongst themselves and with improving their position in the shanty town community than with narrowing status gaps between themselves and other class groups in the metropolis.

(Safa 1974: 25–6)

Much was written about the process of movement between wage labour and self-employment, which was said to impede the development of a proletarian consciousness. One idea was that workers' responses to particularly exploitative working conditions were modified by the fact that such jobs were seen as stepping stones rather than culs-de-sac. Another was that even when workers were employed in classic proletarian conditions, they retained an element of petit bourgeois consciousness because their ultimate aim was self-employment (cf. Laite 1981). Some authors maintained that the reliance on kin networks in migration and mobility produced vertical ties of allegiance that could crosscut class loyalty (Campaña and Rivera 1984). Yet it was also argued that the tenuousness of the link to the wage labour market could make semi-proletarianized workers *more* militant than fully proletarianized ones (Peace 1979).

The focus on migration and mobility produced a very different picture of Latin American society from that based on differentiation. It stressed movement and integration rather than stasis, inequality and exclusion. Each focus provided very different conclusions regarding consciousness and action. At one level, these two approaches were irreconcilable for they made different assumptions about the basic constituents of class and their relationship to action. Some Marxists did accept that mobility was taking place, but maintained that the appropriate focus for class analysis was structural categories not individual experiences (Portes and Walton 1981: 105).

Differences of interpretation also hinged on the question of *how much* mobility was actually taking place, the argument being that if mobility only affected a small minority it was of little consequence for the majority of workers. Unfortunately, there have been very few aggregate level mobility studies which could show how extensive mobility processes were. One path-breaking study was carried out in Monterrey, Mexico in 1965 (Balan *et al.* 1973) which provided evidence of extensive vertical and lateral mobility amongst all classes. However, it was suggested that Monterrey was unusual compared with many other Latin American cities. A major national study appeared in 1982 in Brazil and this too provided evidence of substantial upward mobility (Pastore 1982; see also Morley 1982).

In this book I show that there was considerable mobility in Lima in the early 1970s. The speed of change had expanded the absolute size of the urban middle classes, providing ample opportunity for upward mobility. In 1974, 60 per cent of the urban middle class were of labouring-class or peasant extraction and 46 per cent of manual workers were from peasant families (see chapter 3). There was also substantial movement amongst manual workers between formal and informal sectors and this was generally associated with increasing earnings (see chapter 6). These mobility processes were far too widespread to be of 'little consequence' to the majority of workers. The question is how did mobility affect consciousness and action?

Most of the questions that were raised about the social and political effects of mobility referred to *individual* consciousness and action; little was written about the structural effects of mobility on class. At the structural level, mobility affects the permeability of class boundaries and the homogeneity of classes. It can have a disintegrating effect on class cultures and institutions, which normally give coherence and stability to class identities. On the other hand, it can also be argued that when migration and mobility occur on a mass basis, they form part of emerging class identities and give rise to institutions which communalize mobility experiences. Migrant associations in Lima are one such example (e.g. Altamirano 1984). Mobilization around consumption issues in the shanty towns can also be seen as an expression of class mobility projects.

The analysis of class formation in Latin America must therefore take account of mobility processes, not just for the effect on individuals, but for its wider social and structural effects. The exploration of such issues requires a theory of class that goes beyond a static analysis of economic positions.

GENDER, CLASS AND THE INFORMAL SECTOR

During the 1970s, women were an ignored category in research on class and the labour market in Latin America. Concepts of class were mainly based on studies of men and reflected their situation. Labour market surveys did not specifically investigate the position of women and one famous study even commented that there were surprisingly few women in the informal sector (Sethuraman 1981: 190). Most mobility studies excluded women; no-one noticed that the 'typical' career pattern of urban workers, which emphasized increasing income over the lifetime, was a male career (e.g. Balan *et al.* 1973, Pastore 1982), and the very different non-career oriented trajectories of women were not mentioned. Analysis of the political participation of workers traditionally focused on unions and formal organizations in which men predominated and theirs was the only consciousness that figured in political analysis. Women's work, consciousness and action was assumed to be of marginal importance both to the class structure and the wider economic and political system.

Since the mid-1970s there has been an enormous growth in research on women's urban employment, consciousness and action. This work has shown evidence of (a) a disproportionate concentration of women in the informal sector, compared with men, (b) extensive gender segregation within both formal and informal sectors, and (c) significant male–female earnings differentials. In Lima in 1974, 61 per cent of women were in the informal sector compared with 38 per cent of men, and women's earnings were half of men's. Two-thirds of the labour force worked in occupations that were over 90 per cent 'male' or 'female', and most of the rest worked in ones that were heavily dominated by one sex or the other (see chapter 3).

Early interpretations of this phenomenon were located within the 'dependency' framework, drawing on the concept of marginality that was associated with it. It was argued that women were suffering a dual marginalization: first they were being relegated to secondary-earner status because of changes in family structure associated with the separation between home and work under capitalism, and second, they were suffering from the general marginalization of the labour force within dependent capitalism produced by its inability to absorb the labour surplus. Women's concentration in the informal sector was thus a reflection of the general dualist structure of the economy and their weak position in the labour market (Schminck 1977, Scott 1986c).

Later theories focused on marginalization *within* production, i.e. the structure of segregation within the formal and informal sectors. In the formal sector there were issues to do with 'male' technologies replacing women workers (Chaney and Schmink 1980) and a specific demand for female labour in 'world market factories' (Elson and Pearson 1981, Nash and Fernandez-Kelly 1983). Humphrey (1987) produced a particularly nuanced analysis of the way in which employer discrimination, labour supply and sex-role stereotyping interacted within Brazilian factories.

In the informal sector, the focus has been on the way women's activities complemented and replicated their domestic roles; much of women's informal work was carried out in the home (e.g. outwork, front-room shops, laundry work). Many observers noticed that this confined them to less lucrative jobs within the informal sector (Moser 1981, Chant 1991). However, there is as yet little analysis of gender segregation within this sector. Few explanations have been put forward to account for the differences between men's and women's work within this sector, other than women's domestic roles. Therefore the male bias in informal production has gone unnoticed. Most studies of women's informal sector work have focused on married women's work, but a significant proportion of it is of a very different type: employment of young girls as living-in domestic servants. Bunster and Chaney (1985) have shown that one feeds into the other, since domestic servants usually turn to retail sales or outwork after marriage.

Women's contribution to household survival strategies has become a common topic for study (for a review see Schmink 1984). How far does the 'male breadwinning wage' actually cover domestic consumption? What role does women's work play in making up the deficit? A common assumption is that women's labour force participation is negatively associated with household income, rising as the income level goes down. Another idea is that women 'dovetail' their economic activities with that of husbands who work in seasonal or casual work, for example construction work, to offset periods of unemployment (Moser and Young 1981: 58). These ideas have often rested on narrowly based case studies, so it is difficult to know how widespread they are. Chapter 8 shows that they were a minority pattern within the labouring class of Lima in the 1970s.

The concern with women's contribution to the household illustrates a prominent feature of current research: it is focused on women rather than gender, and it concentrates on the family for its main explanations. Yet important as domestic constraints are for women, they are only one aspect of gender segregation in the labour market and demand factors have to be considered too. Moreover, the family itself is in need of some theoretical attention, with more careful analysis of the variety of ways in which structural and ideological variables constrain women. In chapters 4 and 8, I make some suggestions.

The implications of women's work for class is another neglected area; only the Marxist feminists have considered the issue in any detail. However, problems arise from the fact that class is equated with paid work and theorized with reference to the overall system of capital accumulation. In the Latin American context, the problem is not just how to treat women's unpaid labour within this framework, but how to deal with the fact that most women's paid work is outside capitalist relations of production. This is akin to the general problem Marxism has had with theorizing class in developing countries. Some writers have adopted the solution of world systems theory, invoking the concept of 'social reproduction' to identify the relationship between capitalist and informal labour within the accumulation process. Thus it is argued that women's informal activities contribute to the social reproduction of labour power, by 'subsidizing' it.

For example, Roldán argues on the basis of her study of outworking in Mexico that this was not merely a subsistence strategy of the poor, but a specific 'subsidy' to wage labour, enabling it to fall below the level required to maintain a working-class family.

> industrial outworking was identified as an important component of the reproduction of labour power in what is clearly a stable section of the working class, parallel and complementary to the more familiar process of the reproduction of labour power which is assured by capital itself....

In other words, the analysis of the above factors made it possible to identify a source of 'additional benefit' or 'subsidy' for capital.

(Roldán 1985: 270)

The concept of reproduction has been much discussed within Marxism and Marxist feminism and is not unproblematic (see Meillassoux 1972, O'Loughlin 1977, Harris and Young 1981, Benería 1979, Bennholdt-Thomsen 1981, 1982, Humphries and Rubery 1984, Mingione 1985). It generally refers to two overlapping functions, both of which occur within the family: first, the production and maintenance of human beings (biological reproduction, childcare, nutrition, medical and welfare activities etc.), and second, the regeneration of social and economic structures (the transmission of property, the supply of labour to the labour market, education and socialization etc.). The family is thus the site for the physical care of its members and the reproduction of its economic and social conditions of survival. The important point for Marxist theory is that the family ensures the reproduction of labour power, and hence production and accumulation. This link between production and reproduction provides a role for women's work (paid or unpaid) through its indirect contribution to the accumulation process.

However, it is not clear how this role relates to class structure. Marxism is unambiguous about the centrality of *production* as the basis for class position, and reproductive activities are outside it unless they involve wage labour. In world systems theory, subsistence producers are given a specific class location separate from wage labour, despite the fact that they 'subsidize' it and thus contribute to its reproduction. By extension, this should mean that informal sector women are in a different class from formal sector men. However, Roldán's analysis implies that men's class position extends to their wives, since the latter's activities contribute to the reproduction of labour power at the level of the class itself. It is unclear whether women's membership of the working class in this case is as wives of wage labourers, or as outworker-wives. Would wives of factory workers who do not work be members of this class? And what about female outworkers who are wives of informal sector producers? How do we relate the class position of working wives derived from their own independent production with that which they can claim through the subsidy link with their husbands? A woman petty trader, for example, would be a member of the 'informal petty bourgeoisie' in her own right, yet a member of the working class if her earnings were 'subsidizing' her husband who was a factory worker.

These ambiguities go to the heart of the central problem in class analysis: how to relate individual and collective determinations of class position. Is the individual production role the unit of class or is it the family? This problem is not confined to Marxism, as can be seen in the tortuous debate about cross-class families in British sociology (e.g. Heath and Britten 1984). This issue has great significance for the analysis of class and gender, for if families can have a common class position by virtue of the link between production and reproduction, then in certain circumstances, differences of gender could be subsumed under class. But if class locations are based on individual economic roles alone, then potentially the family can be the site of class conflict and large numbers of women who are not in paid work have no class location at all. I believe that the concept of class has to be reformulated to resolve this ambiguity.

The analysis of women in poverty has focused on their important roles in the sphere of consumption. The literature on survival strategies places particular emphasis on women's networks of reciprocity within the neighbourhood, which are an important resource in the struggle for survival (e.g. Lomnitz 1977, Blondet 1990). It has been argued that women's responsibility for consumption extends into wider roles as 'community managers' which provides a space for them to mobilize politically (Moser 1987, 1993). However, such activities have been interpreted as social movements rather than as class action. This raises the question of whether the concept of class could be extended to include consumption-based activities. In this book I argue that it should.

However, it would then have to be asked whether women's activities in defence of consumption were to further the interests of gender or class, or both? Women's activities in support of basic subsistence needs such as health, housing, food and education have been seen as manifestations of gender interests because they reflect women's specific responsibilities within the domestic division of labour, women more frequently express these needs and they stand to benefit from them the most. Molyneux sees these as promoting 'practical' rather than 'strategic' gender interests because they are aimed at improving women's position within the existing sexual division of labour, rather than changing the division of labour itself (Molyneux 1985).

However, as Molyneux herself says, since gender and class are closely intertwined, 'practical interests, therefore cannot be assumed to be innocent of class effects' (Molyneux 1985: 233). The point here is that 'practical' gender needs are specific to the economic situation of women in a particular class; and the satisfaction of these needs may benefit men as well as women. In many cases, the consumption goods that women struggle for are *collective* goods such as housing, schools and community services, from which the family as a whole stands to benefit. Indeed, the rallying call in these mobilizations is usually in the name of the family. A concept of class that included consumption as well as production and that saw the family as a source of common class identity could justifiably claim that these actions were class actions. What we have here, in other words, is a situation where the interests of class and gender converge.

And what of women's consciousness of class and of gender? The common assumption is that women's relative confinement to the home and to the informal sector has isolated them from the main source of class consciousness, formal sector work. As a result they have a passive, diffuse consciousness, with little perception of the causes of their poverty and little disposition to political activism. However, as already indicated, this picture conflicts with recent evidence of women's participation in a broad range of activities, within the formal and informal sectors as well as in the community (Andreas 1985, Eckstein 1989).

The fact is that with the exception of the 'world market factories', very little research has been done on women workers in the formal sector, far less on their participation in trade unions. As mentioned above, little is known about the consciousness and action of informal sector workers generally, never mind the women there. In this book I shall be arguing that despite women's marginalization from formal sector employment, they *did* have a clear image of class inequality, it was not passive or quiescent, and it was very similar to men's. Thus despite profound gender divisions in the family and the labour market, men and women shared a common class identity and consciousness. Women's consciousness of class was more salient than that of gender, and their definition of gender interests was framed in these terms. In my view this was because the family was the basic unit in the struggle for survival and at the same time a major class institution.

CONCLUSION

The analysis of class and gender in Latin America has mainly centred on the division between formal and informal sectors of the economy, and the theories that have been developed to explain this division. Class analysis has been influenced by Marxist theory which prioritizes production relations as the principal source of class identity, and Marxist theory itself has absorbed aspects of the informal sector model into its framework. This has produced a highly formalist analysis which has great difficulty in predicting forms of consciousness and action, especially those that arise outside the sphere of production.

The analysis of gender has tended to focus on women rather than gender and has also worked within the general informal sector paradigm. There has been little analysis of women's class position in their own right, i.e. as a result of their own position in the labour market, or of the wider class implications of their work (but see Benería and Roldán 1987). Most research has concentrated on the relationship between women's work and the family, within a framework of 'survival strategies' or 'social reproduction', neither of which has any specific concern with class. The analysis of women's roles within the sphere of consumption has also taken place outside a class framework, and has tended to see this as *women's* mobilization rather than *class* mobilization.

In general therefore, the links between class and gender have not been fully explored in the literature reviewed in this chapter. The early work on class ignored gender and the recent work on gender does not consider class. One conclusion to be drawn here is that if this interrelationship is to be analysed systematically, existing concepts of class have to be reformulated so that they are less individualistic and production oriented. Even within the sphere of production itself, the links between gender and class still have to be spelt out. In particular, the role of the formal/informal sector division as the dominant source of differentiation within the labouring class must be challenged.

3   Growth, inequality and mobility

In the 1970s, Peru was a highly unequal society with a rapidly growing economy. It had great economic, cultural and ethnic diversity combined with a high concentration of power and wealth. Historically, Peruvian society was polarized between two main classes: the 'oligarchy' – a set of urban-based elites linked by kinship, landownership and political power – and the peasants. These class divisions were intertwined with ethnicity, and with cultural, linguistic and regional differences.

This situation was rooted in Spanish colonialism: the conquest involved a clash of cultures, institutions and language between the white, hispanic, urban-based elites and the colonized Aymara and Quechua peasantries. These divisions were sustained over the centuries, albeit in modified form, because of the relative economic and cultural independence of the peasants. Class relations throughout colonial and post-Independence period were characterized by exploitation, antagonism and occasional political violence. These relations strongly coloured the status order of Peruvian society, producing a high degree of derogation towards the rural and urban poor and resentment amongst the latter towards the rich and powerful (see, for example, Bourricaud 1970 and chapter 9).

Within broad social classes there were finer distinctions – subgroups within classes, regions and ethnic groups. Indian villagers situated in the remote Andean mountains were light years away from the modern, bustling coastal city of Lima, but they also distinguished themselves from other communities nearby who had perhaps a slightly different kinship system, dialect or communal traditions. On the coast, class relations had a different character again, originating in imports of African slaves and Chinese and Japanese bonded labour and more proletarian relations of production.

The post-world war economic growth introduced enormous changes into Peruvian society, breaking down many of these structural divisions through migration, miscegenation and social mobility. The rapidly expanding cities were being peopled by migrants from a very different rural background, while rural areas were being permeated by urban institutions and values. Growth was producing two new urban classes, the middle class and the labouring class, both shaped in various ways by the old social polarities, the oligarchy and the peasants. One of the questions to be addressed in this book is the extent to which the old social antagonisms were resurfacing in the consciousness of these new classes.

Much of the growth was concentrated in Lima, increasing inequality and social polarization there. However, there was progress for most social groups. There was a rise in the incomes and living standards of the poor, dynamic growth within the informal sector, considerable upward occupational and social mobility, and expanding opportunities for many women. Our analysis of the labouring class therefore needs to be set within this larger picture of growth, diversification and mobility.

This chapter provides evidence that will cast doubt on simplistic models that divide the labour market into a single formal/informal polarity or contend that women were marginalized from the growth process. The picture was much more complex than that. There were important subdivisions within the formal and informal sectors and amongst men and women, and there was income growth and mobility in all of them. Much of the informal sector literature assumes that Third World cities were 'swamped' by a labour surplus that vastly exceeded demand – a labour surplus harboured by the tertiary and/or informal sectors, where two jobs were 'created' where only one was needed and where incomes were depressed and could only deteriorate further. This chapter shows that the tertiary sector in Lima did not grow uncontrollably during the growth period, nor was its growth primarily associated with petty commerce and personal services. It was already large before industrialization took off and it grew because of expansion in formal sector employment there. The most dynamic category in the labour market was not self-employment but white collar labour.

In order to identify the labouring class and differentiate it from the middle class, it is important to distinguish between manual and non-manual occupations.[1] In 1974, about a third of the metropolitan labour force were non-manual and two-thirds manual. Non-manual employees earned more than twice as much as manual workers, on average, and had double the amount of education (Scott 1986a: 352). Non-manual employment expanded greatly during the growth period, fuelling a widespread process of upward occupational mobility. In 1974, 60 per cent of the middle class and 59 per cent of the labouring class had experienced cross-class upward mobility. This mobility process reached down from the middle class to the peasants and included women as well as men. It provided a broad framework for mobility within the labouring class, as we shall see in chapters 6 and 7.

The manual/non-manual distinction also sheds important light on the structure of the formal and informal sectors. In particular it points up the importance of occupational composition in differentiating the two sectors. Non-manual work was over half of formal sector employment but only 15 per cent in the informal sector. In the formal sector, a good third were in the two top occupational groups with the highest education and earnings and working conditions very different from the factory workers with whom they are usually lumped together.

Within the informal sector, some groups were earning relatively high incomes, on a par with factory workers. This does not sit easily with a picture of the informal sector as a depressed, marginalized group, and it is testimony to the fact that it too was participating in the processes of growth and mobility. There was considerable diversity within both sectors, even after controlling for occupation, which points to the need for further disaggregation. In particular there was significant segmentation by gender. The growth process differentiated opportunities between men and women, increasing gender inequality in employment. However, a substantial number of middle-class women did benefit from the growth process and there was thus an increasing class division *amongst* women.

This chapter does not deny that growth increased inequality in Lima. On the contrary, the argument is that it produced *both* increasing relative inequality *and* an absolute improvement in the situation of the poor. The interaction between these two aspects of inequality was an essential component of the dynamics of class and gender at the time.

THE PATTERN OF GROWTH 1940-72

At the beginning of the 1970s, Peru was at an intermediate level of development compared with other Latin American countries, yet much more developed than most parts of Africa and Asia (World Bank 1979a). It still had a relatively large peasantry, with 40 per cent of the labour force in agriculture. Two-thirds of the population were classified as 'urban', although many of them were living in small towns and villages.[2] The industrial sector was relatively well developed, able to meet most of the demand for consumer durables and much of that for capital and intermediate goods.

Peru is not naturally well endowed with good agricultural land; much of it consists of high altitude plains, precipitous mountainous slopes, infertile rainforest or coastal desert. However, it has rich mineral and maritime resources, and – in those areas where commercial agriculture did develop – a variety of crops. For the major part of this century, Peru has thus benefited from an unusually diverse export package,[3] which has ensured it a relatively sustained pattern of growth.

Because of the strength of its exports, Peru had generally been an open

economy and came late to protectionism and import-substituting industrialization, compared with other Latin American countries (ECLA 1959, GIECO
1972).[4] Industrialization started in a limited way at the turn of the century,
although it suffered from the depression of the 1930s and from competition
with import houses linked to the export trade (Thorp and Bertram 1978). A
major change in the pace of industrial growth began after the Second World
War as a result of increased foreign investment, particularly in export-processing[5] and import-substituting industries.[6] This produced a general
acceleration of growth throughout the economy and profound changes in the
social and political structure.

In 1968, a military coup led by General Velasco ushered in a period of
major economic and social reform involving land reform, expropriation of
foreign enterprises, industrial promotion and pro-labour legislation. Despite
the threat to private interests, economic growth continued through the period
of this research. The programme went into crisis from 1975 onwards as a
result of a variety of factors connected with a decline in export markets,
mounting public sector debt and rising inflation (Fitzgerald 1979, Thorp
1987).

Between 1940 and 1972 real growth in GDP averaged around 5.5 per cent
per annum, and per capita GDP doubled in spite of population growth (World
Bank 1979b: 163A). Manufacturing output rose at approximately 7 per cent
per annum, with spectacular rises in some years.[7] As a result, its share of GNP
increased from 14 per cent in 1950 to 22 per cent in 1972 (Central Bank 1966,
1976). The commercial sector showed strong growth as a result of the
flourishing import–export trade and urban property development. The public
sector also expanded with broad increases in welfare services, central planning and defence expenditure.[8]

Regional imbalances in the pattern of growth

The regional pattern of growth has always been very uneven in Peru. During
most of its history, the majority of the population has lived in the mountainous
region known as the *sierra*, while the growth sectors of the economy
associated with export industries were located in areas of sparse population.
Sugar, cotton, fishmeal and oil were mainly concentrated on the coast, while
rubber, coffee and tea were in the eastern Andean rainforests. Mining and
wool production, although located in the *sierra*, were concentrated in very
specific areas of it, usually at high altitudes away from the main settlements.
Export industries were very regionally specific, separated by considerable
distances from each other and from the peasant communities. Over time, a
symbiotic relationship developed between areas of labour supply and those
of export production involving cyclical flows of labour and resources in both

directions. This generated a process of growth and differentiation within the peasant communities (Favre 1977, Long and Roberts 1978, 1984, Laite 1981, Webb 1977).

With the post-1940 spurt in industrialization, the regional concentration of growth shifted decisively to Lima. Most of the new capital and intermediate goods industries, wholesale trade and government services were located there.[9] Although some provincial cities grew considerably during this period, none of them could match Lima in terms of population or resources.[10] Between 1940 and 1972 the population of Lima[11] rose from 645,172 to 3,302,523 and its share of the national population rose from 10 per cent to 24 per cent (National Censuses). The economically active population in Lima[12] grew at an average of 4.5 per cent per year, reaching 1,077,335 by 1972. The rapid expansion of Lima's population was visible in the growth of shanty towns around the outskirts of the city. The proportion of the population living in shanty towns rose from less than one per cent in 1940 to 25 per cent in 1972 (Collier 1976a: 144).

Migration

Peru has a long history of migration, which reaches back into colonial times. However, the industrialization period produced a sharp acceleration in migration to Lima. The proportion of immigrants in Lima rose from 33 per cent to 41 per cent, and the net immigrant population, which was barely 200,000 in 1940, rose to over a million in 1972 (World Bank 1979b: 87). Because more migrants were of working age than the Lima-born, they were a larger proportion of the metropolitan labour force (69 per cent) and larger still of the manual labour force (72 per cent) (Ministry of Labour 1974).

A high proportion of immigrants were of rural or semi-rural origin; 45 per cent came from district capitals most of which had populations under 2,000 and a further 14 per cent came from more isolated areas (Martinez *et al.* 1973: 79–81). Many of those who came from larger towns were only one generation removed from the countryside and still had kin relations with peasants. However, the migration process was highly selective, drawing in the young and able-bodied, the better educated and those with previous experience of urban employment and wage labour – especially in mines and on plantations. Because of the long-standing tradition of migration, the process was highly institutionalized, with information and resources passing between the city and places of origin via kinship networks and migrant associations (Figueroa 1984, Radcliffe 1986a, Altamirano 1984, Smith 1984). This had an important effect in regulating the supply of labour to Lima and facilitating migrants' incorporation into the metropolitan labour market, as we shall see in later chapters.

INCOME INEQUALITY

According to the World Bank data, Peru had one of the most unequal distributions of income in the world in 1972 (World Bank 1979a: 86). The degree of poverty amongst those living at the bottom of this distribution was dire. Peru's daily per capita calorie supply was the second lowest in Latin America, at the level of the mean for sub-Saharan Africa. The infant mortality rate was the highest in Latin America after Bolivia and Haiti (World Bank 1979a). The lowest incomes were amongst the peasants, especially in the *sierra*, where plots were small, the land unproductive and the methods of cultivation very rudimentary.

High incomes were generally associated with property ownership, formal sector production, and the regions in which these activities were located. Property income was an unusually high proportion of national income in Peru – around 23 per cent – comparable figures for the period in Argentina, Brazil and the USA were 12 per cent, 14 per cent, and 17 per cent respectively (ECLA 1971: 92). The distribution of property income was extremely unequal, almost all of it being concentrated amongst the top one per cent of income recipients. Webb says that in 1961 this meant only 100 or so families (Webb 1977: 8, 209).

The concentration of growth in Lima and other cities, together with the persistence of peasant agriculture, greatly increased rural–urban income inequality. On average, urban wage earners earned twice as much as peasants, and urban white collar workers six times as much (Webb 1977: 10–11). 'In 1961, the average resident income of Lima was almost three times the national average and five times higher than that of the *sierra*; around half the total national wages and salaries were paid out in Lima' (Webb 1977: 16). There was increasing inequality between the rich and the poor within Lima. This was evidenced in the expansion of wealthy suburbs with immense mansions surrounded by high walls, and the sprawling, crowded shanty towns. In terms of labour income, the top one per cent of the workforce in 1973 had earnings that were twenty-five times that of the lowest 10 per cent and ten times the minimum wage. The earnings distribution had a Gini coefficient of 0.47 which is extremely high (Ministry of Labour 1973, author's calculations). According to the 1974 figures, 35 per cent of the Lima workforce were earning less than the minimum wage (Ministry of Labour employment data, unpublished). On average, professionals and managers earned four times the minimum wage, while unskilled and service workers did not even reach this subsistence level. These earnings differentials underpinned the visible contrast in life styles and living standards in the city.

However, most social groups, even the urban poor, enjoyed an increase in real incomes up to around 1975. There is ample evidence that real wages and salaries rose between 1940 and 1975 (Payne 1965: 20, Hunt n.d.). The real wages of unskilled construction workers rose by 138 per cent between 1945 and 1971 (SERH 1971b: table 4). Between 1957 and 1971 real wages in manufacturing rose by 21 per cent and construction by 25 per cent (Sulmont 1977); the real minimum wage rose by 30 per cent between 1962 and 1972 (Sulmont 1974). The average income of households in the shanty towns studied by Lewis between 1956 and 1967 increased in real terms by about 33.5 per cent (Lewis 1973). The widespread construction of houses in these areas and their gradual upgrading in terms of physical amenities bore witness to this income growth (Mangin 1967, Turner 1963, Lobo 1982). According to Lewis, almost two-thirds of the growth in squatter incomes was due to a general increase in the wage rate; only 26 per cent was due to an increase in the number of employed persons per household and 12 per cent to a shift into white collar work. Only the tenth percentile of his sample had stagnant real earnings.

FORMAL AND INFORMAL PRODUCTION

The Peruvian economy had a high degree of polarization between formal and informal production. For centuries, this polarization had been epitomized by the *latifundio–minifundio* system whereby extremely large estates (*haciendas*) and plantations had contrasted with tiny peasant plots. In 1963 the agricultural census showed that 83 per cent of farms were less than 5 hectares in size yet accounted for only 6 per cent of the farmed land, while 0.1 per cent of the farms were over 2,500 hectares and accounted for 60 per cent of the farm land (Agricultural Census 1963). Most of the traditional export industries had been labour-intensive, especially in the mines and plantations, but after the Second World War these industries became progressively more capital-intensive, resulting in substantial shedding of labour (C. Scott 1979, Laite 1981). The new postwar industries, on the other hand, were capital-intensive from the start. They were associated with modern technology and high levels of productivity and wages, contrasting greatly with the small-scale, low-income and labour-intensive sector of the economy. Such contrasts were already noted in 1948: 'In agriculture, industry and to a lesser extent in mining, there is a noticeable discrepancy between a relatively small sector which has attained considerable development and a large majority operating with very primitive methods and organization' (Pan American Union 1950: 195).

The 1963 Economic Census showed that 83 per cent of manufacturing enterprises had less than five persons per establishment and accounted for only 2 per cent of output, while 6 per cent of them, which employed over twenty persons per establishment, produced 92 per cent of output. In retail commerce, 96 per cent of enterprises employed less than five persons per establishment and accounted for 39 per cent of the value of sales, while the remaining 4 per cent of enterprises accounted for 61 per cent. Large state bureaucracies contrasted with a wide variety of personal services yielding some of the lowest incomes (1963 Economic Census, preliminary results).[13]

The 1974 manufacturing census shows continued polarization between large and small establishments. Even excluding establishments with less than five workers (which were not adequately covered by the census), small enterprises dominated manufacturing production in terms of numbers but accounted for only a small proportion of remunerations, value added and output.[14] Fitzgerald's figures, based on the national accounts, show the contrast in productivity between the two sectors at the level of the whole economy (table 3.1).

Table 3.1   Distribution of value added and workforce size in modern and traditional sectors of the economy, Peru 1972

	% workforce	*% value added*
Modern (5+ persons)	36	61
export production	18	19
industry	5	11
government and tertiary	13	31
Traditional (<5 persons)	64	39
food agriculture	33	10
small industry	11	9
petty tertiary	20	20

Source: Adapted from Fitzgerald (1976: 13)

Economic growth and the informal sector

The growth process had produced an increasing polarization between formal and informal production, and an accompanying differentiation in productivity and incomes (Webb 1977, Beaulne 1974). However, earnings in both sectors were rising; the polarization was the result of differences in the rates of growth rather than because of stagnation in the informal sector. Webb shows that although growth was concentrated in the modern sector, the incomes of the poor were rising, even in rural areas (table 3.2).

The rise in incomes within the informal sector casts doubt on the notion of an 'oversupply' of labour and internal involution there. This is corroborated by data on the changing structure of employment over the 1940–72

Table 3.2   Trends in per capita real income in Peru 1950–66

	Average income (US$ 1961)	Annual income growth per capita 1950–66
*Modern sector**	*1,126*	*4.1*
wage earners		4.9
government employees		3.6
white collar		3.3
*Urban traditional***	*407*	*2.0*
wage earners		2.5
self-employed		1.9
salaried workers		1.8
domestic servants		1.6
*Rural traditional***	*264*	*1.3*
coastal wage earners		4.1
sierra and jungle wage earners		1.5
small farmers		0.8

Source: Adapted from Webb (1977: 10–11, 39)
*   Modern sector = establishments with 5+ employees (formal)
** Urban/rural traditional = <5 employees (informal)

period,[15] which show little evidence of an 'excessive' growth in commerce and services or in self-employment. On the contrary, what is noteworthy is the stability of the distribution of employment between economic sectors (see table 3.3). Although commerce and services did account for slightly over half of the net increase in employment between 1940 and 1972, this was not because of any spectacular rates of growth relative to other sectors, but was the product of an average rate of growth in an already large sector. Only commerce was slightly out of line with the overall growth rate: it grew more during the early period but *less* during the second.

Similarly, the data on employment status provide little support for the notion that the dynamic growth in employment came from the informal sector (table 3.4). If we aggregate self-employment, family labour and domestic service[16] we can see that the overall proportion *fell* slightly from 33 per cent to 30 per cent. Most of this fall was due to the relative decline in domestic service (whose share almost halved), and although self-employment rose, it did so only slightly and by 1970 represented merely a fifth of total employment. The high rate of growth in this category in the first intercensal period was a product of the low base in 1940 and it was not sustained in the second period. In fact, self-employment was only responsible for 22 per cent of the net increase in employment between 1940 and 1972, less than wage labour (27 per cent) and almost half that of salaried employment.

Table 3.4 shows that the most dynamic growth in Lima's workforce during

Table 3.3   Distributions of total non-primary employment* by economic sector, Department of Lima & Callao, 1940–72

Economic sector**	Percentage distributions			Annual compound growth	
	1940	1961	1972	1940–61	1961–72
Manufacturing	25	26	26	5.1	3.8
Construction	8	7	7	4.5	4.0
Transport	8	7	9	3.9	6.2
Commerce	16	20	17	5.9	2.5
Services	38	35	37	4.4	4.5
Unspecified	4	4	4	5.2	4.0
Total	99	99	100	4.8	4.0

Source: Adjusted worksheets based on National Population Censuses (see Scott 1988)
* Economically active population of 6 years and over, unemployed excluded in all years
** The classification of economic sector has been adjusted in order to permit maximum comparability between censuses

Table 3.4   Distributions of total non-primary employment* by employment status, Department of Lima & Callao, 1940–72

Employment status	Percentage distributions			Annual compound growth	
	1940	1961	1972	1940–61	1961–72
Wage labour	37	37	29	5.1	1.5
Salaried employees	27	27	39	5.0	7.3
Self-employed	17	21	21	6.0	3.5
Family labour	1	1	1	4.3	2.9
Domestic servants	15	11	9	3.7	1.2
Unspecified	3	2	1	3.5	−4.5
Total	100	99	100	5.0	3.7

Source: Adjusted worksheets based on National Population Censuses (see Scott 1988)
* Economically active population of 6 years and over, excluding the unemployed except in 1961

the period under review came from *salaried* employment. As a proportion of overall employment, it rose from 27 per cent in 1940 to 39 per cent in 1972 and it contributed 43 per cent of the total net increase in employment. This offset a relative decline in wage work so that the overall proportion in formal employment[17] grew from 64 per cent to 69 per cent, representing nearly three-quarters of the new jobs created between 1940 and 1972. A cross-tabulation of sectoral employment by employment status shows slight evidence of a decline in self-employed manufacturing and none for the uncontrolled growth of petty commerce (Scott 1988: appendices).

The effects of the growth in salaried employment on the occupational structure can be seen in table 3.5.[18] The three top occupational groups accounted for over a third of the net increase in employment between 1962 and 1972. Of the three groups, the most spectacular increase was amongst professionals and technicians, whose share of total employment doubled and whose rate of growth was twice that of the two next fastest growing groups, clerical and sales workers. Unfortunately, the latter category lumps together street pedlars and sales assistants in modern department stores, but more disaggregated analysis shows that it was the latter subgroup that expanded most (Scott 1988).

Table 3.5 Distributions of total non-primary employment* by occupational group, Metropolitan Lima, 1961, 1972

Occupational groups	Percentage distribution		Annual compound growth rate	% share of net increase
	1961	1972	1961–72	
Managers & administrators	4	1	−7.4	−3.4
Professionals & technicians	6	12	10.4	20.9
Clerical workers	13	14	5.6	16.8
Drivers	5	4	1.8	1.8
Artisans, workers in production & construction	31	32	4.5	31.8
Sales workers	13	14	5.5	17.0
Service workers	19	17	3.2	12.8
Unspecified	9	6	1.3	2.3
Total	100	100	4.4	100.0

Source: National Population Censuses: 1961 table 38, 1972 tables 27, 28
* Economically active population of 6 years and over, including the unemployed

It should be noted that the single largest occupational group, which continued to grow at about the rate of the labour force as a whole and accounted for almost a third of the net increase in employment, matching white collar work, was that of artisans, and production and construction workers. Most of these workers would have been in the secondary rather than the tertiary sector. On the other hand service workers had one of the slowest rates of increase of any group, and their share of total employment actually declined. Thus when white collar work is extracted from commerce and services we can see just how little of the growth in these sectors was due to jobs typical of an 'urban labour surplus'. This analysis indicates that the expansion of tertiary sector employment was in large part due to the state and formal commercial and financial enterprises, which greatly expanded white collar occupations. This created opportunities in the upper part of the occupational structure, facilitating upward mobility for those below. The informal sector did expand during the growth period, but it had a more dynamic and positive role in the economy than is usually assumed and, as a result, was capable of participating in the rise in earnings, albeit at a lower rate than the formal sector. Let us now look more closely at the structure of these sectors in Lima in 1974.

The informal sector in Lima, 1974

In the early 1970s, the polarization between formal and informal sectors in Lima was visible to the most casual observer. Large modern factories coexisted with small workshops and repairmen operating on street corners, construction companies erecting modern skyscrapers were complemented by individual and communal building in the shanty towns, modern articulated buses capable of carrying 200 passengers travelled the same routes as ramshackle taxis and dormobiles crammed with people, large modern supermarkets and department stores were to be found not a stone's throw from street markets, and the entrances to huge ministerial buildings were swarming with shoeshiners, food sellers and car washers.

Household surveys show that the Lima labour force was divided roughly equally between the formal and informal sectors in 1974. However, definitions vary: if we take self-employment together with unpaid family labour as the basis for informal employment, as was suggested by some of the earliest models (e.g. Hart 1973) this amounted to 24 per cent. If wage workers in enterprises with less than five workers are added, e.g. apprentices, paid relatives etc., the figure rises to 37 per cent. When domestic servants are included, the figure reaches 45 per cent. If we allow for some underestimation of unpaid family labour, the figure might have reached 50 per cent.[19] This corresponds to the total labour force in enterprises with less than five workers, which is the conventional definition of 'informal sector' and the one used throughout this book. Within this sector, just over half were self-employed, 28 per cent were wage workers and 20 per cent were domestic servants. A tiny proportion were unpaid family helpers.

Average earnings in the formal sector were double that in the informal sector (6,925 and 3,427 soles respectively, the minimum wage being 3,000 soles at the time of this survey). However, there were high coefficients of variation in both sectors. This was partly due to the different occupational composition of each sector. As mentioned, over half of formal sector employees were in non-manual occupations, compared with only 15 per cent in the informal sector. Moreover, a third of these employees were in the very highest income groups – professionals and managers. When non-manual employees were subtracted from both sectors, average formal earnings dropped by a third and informal earnings as a proportion of formal rose from 49 per cent to 65 per cent.

Table 3.6 shows the large class difference in the distribution of formal and informal employment: over four-fifths of the middle class were in formal employment whereas nearly two-thirds of the labouring class were in informal work. Within all occupational groups (with the exception of drivers) average earnings were higher in formal enterprises than in informal ones. However, the discrepancy between the two sectors was much less in non-manual occupations. Therefore not only did the middle class benefit from their greater access to jobs in large enterprises, but they were much less disadvantaged by working in small ones, compared to manual workers. The latter suffered a substantial penalty for their concentration in the informal sector.

Substantial differentials remained within the two sectors even after controlling for occupation. This internal diversity casts doubt on the usefulness of the simple dichotomous version of the informal sector model and on the validity of the behavioural assumptions associated with it. Further analysis revealed that many of these assumptions were inapplicable to the Peruvian case. In brief, there was less polarization between the two sectors, more diversity of skill and earnings within them, uneven institutional protection within the formal sector, relatively little subcontracting and little confinement of informal producers to low-income markets. In sum, the informal sector was much less depressed and excluded than is normally assumed and the formal sector less privileged. Since this interpretation is somewhat controversial, it is necessary to provide further evidence on these points here.

The extent of formal/informal polarization

Conventionally, formal and informal sectors have been defined in terms of firm workforce size, 'formal' being equated with 'large' and 'informal' with

Table 3.6   Occupational groups and levels of earnings by enterprise size, Metropolitan Lima 1974

Occupational groups	% informal	Average monthly earnings		% of workforce
		< 5 workers	5+ workers	
Managers	24	10,866	14,954	6
Professionals	17	11,141	11,625	5
Technicians	8	5,139	6,965	8
Office workers	14	4,039	5,478	13
Total non-manual	*16*	*6,946*	*8,240*	*32*
Drivers	47	6,407	5,555	5
Skilled & semi-skilled workers	38	3,725	4,589	29
Sales workers	91	3,132	5,316	14
Unskilled & service workers	70	1,548	3,632	20
Total manual	*61*	*2,942*	*4,495*	*68*

Source: Scott (1986a: 352)
Notes: Author's classification of occupations differs from that of the census (see footnote 1); minimum wage = 3,000 soles

small. Although the usual practice has been to use five, ten or twenty employees as the cut-off point for the division between the two sectors, the literature implies that 'large' actually means considerably more than this (something like 100 plus), with relatively few enterprises in between. However, this dichotomous measure greatly overestimates the extent of polarization between small and large enterprises. In Lima, there was a significant medium-sized sector with five to ninety-nine employees, whose working environment and earnings levels were much inferior to those in the larger category. Workers in these enterprises were more like sweated labour than a privileged elite. In 1974, 41 per cent of all formal sector employees and 54 per cent of manual ones were in this middle group; women wage workers were particularly concentrated there.

Firm size, capital intensity and technological skills

It is normally assumed that there is a strong relationship between large-scale production, capital intensive production techniques and high skill levels, this being a major reason for the high incomes in the formal sector. In Lima, although this association was present, it was weak.[20] Manufacturing firms were more capital-intensive than commercial ones, and within manufacturing, engineering industries were more so than consumer-goods industries (Ministry of Industry and Tourism 1973). Consequently labour productivity varied amongst large firms, being lower in industries such as footwear and clothing than in the white goods industries (cf. Schmitz 1982).[21]

All formal enterprises employed unskilled as well as skilled labour, but the proportions differed considerably. For example, in the chemicals industry, a sector with many foreign firms and large plants, the majority of the manual workforce was unskilled, whereas in the mechanical industries it was skilled (SERH 1970). Unskilled and semi-skilled jobs were an important entry port into formal sector employment, and one where relatively few credentials were required. This factor has been underrated in formal sector models and has led to an exaggeration of the role of barriers to entry in the sector. Skill diversity in both sectors is examined in chapter 5.

Institutional protection

In Peru, although institutional protection of labour (unions, labour legislation, social security) was largely associated with the formal sector, the quality and quantity of protection was variable. Moreover, it was not confined exclusively to the formal sector – there were some important workplace associations and a degree of social insurance coverage in the informal sector too. Therefore it is unlikely that avoidance of institutional protection was a major reason for informal sector growth.

Legally, a minimum of twenty employees in the workplace was required before a union could be recognized and most labour legislation and social security provision was also based on this cut-off point. This meant that over half the total metropolitan workforce and almost three-quarters of manual workers were excluded from any form of protection by unions or the state. Many of these were wage earners in enterprises with six to nineteen workers, which usually would be included in the formal sector.

Although unionization had increased considerably during the 1960s, it was very patchy. The membership rates were low: in 1974, only half of those eligible for membership were actually affiliated to unions.[22] Although the membership rate was highest in the largest enterprises, even there, only 61 per cent of manual employees were unionized. The organized labour movement was very fragmented by political divisions and the fact that collective bargaining was usually plant based rather than industry or trade based (Payne 1965, Chaplin 1967, Sulmont 1977, Haworth 1984). Payne (1965) maintains that organized workers were more successful in obtaining real wage increases than unorganized ones during the 1950s and 1960s. However, scattered evidence suggests that there was considerable variation in union militancy between formal sector firms.

It appears that employers were more worried about intervention by the state than by unions. Labour legislation and social security provision were much more widespread than unionization.[23] During the 1960s there were many complaints about the high social costs of labour (i.e. employers' contributions to social security, paid holidays, sickness benefit, etc.) which were said to amount to between 50 and 100 per cent of the basic wage (Reichmuth 1978: 38, 119, US Dept of Labor 1968, Little 1960). Employers also complained about labour stability laws and maternity legislation which limited their flexibility in labour use. However, the most vociferous complaints came from the most advanced sectors of the economy, where firms were more exposed to public scrutiny: smaller sweatshops were able to avoid the legislation. Most firms complied with the basic social security requirements, but provided little else.

It is difficult to assess whether these factors limited the size of the formal sector and artificially inflated the informal sector, as claimed by De Soto (1986). Reichmuth's study of the clothing industry in 1975 showed less than one per cent of small enterprises were in the 'large informal' or 'small formal' category just below the twenty-worker legal limit (Reichmuth 1978: 92). He found little evidence of institution-avoidance strategies apart from subcontracting (see below).

Finally, institutional intervention in the *informal* sector may have been underestimated by neo-liberal theory. Producer associations were frequent in parts of the informal sector, such as market traders and bus drivers. In 1973, about a quarter of informal sector workers had social security coverage.[24] Informal sector workers were not free of bureaucratic control: there were frequent complaints about state intervention, particularly licensing, price controls and police harassment.[25] In my survey, 80 per cent had some form of documentation.

The point here is that institutional intervention was more widespread than is posited by recent informal sector theory, but at the same time more uneven. Although formal sector workers were generally more protected than informal ones, there were variations in the nature and impact of intervention there.

Subcontracting

Many have argued that subcontracting between formal and informal enterprises occurs in order to avoid unions and labour legislation and is a major reason for the persistence of the informal sector (e.g. Portes and Walton 1981: 98–100). The data from Lima suggest that this factor can be exaggerated. Certainly, subcontracting did exist during the 1970s (see Scott 1979), although it is difficult to assess the precise extent. Reichmuth's analysis of the 1973 manufacturing census shows that industrial subcontracting was restricted to only a few branches of industry, particularly clothing. It existed in other branches but was not widespread. We cannot discount under-reporting here because of the poor coverage of establishments with less than five workers, but even in the next size group (five to nineteen workers), which was better covered, was not unionized, and made the most use of subcontracting, the proportions were not large (Reichmuth 1978: 87–9).

Other studies suggest that fluctuations in demand or the small size of the market were a more important reason for subcontracting; for example, it was used by department stores in the 1950s because of shortages of supply or a desire for product exclusivity (Fritsch 1962). This would be consistent with the fact that such workers were sometimes paid a comparable wage to stable wage earners and even had access to social security, paid for by their employers.[26]

Most of the evidence on subcontracting in Lima relates to the use of domestic outwork by clothing manufacturers. The reasons for this practice had less to do with unions and the avoidance of social security costs than with the existence of a large supply of skilled housebound women willing to work for low wages. However, these women were only a small proportion of total small-scale manufacturing employment and an even smaller proportion of the whole informal sector.[27]

Confinement to low-income consumer markets

The majority of informal producers in Lima in 1974 were operating autonomously and selling directly to the market, especially in commerce and services where they predominated.[28] Most were producing for a variety of markets and were not confined to low-income customers (Vega-Centeno 1973, SERH 1971).[29] Some produced mainly for a middle- and high-income market (e.g. artisans and domestic servants). Many could rely on custom markets which enabled them to charge *above* the price of comparable factory-made products.[30] Small traders in the shanty towns were limited by the income levels of the neighbourhood, but even here there was great variation.

The existence of some high-income informal producers suggests that this sector survived and expanded in the 1970s because there was a demand for their products or services in particular niches of the urban economy created by rapid change and income growth. Their comparative advantage was flexibility, mobility, low fixed overheads and the high personal service content of their products. However, some were better placed than others to take advantage of this situation. They had had the benefit of long apprenticeships, savings and family loans for starting up, a good location and networks of regular clients. These were the crucial components of success in the informal sector, but for those who could not get access to such resources, particularly women, they were formidable obstacles. Thus, contrary to many assumptions, there were significant barriers to entry in the informal sector and these were strongly related to earnings variation there. As a result of these barriers there was a depressed group within the sector who did conform to the traditional stereotype, but in the booming years of the 1970s they were the minority (see chapter 5).

In summary, the Lima data show that within the formal sector there were important variations in enterprise size, skill mix, degree of institutional intervention and earnings. In the informal sector, there were variations in economic success, which related to access to crucial productive resources rather than exploitation through subcontracting or confinement to unprofitable markets. The fact that the informal sector was not 'overextended' or depressed in economic terms meant that it was not a drag on income growth and occupational mobility. On the contrary it was part and parcel of both processes.

GENDER DIVISIONS WITHIN THE LIMA LABOUR MARKET

The changing gender distribution of employment 1940–72

Early analyses of the post-1940 period in Latin America held that women were marginalized from the growth process: they were either relegated to the informal sector or pushed out of the labour market altogether. The situation in Lima was rather different from this. In general, women benefited from the expansion in education and employment, although less so than men. Hence their overall situation improved, although relative inequality between men and women increased. However, the situation was different for middle-class and labouring-class women, opportunities increasing for the former but less for the latter. The marginalization thesis thus holds for *manual* women, but not for all women; and even in this case, many of the women were benefiting from the rise in informal sector incomes. This analysis has been published in Scott (1986a and b), therefore only a brief summary is presented below.

In Lima, labour force participation rates generally declined between 1940 and 1972 because of the rise in full-time schooling, the fall being more pronounced amongst men than women.[31] The male participation rate (based on a population of 6 years and over) fell from 66 per cent to 56 per cent and the female rates from 26 per cent to 22 per cent. There was an increase in labour force participation amongst highly educated women, particularly after marriage, but this was offset by a decline in the proportion of illiterate women, who generally had higher rates. Overall, women's share of metropolitan employment remained stable at 28 per cent.[32]

Already in 1940, women were distributed in the labour market very differently from men. They were more concentrated in the tertiary sector, especially in domestic service, and had less wage work. These discrepancies increased over time. Women were much more affected by the relative fall in wage work than men, but they benefited more from the expansion in white collar work. This resulted in a shift towards non-manual employment especially in commerce and services. However, because women were only a small proportion of total employment, the male predominance in almost every sector of employment persisted, and in some cases (e.g. the professions) it increased. An overall improvement in the occupational composition of female employment therefore existed alongside increasing inequality between men and women.

Between 1940 and 1972, women received only 6 per cent of the net increase in wage work and their share of it fell from 20 per cent to 9 per cent. The predominance of men here, which was already large in 1940, therefore increased to 90 per cent. The proportion of women in tertiary employment rose from 71 per cent to 78 per cent. However, this was by no means associated with informal employment or menial services as is often implied. On the contrary, within services there was a fall in the proportion of domestic and other personal services and a rise in white collar work. Although domestic service increased in absolute terms between 1940 and 1972 (from 26,230 to 78,389) its *share* of service employment fell from 66 per cent to 49 per cent, and of total female employment, from 38 per cent to 27 per cent. Self-employed women in commerce and services crept up from 11 per cent to 14 per cent of all employed women – hardly a staggering increase (Scott 1988: appendix). The proportion of all women in self-employment increased only marginally (from 17 to 19 per cent) but so did that of men, so the ratio of women to men in this category actually fell slightly (Scott 1986a: table 8.10).

The most notable change for working women was the increase in white collar work: it rose from 20 per cent to 43 per cent of total female employment, representing half the net increase in women's jobs. Its rate of growth was two and a half times that of total female employment, higher than any other form of employment and exceeding the male rates as well. The rise in women's salaried labour took place in every sector. Within manufacturing the proportion rose from 9 per cent to 29 per cent; in commerce from 35 per cent to 40 per cent and in services from 20 per cent to 43 per cent. By far the highest proportion of white collar women were concentrated in the services sector (57 per cent) and the majority of them were employed in state bureaucracies.

As a result of the expansion of female white collar work there was an upward shift in the overall distribution of female employment between manual and non-manual jobs, indeed the relative shift towards the top three occupational groups was *greater* amongst women than men over the inter-censal period. This represented a significant increase in mobility opportunities for women, especially the younger ones.

However, the situation was rather different for manual women. The fall in women's industrial wage work signified a decline in better paying jobs for labouring-class women and they had to turn to small-scale retailing and personal services. Few were able to move into non-manual work because of their age or low level of education. In 1973, three-quarters of manual women were employed in small-scale retailing and personal services. Thus *relative* inequality between middle- and labouring-class women was increasing.

In terms of inequality between men and women, the data show increasing segregation and inequality. Because of their majority in the labour force as a whole, in all cases more jobs went to men than to women. Even where women did make rapid gains, such as in white collar work, men still predominated there. Moreover, the jobs that expanded fastest for men tended to be at the top of occupational hierarchies, whereas for women, they were at the bottom. As far as non-manual employment was concerned, more women were concentrated in low-grade clerical work than men, and even within the professions women tended to concentrate in low-status occupations such as teaching and nursing, while men went for the high-status ones such as medicine, law and engineering. Amongst manual workers, men's relative concentration in manufacturing, construction and transport meant employment in relatively high-wage jobs whereas women's increasing confinement to personal services and retailing meant concentration in the low-wage region. Since two-thirds of all women in paid work were manual workers, and the majority of these were at the bottom of the manual labour market, their situation strongly influenced the aggregate profile of gender inequality.

In summary, the major effect of growth was to improve the overall occupational composition of the female labour market (as measured by an upward shift into higher paying and less arduous occupations), while at the same time differentiating the relative positions of manual and non-manual women and that of women vis-à-vis men within these classes. Therefore although in *absolute* terms the position of most women did improve, *relative* inequality between men and women, and amongst women themselves, increased.

Gender and employment in 1974

In 1974, women's average earnings were about half of men's. This was partly due to the concentration of women in the informal sector and in low-level occupations. However, there were also wide gender differentials *within* occupations and sectors, especially in the manual workforce. As a result, the sex differential in earnings amongst manual workers was much greater than amongst non-manual employees.

Survey data show that women were much more concentrated in the informal sector than men – 61 per cent compared with 38 per cent. However, as already mentioned, there were important class differences: 84 per cent of manual women worked in informal establishments, whereas 88 per cent of non-manual women worked in formal ones (table 3.7). In fact, this gap was bridged directly – a large number of manual women were employed by middle-class women as servants.

The formal/informal earnings differential was greater for women than men, but sex differentials in earnings *within* formal and informal enterprises were also very large. Men earned substantially more than women whichever sector they were in; in fact they earned more in informal enterprises than women did in formal ones. The final column of this table shows that although

Table 3.7   Distribution of men and women by enterprise size and manual/non-manual class, earnings and educational differentials, Lima 1974

Workforce	% distribution		$\bar{x}$ earnings*		$\bar{x}$ education*	
	<5	5+	<5	5+	<5	5+
Non-manual workers	*16*	*84*	*6,946*	*8,239*	*9.1*	*10.7*
men	17	83	7,745	9,369	9.1	10.4
women	12	88	4,315	5,779	9.0	11.2
Manual workers	*61*	*39*	*2,942*	*4,495*	*5.0*	*6.1*
men	49	51	3,990	4,715	5.8	6.1
women	84	16	1,689	3,047	4.2	6.1

Source: Ministry of Labour employment survey 1974
*   Average monthly earnings, average years of education

there was a slight association between education and sector in both classes, the earnings differentials were much larger.

Turning to the occupational structure, table 3.8 shows that women were concentrated at the bottom of the overall occupational hierarchy, as well as on the bottom rungs of the manual and non-manual hierarchies. Over half of all women were concentrated in the bottom two groups, compared with only a quarter of the men. Amongst manual workers, unskilled and service work constituted 53 per cent of female employment compared with only 17 per cent of male employment; and amongst non-manual employees, 52 per cent of women were employed in clerical work compared with only 34 per cent of men.

Women's concentration at the bottom of occupational hierarchies was a major cause of earnings inequality; however, there were high sex differentials

Table 3.8 Distribution of men and women by occupational group, and sex differentials in earnings and education, Lima 1974

Occupational groups	% distribution		% women in group	Women's average as % of men's:	
	Men	Women		earnings	education
Managers & senior administrators	9	2	10	53	95
Professionals	6	3	24	65	99
Technicians	8	9	35	87	119
Office Workers	11	15	39	83	109
Subtotal non-manual	*33*	*29*	*30*	*62*	*107*
Drivers	7	*	1	*	*
Skilled & semi-skilled workers	35	15	17	60	104
Salespersons	13	18	40	53	154
Unskilled & service workers	12	37	60	48	82
Total manual	*67*	*70*	*33*	*43*	*76*
Total	101	99	32	51	88

Source: Ministry of Labour employment survey 1974
* Numbers too small to be meaningful

in earnings within occupational groups, especially in manual work. Once again, sex differentials in education were lower than the earnings differentials within these groups. In fact, in many groups women had marginally *more* years of education than men, particularly in the middle of the occupational hierarchy.

Much of the occupational inequality between men and women was linked to gender segregation at the micro level. Table 3.9 provides a 'map' of occupations identified at the three-digit level, arranged according to the type and degree of gender segregation and their location in one-digit occupational groups. It shows a very high polarization of occupations at the extreme edges of the male–female continuum, and a heavy clustering of occupations at the male end. There was a much larger number of exclusively 'male' occupations than 'female' ones in all broad occupational groups. In contrast, there were very few exclusively 'female' occupations and women were heavily concentrated in them: 63 per cent of all women were employed in just fifteen out of a possible 107 occupations. These occupations had mainly to do with education and welfare, cooking, cleaning, clothing and provisioning.[33]

The confinement of women to 'female' occupations[34] was high in all occupational groups, even at the bottom of the occupational hierarchy. Indeed the degree of segregation was *greatest* there. Moreover, the concentration of women in 'female' occupations was strong in formal and informal sectors: 64 per cent of women working in informal enterprises and 60 per cent of the women in formal ones were employed in 'female' occupations (Scott 1986a: table 8.18). However, a much greater proportion of the workforce was employed in male-dominated occupations than in female-dominated ones (Scott 1986a: table 8.13). The workforce was thus very polarized between 'male' and 'female' occupations. Four-fifths were employed in occupations that were heavily biased in one direction or the other, and nearly two-thirds worked in ones that were exclusively 'male' or 'female'.

The most striking pattern is the diagonal polarization of the workforce between 'male' jobs at the top of the occupational hierarchy to 'female' jobs at the bottom. This diagonal shift occurs within manual and non-manual classes although it is less pronounced in the former because 'clerical workers' included some male jobs.[35] Note that the apparent lack of segregation amongst salespersons is misleading, for sales work is differentiated by gender according to type and scale of commercial activity rather than occupational titles (Moser 1977, Bunster and Chaney 1985).

Employment in Lima was thus highly segregated between 'male' and 'female' jobs and this segregation crosscut the manual/non-manual and the formal/informal divides. It is difficult to say whether gender segregation increased or decreased during the period of growth, although it would be hard to imagine a more extreme segregation than that of 1974. It appears that the

Table 3.9 Degrees of male/female concentration within occupations and occupational groups, Lima 1974

Occ. group	Almost all men M = 90–100%	Disproportionately male M = 69–89%	Slight female overrepresentation F = 32–49%	High female overrepresentation F = 50–89%	Almost all women F = 90–100%
I	Architects, engineers, agronomists, doctors, dentists, lawyers, accountants	University academics	Chemists	Secondary school teachers	Obstetricians
II	Diplomats, ministers, senior civil servants, directors and managers in commerce, production and service firms, construction contractors, senior admin., bankers and insurance agents	Senior executives, self-employed wholesalers, branch directors in commerce			
III	Animal and farm technicians, officers of the armed forces, photographers, engine drivers, pilots, navigators, policemen and security officers, misc. technicians	Draughtsmen, artists and journalists, foremen, computer operators	Laboratory technicians, teachers in private schools, translators, librarians	Dieticians, primary school teachers, teaching assistants, social workers	Nurses, midwives
IV	Inspectors, depot workers, expediters, sales representatives, customs officials	Cashiers, storemen	Telephonists and radio operators,* xerox operators		Secretaries, typists
V	Bus, lorry and taxi drivers				

Table 3.9 (continued)

Occ. group	Almost all men M = 90–100%	Disproportionately male M = 69–89%	Slight female overrepresentation F = 32–49%	High female over-representation F = 50–89%	Almost all women F = 90–100%
VI	Tailors, shoemakers, carpenters, bricklayers, painters and decorators, metal workers, plumbers, electricians, mechanics, radio and TV engineers, jewellers, typesetters, potters and glass workers, brickmakers, chemical workers, vulcanizers, butchers, bakers, milkmen, tanners and leather workers	Textile workers, misc. production process workers	Cigarette and tobacco workers, packers, labellers and bottlers		Dressmakers
VII			Shop assistants, retail sales street sellers		
VIII	Postmen and messengers, apprentices, caretakers, stevedores, barbers, shoeshine boys, gardeners, cleaners and sweepers	Waiters and waitresses*		Chambermaids, lodginghouse-keepers, cooks, nursing auxiliaries	Domestic servants

I = Professionals; II = Managers and administrators; III = Technicians; IV = Office workers; V = Drivers; VI = Skilled and semi-skilled workers; VII = Sales workers; VIII = Unskilled and service workers

Source: Ministry of Labour employment survey 1974, published in Scott (1986a)

*This group is subject to internal gender specialization

growth process had expanded traditional 'male' and 'female' jobs and created new ones. The expansion of the state was important in augmenting traditional female occupations such as teachers, nurses and welfare workers. The growth in government offices and private firms created jobs for female clerical staff. The rise in middle-class incomes together with cultural tastes for personal services increased demand for domestic servants, hairdressers and dressmakers. Some 'female' jobs were disappearing, particularly in the manufacturing sector, but others were taking their place. In general then, the growth process offered increased employment and rising incomes[36] for both men and women, but within very segregated labour markets.

EDUCATIONAL INEQUALITY

Before turning to the analysis of occupational mobility, I want first to consider the pattern of educational qualifications in Lima, since education was the main vehicle for mobility. It was also a contributory factor to the pattern of gender segregation discussed in the previous section.

In Peru, educational inequalities were traditionally associated with class, gender and ethnicity. This situation changed dramatically during the growth period because of the clamour for education in all social classes, changing attitudes towards girls' education and high investment by the state in education.[37] Even so, inequalities persisted to some extent, particularly amongst the older age groups.

Educational inequalities were far less marked in Lima than at national level because a high proportion of the expansion in educational resources had been concentrated there and because the migration process had been very selective in educational terms. Migrants were generally better educated than those who stayed at home (Martinez *et al.* 1973, World Bank 1979b, Bradfield 1965, 1973). Moreover, after their arrival there was continuing enthusiasm for education, reflected in night school attendance and the enormous efforts – often at considerable cost in time and money – to secure better opportunities for their children. In all social classes there was a desire for upward mobility and a recognition that education was the principal mechanism to achieve it. This is reflected in the fact that 80 per cent of the Lima sample desired a professional or technician's job for their eldest son, and this percentage was almost as high amongst the offspring of peasants as it was amongst the middle class.[38] Education was a vehicle for the assimilation of urban middle-class values, a major source of middle-class employment and a panacea for the poor in their efforts to escape from poverty.

They look to the future for their children with hope... they have immense faith in the value of education for social betterment.

(Caravedo *et al.* 1963: 180)

Between 1940 and 1972, school and university enrolments in Lima exceeded population growth, the proportion of the adult population with post-primary education more than doubled and the proportion of illiterates nearly halved. By 1973 the degree of illiteracy in the metropolitan labour force was less than 4 per cent and consisted mainly of older workers. Increased emphasis on credentialism in the labour market had produced a keen interest in vocational courses. This was reflected in a proliferation of small private 'academies' providing a range of certificates and diplomas, and enormous pressure on university places.

Class and gender differentials in access to education persisted to some extent, however. The labouring class clearly participated in the educational expansion, but it did so to a lesser degree than the middle class. A comparison of the educational levels of the manual and non-manual workforces in 1974 shows significant differences in levels of achievement. On average, non-manual employees had 10.7 years of education whereas manual workers had 5.5 years.

Table 3.10 shows significant gender differentials in education within and between both classes, with a particular discrepancy between non-manual and manual women.[39] In fact, women had participated strongly in the educational expansion with a marked improvement in educational levels during the period. The rise in women's levels was actually *faster* than men's, so gender inequalities in education were reducing (Scott 1986a: table 8.1). However, although there was much support for increasing women's access to education, it still took second place after men's. For example, fewer parents aspired to a professional job for their daughters than for their sons, and most expected them to enter the lower levels of white collar work (cf. Sara-Lafosse 1983: 11, Raffo 1985: 28–33).[40]

Women's increased access to education was partly conditioned by segregation within the educational system. According to Ministry of Labour data (1973), manual women who had done vocational training at secondary school had concentrated overwhelmingly in secretarial and domestic science courses while manual men had done bookkeeping and mechanical and electrical courses. Gurrieri (1971: 141) says that the vocational courses followed by women in the shanty towns were narrow in range and oriented towards 'female' occupations. These were, in order of popularity, dressmaking, secretarial, hairdressing, nursing, languages and bookkeeping. Similar findings have been reported in a host of more recent studies (Raffo 1985: 30, Anderson *et al.* 1979: 33–4, Chueca 1982: 12).

Table 3.10   Educational levels of the manual and non-manual workforces by sex, Lima 1974

	Non-manual		Manual	
	Men	*Women*	*Men*	*Women*
Higher	39	39	2	1
Secondary	45	56	42	27
Primary	15	5	55	60
Illiterate	1	*	2	12
Total	100	100	101	100

Source: Ministry of Labour employment survey 1974
* = <0.5%

This segregation by field was also present in higher education. In 1974, 78 per cent of men with higher education had specialized in engineering, economics, medical or pure sciences and law (compared with only 22 per cent of women). Women tended to specialize in education, social sciences (especially social work), the humanities, nursing and pharmacy. These fields accounted for just over two-thirds of women's professional training, and education alone was one-third of it (Ministry of Labour 1974 survey). Thus, although women were participating in the educational process as much as men, the sex-specificity of their courses tended to direct them to very different parts of the labour market.

There were strong generational differences in educational achievement in both classes, especially within the labouring class. Educational mobility data shows a 'ratchet effect' across the generations. Each successive generation usually managed to achieve a higher level than the preceding one, but only to the next level. Thus, the children of illiterate peasants usually managed to obtain primary education, while their children in turn went through to secondary education. On the whole, most of those who obtained access to higher education came from parents who already had secondary levels of education, and these were not usually peasants or workers. This 'ratchet' effect was much less developed amongst women than men, although it was present to a degree.

Economic growth and social change had produced an enormous desire for education amongst a population that saw it as the principle mechanism for upward mobility. This was matched by an increasing tendency towards educational credentialism in the labour market. There was a marked educational improvement in the whole population during the period of growth, amongst the labouring class as well as the middle class and girls as well as boys, but class and gender differentials did persist to some extent. However, educational changes were mainly intergenerational and therefore took time to work their way through the labour market. Because of this the mobility process was inter- rather than intragenerational, as we shall now see.

OCCUPATIONAL MOBILITY IN LIMA[41]

Peru may have been a highly unequal society, but it was also a very mobile one. This mobility was produced by the expansion of opportunities in the city, especially in middle-class occupations, coupled with migration and rising levels of education. We have already noted the rapid growth of white collar employment in Lima between 1940 and 1972. Table 3.11 shows that the proportion of employed men and women in non-manual employment was nearly double that of their fathers. While a very high proportion of non-manual fathers managed to secure similar employment for their offspring (69 per cent), the massive expansion in white collar jobs meant that these offspring were actually in the minority within the middle class. In fact, 61 per cent of non-manual employees in 1974 were upwardly mobile and just over a third of them were the sons or daughters of peasants.

Mobility between occupational groups, rather than across the broad non-manual/manual classes, shows even greater movement. For the sample as a whole, only 18 per cent were occupationally stable between generations; 61 per cent were upwardly mobile and 21 per cent downwardly mobile. The stable proportions within each group were generally less than 20 per cent and

Table 3.11 Intergenerational mobility between non-manual, manual and peasant classes, inflow and outflow, men and women, Lima 1974

Father's class position	Respondent's current class position				N
	Non-manual	*Manual*	*Total*		
non-manual	69	31	100		620
	39	8	18		
manual	29	71	100		1,435
	39	45	43		
peasants	18	82	100		1,285
	22	47	39		
total	32	68	100		
	100	100	100		
N	1,081	2,259			3,340

Source: Ministry of Labour employment survey 1974
Note: lower figures in each row = inflow; upper figures = outflow

in some cases less than 10 per cent. The only exceptions were skilled and semi-skilled workers who reached 31 per cent (see table 3.12). Because of the structural expansion at the top, upward mobility was particularly high there. However, it was also significant at the bottom because of migration from the peasantry. In fact, mobility from peasant fathers accounted for 63 per cent of total occupational mobility and just under half of all urban manual workers were of peasant origin.

Table 3.12   Proportions of stable, upward and downward intergenerational mobility, * by current occupational group, Lima 1974

Occupational group	Stable	Upwardly mobile	Downwardly mobile	Total	N
Managers	13	87	—	100	219
Professionals	16	76	8	100	157
Technicians	12	73	15	100	279
Office workers	13	64	23	100	426
Drivers	9	77	14	100	163
Skilled & semi-skilled workers	31	54	15	100	968
Sales workers	19	51	30	100	480
Unskilled & service workers	6	57	37	100	648
Total	18	61	21	100	3,340

Source: Ministry of Labour employment survey 1974
* Men and women in current job compared with father's job

Unusually, a high proportion of all upward mobility was medium- or long-distance mobility.[42] Only 29 per cent of all upwardly mobile persons moved into the adjacent group; 47 per cent moved two or three groups and 24 per cent moved four or more. This means that a high proportion of all mobility was across the broad categories of non-manual, manual and peasant employment; on this definition, 84 per cent of all upward mobility was *cross*-class mobility. On the other hand, downward mobility had a different pattern. At 21 per cent, the general rate of downward mobility was low and most of this was *intra*-class mobility. Thus non-manual employees who were downwardly mobile did not usually leave white collar employment altogether and manual workers who were downwardly mobile usually only came from skilled manual work. Much of this downward mobility was associated with sex and age. Women tended to enter lower status occupations than their fathers although they remained within the same class, and many old manual workers would take up lower status jobs towards the end of their working lives.

Turning to occupational mobility *within* generations, i.e. over the lifetime, we find much less mobility. However, the extent of overall movement over the lifetime may be disguised by the exceptionally high number of people (70 per cent) who were still in their first jobs at the time of the survey.[43] Amongst the remaining 30 per cent of the workforce who had been in more than one job at the time of the survey, there was a higher level of occupational stability compared with the intergenerational figures (table 3.13), although the mobility figures were still high. Almost half the workforce were currently in a different occupational group from their first one.

Table 3.13 Proportions of stable, upward and downward intragenerational mobility, by current occupational group, excluding first-time job-holders, Lima 1974

Occupational group	Stable	Upwardly mobile	Downwardly mobile	Total	N
Managers	9	91	—	100	80
Professionals	23	77	—	100	43
Technicians	20	76	4	100	70
Office workers	40	54	6	100	121
Drivers	22	66	12	100	65
Skilled & semi-skilled workers	47	45	8	100	350
Sales workers	14	43	43	100	120
Unskilled & service workers	57	8	34	100	169
Total	37	48	15	100	
N	373	490	155		1,018

Source: Ministry of Labour employment survey 1974

The biggest difference was the reduction of mobility amongst the labouring class – only 10 per cent of those currently in manual jobs had previously held agricultural jobs (the intergenerational figure was 47 per cent, and in the case of unskilled and service workers, 57 per cent). This reflects the fact that most migrants travelled to Lima at an early age and took up their first jobs in the city (see chapter 6). There was greater stability within skilled and semi-skilled work and a significant movement from skilled manual work into sales work – which is represented here as downward mobility.[44] Compared with the intergenerational figures then, there was much less movement into the labouring class from the peasantry, less movement from unskilled into skilled work and more downward (or lateral) mobility into sales work. The greater stability amongst office workers also suggests less intragenerational movement out of the labouring class into the middle class.

A crosstabulation between first job and current job, *including* first-time job-holders, shows a high degree of direct entry into both manual and non-manual employment: 86 per cent of those currently in non-manual jobs started there and 95 per cent of those in manual jobs did so too. Comparable figures for intergenerational movement were 40 per cent and 45 per cent respectively. This shows the power of education to effect direct entry into middle-class employment, even for those whose parents came from a different class. Most job changing was therefore restricted to movement *within* the broad manual and non-manual classes. Although a relatively high proportion of office workers were upwardly mobile from manual jobs, they were a small proportion of the total currently in non-manual employment (13 per cent), and an even smaller proportion of those who had started out in manual employment (6 per cent).

Taking both inter- and intragenerational figures together, the indication is that most cross-class mobility in Peru was achieved through migration and education rather than through job changing. The latter was mainly a means for mobility *within* classes.

GENDER AND OCCUPATIONAL MOBILITY

Before analysing whether women experienced the same amount of mobility as men, the methodological problem of measuring female mobility has to be addressed. Problems arise from the discontinuity in women's working lives and the high degree of occupational segregation. Under these circumstances, it may be appropriate to compare mobility between daughters and their mothers rather than their fathers. However, conventional practice has usually assumed that only the father's occupation is significant for mobility analysis and does not collect data on the mother. This was the situation with the Ministry of Labour 1974 survey. In the following analysis therefore, we have no alternative but to compare the occupations of fathers and daughters.

However, there is some justification for this procedure. Let us consider what such comparisons may or may not be useful for. The analysis of occupational mobility tells us about two things: (a) the movement of individuals between positions and (b) the transmission through the labour market of the class privileges and disadvantages of families. Much of the debate about the mobility of women has concerned this second aspect. The conventional argument is that since husbands and fathers are assumed to be the main breadwinners in the family, their occupation is the main determinant of family class position and the most meaningful basis for the study of family mobility. This assumption has been hotly contested in recent sociological debate on the grounds that women's occupations make a significant contribution to family welfare (see Goldthorpe 1983a, 1984, Stanworth 1984, Marshall *et al*. 1988). However, in this chapter I am not dealing with this aspect of mobility; the focus is on *individual* occupational mobility.

The question then is whether father–daughter occupational comparisons are meaningful given the high degree of occupational sex segregation. However, this problem may be overcome by using the appropriate degree of aggregation. If by 'position' we mean broad (one-digit) occupational groups, rather than specific jobs, then it is the general character of such groups that is relevant, which men and women in them both share, rather than differences within these occupational groups which may arise from gender segregation.

A second question, still at the level of individual mobility, is whether father–daughter comparisons are meaningful given the very different positions of men and women in the family. Women's mobility might be assessed better when measured against those who faced similar constraints, such as mothers and grandmothers.[45] There is certainly much validity to this position, but equally one can argue that if it is *gender* and mobility we are interested in, rather than just female mobility, it is comparisons of *sons* and *daughters* measured against a common reference point that is of interest. For these purposes, the father's occupation will do.

Looking first at movement between the broad occupational classes, non-manual, manual and peasants, we find that women as well as men experienced substantial upward mobility (table 3.14). The class origin of currently employed men and women was very similar; 18–19 per cent were from the middle class, 42–43 per cent from the labouring class and 39 per cent from the peasantry (table 3.14, cols iii and vi). The structural shift towards middle-class occupations was similar: whereas 19 per cent of their fathers had been in the middle class, 35 per cent of sons and 31 per cent of daughters were now in this class.

In terms of total upward mobility (bottom row, cols iii and vi), both men and women had similar rates (81–2 per cent); however, they were distributed slightly differently in the different classes. A higher proportion of men's mobility was into the middle class while more of women's mobility was into the labouring class. Mobile women thus tended to go less far than mobile

Table 3.14 Intergenerational mobility between non-manual, manual and peasant classes, inflow and outflow, Lima 1974

	Respondent's current class position					
	MEN			*WOMEN*		
Father's class position	Non-manual (i)	Manual (ii)	Total (iii)	Non-manual (iv)	Manual (v)	Total (vi)
Non-manual	70	30	100	67	33	100
	37	8	18	41	9	19
Manual	30	70	100	31	69	100
	37	46	43	43	42	42
Peasants	23	77	100	13	87	100
	26	45	39	16	49	39
Total	35	65	100	31	69	100
	100	99	100	100	100	100
Total upward mobility	63	45	82	59	49	81
(N	810	1,521	2,331	329	736	1,065)

Source: Ministry of Labour employment survey 1974
Note: lower figures in each row = inflow; upper figures = outflow

men. For example, of those from peasant backgrounds, only 13 per cent of the women had gained access to non-manual jobs but 24 per cent of the men had done so; and there was a much higher proportion of upwardly mobile men than women amongst current non-manual employees. On the other hand, women were more susceptible to downward mobility: of those who had non-manual fathers, a slightly higher proportion of daughters had ended up in manual jobs than sons.

At the level of one-digit occupational groups, the differences between men's and women's mobility patterns were more marked: particularly the more constrained distance of women's upward mobility and their greater downward mobility. Overall, women still had high rates of intergenerational mobility, even if slightly below that of men (57 per cent compared with 63 per cent) and a very high proportion of it was cross-class mobility (table 3.15).[46]

However, they were much more likely to move across broad class boundaries into the *lower* stratum of the next, whereas men seem to have been able

Table 3.15 Proportions of stable, upward and downward intergenerational mobility by sex and current occupational group

Occupational group	Stable	Upwardly mobile	Downwardly mobile	Total	N
MEN					
Managers	13	87	–	100	196
Professionals	16	77	7	100	120
Technicians	10	77	13	100	180
Office workers	15	66	19	100	260
Drivers	9	77	14	100	162
Skilled & semi-skilled workers	32	55	13	100	802
Sales workers	21	51	28	100	297
Unskilled & service workers	7	57	36	100	260
Subtotal	*20*	*63*	*17*	*100*	*2,277*
WOMEN					
Managers	13	87	–	100	23
Professionals	16	76	8	100	37
Technicians	16	67	17	100	99
Office workers	10	61	29	100	166
Drivers		*			1
Skilled & semi-skilled workers	28	47	25	100	166
Sales workers	15	53	32	100	183
Unskilled & service workers	5	57	38	100	386
Subtotal	*13*	*57*	*30*	*100*	*1,061*

Source: Ministry of Labour employment survey 1974
* Number too small for meaningful statistics

to leapfrog this group and achieve entry into the higher levels. For example, amongst women of peasant origin just over half were currently in unskilled and service work and a fifth were in sales work. On the other hand, amongst men of peasant origin, just under half were in the upper echelons of the labouring class in skilled and driving work.

Table 3.15 shows that 30 per cent of the women were downwardly mobile compared with only 17 per cent of the men. Most of this was mobility within their class, to office work and sales or service work, but a significant amount was also cross-class mobility – daughters of middle-class fathers who had become dressmakers. This downward mobility contributed to the high educational levels of women in skilled manual jobs.

In summary, women had a surprising amount of intergenerational occupational mobility: not only were the rates high, but they were extensive throughout the occupational structure. Differences between men's and women's mobility patterns were slight compared with the more general trends in absolute levels. These findings are consistent with the fact that women participated strongly in both migration and educational improvement.

This analysis has focused on inter- rather than intragenerational mobility, but the degree of mobility experienced over individual women's lifetimes may have been very different. Unfortunately I have not been able to include a study of intragenerational mobility by sex because the withdrawal of women after marriage reduced the numbers too much for any sensible quantitative analysis. However, the analysis of manual career trajectories in chapter 6 suggests a substantial divergence between men and women, with men achieving upward mobility towards the end of their working lives and women experiencing downward mobility or stagnation. This downward trajectory in the labour market may, however, have been offset by upward *social* mobility through marriage.

INEQUALITY, MOBILITY AND THE CLASS STRUCTURE

We have seen that the mobility process in Lima during the 1970s was extensive; it affected both the middle class and the labouring class, and men and women. Because it was so extensive, the size of the intergenerational core[47] in each occupational group was rather small, and although it was somewhat larger in the broad class categories of white collar and manual work, it was still less than 50 per cent. This means that the intergenerational transmission of class experience was playing a relatively small part in the creation of class identities and organizations. Rather it could be argued that it was the common experience of *mobility* and its consolidation through individual and collective action that was structuring class consciousness in Lima.

Most of the labouring class, for example, had experienced some upward intergenerational mobility. Compared to their parents, many found themselves in vastly different circumstances in the city and they could with some justification aspire to a similar change for their children. Their strategies for mobility therefore involved an enormous stress on formal education and apprenticeships for their children together with strenuous efforts to consolidate their own position within their class. Both of these strategies required some degree of collective action – building schools, improving the neighbourhood etc.

The family, community and regional associations[48] played an important role here. These provided the skills and credentials, the contact networks, the information and the resources necessary for access to higher status jobs. They canalized mobility from the peasantry into the urban labour and housing markets (see next chapter), as well as serving as a basis for the consolidation of class position. Although these institutions had strong rural roots, they were more concerned with achieving urban integration than with reminiscing about their common origins. Effectively, they collectivized the aspirations and experiences of the upwardly mobile and thus played a role in mediating the relationship between individuals and classes. To the extent that they expressed group identities and solidarities within classes, they can be seen as class institutions. However, they sometimes acted as a segmenting force when there was competition between groups for resources, and they could also become cross-class groupings where some of the members had become mobile, creating conflicts of loyalties as regards class.

This chapter has shown how economic growth generated a process of structural expansion and diversification; increasing inequality being combined with rising incomes and occupational mobility. However, while the latter processes were beginning to erode boundaries between classes, especially between the middle and the labouring class, distinctions based on status such as ethnicity and culture continued to perpetuate them.

As we have seen, the middle class expanded extremely fast during the industrialization period in Peru. Unlike their counterparts in the older industrial countries, their economic base was not so much based on private accumulation within family firms, as on the expansion of the state and the rise of middle management in the private sector. Their prime resource was therefore education rather than property or capital. This implied an economic vulnerability that was to become all too evident during the recession when public sector expenditure was cut. Yet in periods of expansion they were able to mobilize politically to protect their market situation.

Although originally recruited from a 'white', urban background, the middle class expanded too fast to be able to maintain this exclusivity. Its reliance on the labour market and education permitted substantial upward mobility from the ethnically and culturally distinct classes below. Despite this, the core of traditional values and behaviour patterns persisted, partly because it was underpinned by the elites, on whose patronage the middle class depended, and partly because the new recruits to the middle class assimilated these values through the same mechanisms. However, the latter retained some loyalty to their social origins, through family links and community associations. In both economic and normative terms then, the boundary between the middle and labouring class was fuzzy.

In other respects, however, a gap remained between the two. Despite considerable labour market heterogeneity within the labouring class, the physical and social conditions of manual work were still clearly differentiated from that of white collar work, and this was true of jobs in small workshops, factories, private homes and on the street. All involved harsh conditions, great strenuous effort, a low level of economic reward relative to their subsistence needs, and the low status of manual work. As we shall see in chapter 9 there was a sense of a shared labouring-class identity based on the common experiences of poverty, hard work and economic uncertainty. A common identity was also promoted by shared deprivation in terms of housing[49] and by cultural and ethnic differences.

Traditionally, the oligarchy and the urban middle class had always exhibited disdain and contempt for the labouring class and the peasants. These attitudes were perpetuated by stereotypes that contained a good deal of class prejudice and racism, as well as ignorance of the real situation of urban workers. For example, they were still characterized as illiterate Indians, rural migrants who lacked 'urban culture' and who were irrelevant to the urban economy and parasites on the state. Such notions persisted despite evidence that migrants readily assimilated urban values and behaviour patterns, were not illiterate (any more), performed an important role in the urban economy and bore more than their share of the costs of infrastructural and social services. This disdain and contempt was expressed in the workplace, in public places, in the press and in casual conversation. It was exemplified by derogatory terms such as 'los recien bajados' (those recently come down from the *sierra*) or 'cholos de mierda' (bloody half-castes). Ultimately it was reflected in the violence and disregard for human life with which workers' protests were met.

One reason for the persistence of these class stereotypes is that classes were to a great extent insulated from one another. On the one hand, a large proportion of the labouring class was self-employed or worked in small workshops and their families lived in clearly segregated residential districts, and on the other, the middle class were largely encapsulated in bureaucracies which employed very few manual workers. The exception to this were middle-class women who employed servants in their homes. My case studies showed that many of these women were guilty of the worst class prejudice and racism.

Such attitudes were a reflection of power relations between classes. The element of domination has always been to the forefront of relations between classes in Peru because of the harshness of traditional landlord–peasant relations. Power was experienced from below as coercion and corruption, while subordination was perceived from above as submission and servility. Notions of representation, participation or consensus were relatively absent.[50] Racism legitimized the arbitrary use of authority amongst the dominant classes, and cultural separatism on the part of the subordinated classes was a defence against it (see Isbell 1978). The status correlates of class were manifestations of this particular quality of power relations between classes and its intertwining with culture and ethnicity, rather than merely differences in life style.

The status divide between the middle and labouring classes affected gender relations, the women within each class tending to identify with their men and their families, rather than with women from a different class. We have seen in this chapter that women participated actively in the growth process, they migrated, obtained better education, better jobs and became occupationally mobile. They benefited from rising aspirations and they reproduced these aspirations in their own children. Relative gender inequality increased because the pace of women's progress was less than men's, not because they were excluded from it altogether. However, while the processes of economic growth and mobility were tending to blur the boundaries between classes, they were augmenting the gap between middle- and labouring-class women. In this case, economic divisions were confirming status divisions, rather than modifying them. In fact, changing attitudes were coming from the political sphere, from feminism, rather than from the economy. However, as we shall see in chapter 9, labouring-class women were wary of approaches from middle-class feminists (see also Radcliffe 1988).

There is a paradox, however, between the persistence of status divisions between classes and high rates of upward social mobility. One might expect that social distinctions would be diluted by mobility and that classes might come to be viewed as open and meritocratic. On the other hand, mobility often provokes an offensive reaction by those anxious to preserve traditional divisions, which in turn creates resentment amongst the mobile themselves. There was still a surprising amount of hostility and suspicion between classes in Lima in 1974, and a perception amongst urban workers that the Peruvian class system was rigid and elitist. Despite the high rates of mobility in Peru, it appears that traditional class attitudes were slow to change.

In summary, although growth, rising living standards and occupational mobility were beginning to modify the economic basis of class in Peru, social and political relations were much slower to change. Heterogeneity within classes and mobility between them increased, preventing the development of stable class cores, but traditional power and status relationships survived these changes, offsetting economic decomposition and preserving class identities and institutions. Thus although the labouring class in Lima did experience some improvement in living standards through migration, mobility and rising incomes, they continued to perceive a deep social gulf between them and the rich and powerful (see chapter 9). The rest of this book will consider the implications of these processes of differentiation and mobility for the labouring class and their families, and the effects on class consciousness and political action.

4   Family, gender and the labouring class

Just as Peru was a highly unequal class society, it was also a profoundly patriarchal one; men enjoyed considerable privilege and power with respect to women. Moreover, just as class was modified by growth and mobility, so also was gender. These processes were not independent of one another, for class relations played an important role in shaping and re-shaping gender inequality in Peru. In turn, gender contributed to the construction and consolidation of social classes. It was manipulated by different classes and ethnic groups as part of the stratification process, e.g. the consolidation of property, the acquisition of labour market advantage, the preservation of status, etc., and was itself changed in the process. The reciprocal influences of class and gender were the product of a wider set of links between family, the economy, and political power. Family and kinship were important for the control and transmission of property (large estates as well as peasant plots), the organization of peasant and informal production, the recruitment of labour in the formal labour market, the acquisition of housing and the consolidation of life styles and access to political office and the distribution of public services.

Peruvian society was strongly familial. The family was a major institution for all social classes, not just for domestic organization, but for economic, political, religious and recreational life. The family had strong ideological force, with the power to invoke moral authority and social solidarity within the nuclear and extended family, and beyond it. This was true of all social classes. Even amongst the poor, where poverty might be expected to threaten the viability of the family, it had retained strength and resilience.

Despite differences in family patterns, certain features were common to all classes: (a) the state and the Roman Catholic Church were the prime legitimators of family roles; (b) there was a patrilineal bias in terms of access to property, although women had significant inheritance rights; (c) although the nuclear family was the normal residential unit, extended kin relations were highly valued; (d) there was a strict separation of male and female roles;

(e) relations within the family were authoritarian; and (f) there was some regulation of female sexuality.

Within this broad pattern, family and gender varied between classes and ethnic groups in terms of the form and content of male/female roles, the degree of female subordination and the nature of the gender ideology that underpinned it. These variations originated in the Spanish colonial situation where a foreign culture and institutions were implanted in an indigenous society that was organized on very different principles. Spanish culture consolidated amongst the urban-resident propertied classes, while amongst the peasants, pre-hispanic structures and ideologies persisted, albeit in modified form. After Independence, this situation continued because of the persistence of class and ethnic divisions and the social institutions associated with them. During the industrialization period, the peasants were increasingly influenced by ideologies emanating from the city, while the growing labouring class combined elements of rural and urban gender relations. Gender, class and ethnicity thus interacted historically to produce variations in family patterns that had their most contrasting elements at the opposite ends of the social structure and various combinations in between.

The labouring-class family was caught between two different traditions and absorbed elements of both, which makes it difficult to interpret their labour market behaviour in terms of a single set of values and preferences. Aspects of the peasant family were reproduced in the city not just because most labouring-class adults had peasant origins, but because the kinship networks that linked peasants and urban migrants played an important role in the urban economy and in local neighbourhoods. On the other hand, the formal institutions of urban society, such as the educational system, state bureaucracies, the media and formal sector employers, whose policies affected the labouring class in various ways, were imbued with the gender assumptions of the elites. For these reasons the analysis of the labouring-class family has to be placed within the context of other class-specific family patterns.

In this chapter I shall describe the 'bourgeois', 'peasant' and 'labouring-class' family in ideal-typical form. An ideal-type is an analytical device constructed by social scientists for heuristic purposes, usually to draw out comparisons of different types of social phenomena. In this case, the purpose is to reveal the sources of different elements of family structure and gender relations in the labouring class. Ideal-types necessarily involve a simplification of reality, based on predominant trends, and cannot do justice to the full diversity which is found in real life. Before commencing the analysis, however, it is necessary to mention some of the theoretical problems involved in analysing the family.

ANALYSING THE FAMILY

Although there is agreement about the central role of the family in the underpinning of gender divisions, there have been many differences of opinion over its analysis – whether it is a benign or conflictual institution and whether gender differences are complementary or exploitative. There is also ambiguity about how the 'family' is constituted – as an ideological construct or as a structure, and how 'family' relates to 'household' and 'kinship'.

In the Latin American literature, three distinct and separate traditions have emerged: (a) anthropological analyses of kinship, usually carried out in rural areas, (b) studies of household structure, particularly in poor urban households and (c) studies of gender ideology, especially *machismo*.[1] Each of these traditions brings different elements to the analysis of the family but only tells part of the story. For example, kinship studies have not usually addressed the question of power relations between men and women,[2] while those that focus on the household relations ignore the role of kinship in underpinning these relations. There is a general tendency to explain inequality in terms of *machismo* in a relatively simplistic, stereotyped way, without showing how this ideology produces structural effects.

In my view there is a need for a systematic framework for analysing gender inequality within the family which combines the three approaches mentioned above. I have found it useful to work with four basic elements: the division of labour, the distribution of resources, the distribution of power, and the legitimating ideology. The *division of labour* refers to the detailed differentiation of tasks and responsibilities that are associated with family roles (gender is not the only aspect here, seniority is also important). The *distribution of resources* refers to the distribution of consumption goods and services necessary for the reproduction of the family on a day-to-day basis (e.g. food and shelter) as well as generationally (e.g. care for the young and the old). Where the family is a production unit, the distribution of productive resources is also important (land, tools, etc.). The *distribution of power* refers to the structure of internal decision-making, forms of control over different family members (children as well as women), and the ways in which the family is represented in the wider community. The *legitimating ideology* of the family consists of the norms, values and symbols that underpin gender divisions within the family and the processes of socialization which reproduce it. Gender ideology does not always reflect the actual division of labour and resources in the family. For example, it is common to find a stress on equality and solidarity amongst family members even in the face of marked inequality. Family ideologies often have a strong naturalistic element, so that gender is represented as an inherent part of the human condition rather than a social product.

In analysing the family, it is important to look at the kinship system as well as concrete structures, such as the household or extended family network. Despite the fact that most family activities may be framed by these structures, it is the kinship system that establishes guiding principles for the division of labour and the allocation of resources there. It thus influences the basic structure of households and the pattern of internal relationships, although there is much that is not laid down by kinship rules. Kinship is essentially a set of organizational principles and has material effectivity through law, the state and the economy, but it also exists as ideology in that it attributes values to these principles. Like all ideologies, however, actual practices may deviate from its normative prescriptions. Thus a kinship system that appears to stress functional complementarity between men and women may coexist with actual relations that are full of tension and conflict.

A second point, which is linked to this, is that the family should not necessarily be seen as a coherent institution, either inherently consensual or inherently conflictual; it may be both. Not only is there the problem of divergence between normative and actual behaviour but there are often contradictions within family structure or ideology itself, for instance, between inequality and complementarity, authority and solidarity. As we shall see, both the peasantry and the labouring class had a strong ideology of kinship solidarity, despite the existence of gender and age inequality and highly authoritarian relations along these axes of differentiation. In the last chapters of this book, I shall argue that the ambiguity between inequality and solidarity within the family was extended to the labouring class as a whole, providing an ideological basis for wider solidarities despite internal differentiation created by the labour market.

ON PATRIARCHY

There has been much debate within feminism over the usefulness or otherwise of the concept of 'patriarchy'. In this book the term is used in a fairly loose descriptive sense to refer to institutionalized patterns of gender relations which involve inequalities of power, sexuality and resource allocation favouring men over women. No assumptions are made here about the universality or transhistorical nature of patriarchy; nor are any claims made for 'original causes' (e.g. men's control over women's labour or sexuality) or for the primacy of patriarchy in relation to other systems of inequality such as class and race.[3] Despite its problems, I use the term because it provides a better summary indication of male–female inequality than any other term produced so far.[4] It captures the gender-specific nature of women's oppression and indicates that this is rooted in, although not necessarily confined to, the family.

ON *MACHISMO*

Most of the literature on Latin America refers to *machismo* in the charac-
terization of gender relations. Entire institutions and Latin American society
and culture as a whole have been characterized by it (e.g. Latin American and
Caribbean Women's Collective 1980). The term has acquired general cur-
rency throughout the western world, but its meaning is far from clear. Like
patriarchy, everyone recognizes it, but no-one can agree on a definition. In
essence, *machismo* is an ideology of masculinity which emphasizes male
dominance and virility. It defines relations between men (aggression, honour,
pride) as well as men's behaviour towards women (sexual conquest, jealousy,
possessiveness). *Machismo* relies on a dual sexual morality which expects
promiscuity of men and chastity of women, and this necessarily involves a
dual categorization of women consisting of 'good' and 'bad' women (see e.g.
Arnold 1978). The former are associated with spiritual purity, fidelity,
passivity and procreation, while the latter are associated with sexual licence
and passion. *Machismo* is underpinned by a patrilineal kinship system, a legal
system that endorses male power within the household, prostitution and
illegitimacy, and a separation between public and private spheres. It is
primarily an ideology, i.e. a set of normative prescriptions and values, and
does not necessarily reflect actual behaviour. However, it has structural
effects which undermine women's position in the family and wider society.

The origins of *machismo* are usually traced to the Spanish Conquest and
Roman Catholicism; the former provided the definition of masculinity and
the latter, femininity (Youssef 1974, Stevens 1973). However, it has altered
over the years, it takes slightly different forms in different Latin American
countries, and above all, it varies in different social classes. Historically, it
was mainly associated with the ruling elites and with urban culture. It is likely
that it reached its apogee amongst the late nineteenth-century bourgeoisie,
whence it was progressively espoused by the petit bourgeoisie and mestizos.
Many claim that it is now most strongly held by the urban poor and peasants,
although this is contested by others (Stevens 1973: 91). Some authors argue
that recent liberalizing trends amongst the urban middle classes have led to
a diminution in *machismo*, others contend that there has merely been a change
in its form (Barrig 1979). Despite these changes and social variations,
however, the stress on male dominance and virility has remained unchal-
lenged as the hegemonic gender ideology. Clearly it is important to include
machismo in the analysis of gender relations in Latin America, but it must be
situated within specific contexts of time and place and linked to family
structures.

THE BOURGEOIS FAMILY

The bourgeois family was the dominant influence on the major social institutions in Peru and hence had repercussions for peasants and the labouring class. It was an urban phenomenon, specifically associated with the oligarchy and the middle classes. (I have used the term 'bourgeois' in preference to 'oligarchic' to denote its wider urban social base.) Its main features were a segregation between public and private spheres, women's confinement to the latter, and their economic and social dependence on men. Gender roles in the bourgeois family were strongly influenced by *machismo*.

The main features of the bourgeois family were laid down during the early colonial period. The hispanic tradition of a patrilineal, monogamous Roman Catholic family was imposed by the Spanish Crown and the Church as part of its regulation of the hispanic settler society.[5] It was further consolidated by the early colonial elites as a means of creating a quasi-aristocracy that was ethnically and culturally homogeneous.[6] The gender ideology associated with it was strongly influenced by Roman Catholicism and Spanish notions of honour (Chaney 1979: 40–3, cf. Youssef 1974: 89–94, Gutiérrez 1984). It stressed the separation of male and female roles; men were associated with war, bravery, and power, and women with the family and religion.

However, women were not necessarily confined to the home at this stage. They were able to inherit and administer property in their own right, were often active as *encomenderas*, landowners, rentiers and money lenders. They were also involved in the welfare institutions run by the Catholic Church, i.e. hospitals, mission schools and orphanages (Burkett 1977, Lockhart 1968: 163, Prieto de Zegarra 1980: chapter 8). There was a disdain for menial work; in the majority of these hispanic families, even those of artisans and small shopkeepers, much of the domestic work was done by household slaves (Lockhart 1968).

Social status was strongly linked to control over women's sexuality while concubinage was widely practised by men, especially with Indian and mestizo women. The particular combination of patriarchal, class and ethnic domination gave Spanish colonists the notion that they were entitled to the sexual services of their subjects and protégées.[7] Thus a predatory tradition towards lower-class women, particularly those in domestic service, was established that survived well into modern times.[8]

During the mid-nineteenth century there appears to have been a greater emphasis on the domesticity of women and a decline in their independent access to economic resources. In part this was the result of a new emphasis in Roman Catholicism on the cult of Maria, which stressed virginity, chastity and the mother role (Barrig 1979: 44–5, cf. Stevens 1973). It was also an effect of Peru's integration into the international economy and the increasing exposure of the Peruvian elites to European gender ideologies.[9] With the rise of new forms of wealth and increased social mobility amongst the urban bourgeoisie, there was a stress on family respectability (*decencia*) as the basis of claims to social status (Barrig 1979: 25, Wilson 1985).[10] Women's access to property was also being redefined during this period. Although marriage was being strengthened as the basis for amalgamating property and social standing, women were being increasingly distanced from productive assets as property owners and were much less able to participate in the growing economy as entrepreneurs (Wilson 1984).[11]

Well into this century, the Catholic Church played a pivotal role both as an independent legitimator of bourgeois family and gender ideologies (e.g. via papal encyclicals) and the agency that transmitted this ideology to other institutions.[12] Many of the daughters of the elites and the middle classes were educated in convents, where the association between femininity, virginity and spirituality was emphasized (Barrig 1979: 53–4). Women were not expected to pursue education for its own sake, but merely to acquire moral virtue and to improve their social skills and hence their stakes in the marriage market (Barrig 1979: 22, 65–7, 81). The only educational skills that were approved for women were those associated with education and welfare. The Church controlled a significant part of the university sector, where the traditional professions were emphasized. 'Working for a living' was considered shameful.[13] The only acceptable occupations were connected with welfare and charity work, and even these were only to be pursued as a hobby or a spiritual vocation. The world of politics was not considered to be appropriate for women (Chaney 1973, 1979).

Much of the contemporary legislation governing women's rights and status, which was formulated during the first thirty years of this century, was influenced by the bourgeois family ideology. Ironically, this period saw a liberalization of many other aspects of Peruvian society, particularly in class relations, but it did not affect the family. Important labour legislation was passed in 1918 and was strongly paternalistic. The Penal Code which still regulates sexuality and legalizes prostitution was passed in 1924. In 1933 came the promulgation of a new constitution, but despite declaring that women and men should have equal rights, women received only limited suffrage (the right to vote in municipal elections). National suffrage was only introduced in 1955 (one of the last countries in Latin America to do so), and even then literacy restrictions excluded large numbers of peasant women (Roca and Rodriguez 1978).[14] This restriction was only finally lifted in 1980. The most important source of family law in the 1970s was the 1936 Civil Code: a clear expression of bourgeois gender ideology. This code recognized civil and religious marriage as well as separation, divorce and concubinage.

The legal state of *sociedad conjugal* established by marriage had a highly patriarchal division of responsibilities.[15]

Barrig suggests that the bourgeois family began to change during the 1960s. Important agents for change were the extension of women's education, especially within the state sector; the increased availability of contraception; the influence of a more 'liberated' international media; the radicalization of the Catholic Church and the growth of feminism (Barrig 1979: 76). The educational levels of middle-class girls were rising and the labour force participation of married professional women increasing. Yet certain features of traditional gender roles remained. For example, the increase in the participation rates of wives was dependent on the employment of servants rather than the participation of husbands in domestic activities (Sara-Lafosse 1978, Seminario 1984), and middle-class girls continued to be oriented towards traditional educational and occupational careers. Women's increased access to education and employment during the 1960s and 1970s, described in the previous chapter, was thus premised on the assumption that they would remain firmly within the female domain. Their improvement in opportunities was a product of the modernization of that domain, rather than an abandonment of it.

THE PEASANT FAMILY[16]

Traditionally, gender relations were structured very differently amongst the peasantry compared with the urban bourgeoisie. Women were much more participant in the economy and had independent access to the major resource, land, through a bilateral inheritance system. Although they were responsible for most domestic activities, they were by no means confined to them. At the symbolic level, there was an emphasis on complementarity of genders and the unity of the sexes in the spiritual world. However, despite this apparent egalitarianism, there was a degree of inequality between men and women and some evidence that this had been increasing in recent years.

The kinship system played a central role in resource allocation in the villages: it was the main mechanism for the transmission of property, the organization of production, and the distribution of consumption goods and welfare services. As peasants were drawn into a wider labour market, the kinship system determined who should migrate and what should be done with their earnings. Gradually kinship networks extended outwards from rural areas to encompass urban informal production and wage work in mines, plantations and factories. As they did so, the structure of the peasant family was transplanted into the city, where it strongly influenced the labouring-class family and manual labour markets.

Kinship relations were not confined to the nuclear family or household, but encompassed a wider network of extended kin, including fictive kin (the *compadrazgo* system which linked parents and godparents of the same child). Because of a high degree of intermarriage between neighbouring peasants and the use of fictive kinship to link persons otherwise unrelated, these networks could be dense and extensive.

In the peasant villages, land and labour were scarce resources. Access to them was maximized through the principle of reciprocity[17] – the mutual exchange of cash, goods, labour and other services – and this was defined through kinship. These exchanges formed an ongoing set of social obligations parallel to and interwoven with the market. Different types of reciprocity were demarcated terminologically and ritually, and close accounts of debts and credits were kept (Mayer 1974). They included individual favours, the organization of collective working parties, and community labour. They occurred between nuclear, extended and fictive kin (*compadres*), and between those living within the peasant community and those scattered by migration. Reciprocity was the key to the peasants' economic survival and the major defence mechanism through which they confronted society (Isbell 1977: 83).

Originally, reciprocity had developed in the Andes as a means of exchanging products between vertically differented ecological zones (livestock from the high altitude plains, agricultural products from the temperate middle regions and *coca* from the subtropical forest (see Mayer and Alberti 1974, Lehmann 1982). However, as peasants were drawn into the wider economy and the family became differentiated geographically and economically, kinship reciprocity was mobilized to exchange goods and services between town and country.[18] For example, a villager might herd the flocks or cultivate the patch of a brother who migrated to the city, while the latter would take the former's son as an apprentice (Smith 1975, 1979, 1984, Mayer 1974, Campaña 1982).[19] Incomes generated in one part of the network were often used in another, and this was crucial for setting up small enterprises in the city. Smith refers to these networks as 'confederations of households' and Campaña as 'diversified family enterprises'. Within them, capital, resources and labour circulated according to the norms of reciprocity.

Reciprocity was as much about the ideology of mutuality as real relations of exchange, and these were not always the same. Reciprocity could conceal class and gender exploitation (Orlove 1977, Sanchez 1982, Brass 1986). Women and children were often used to pay off the debts of male kinsmen, and poor relatives, the debts of rich ones. The literature on debt bondage (*enganche*) has shown how these chains of kinship debts could merge with commercial ones (e.g. Brass 1986).

Compadrazgo was another case where the egalitarian ideology of mutual help could accompany unequal relationships. It was often used for seeking favours for patrons in a different class, and these in return would be able to enjoy the cheap labour of their *compadres'* kin (Orlove 1974, 1977). *Compadrazgo* relations were commonly used as a means of recruiting domestic servants (Bunster and Chaney 1985, Sindicato de Trabajadores del Hogar 1982). Young girls would be taken to 'ayudar en casa' (help in the home) in return for education. This occurred amongst labouring-class families as well as amongst the middle and upper classes, the status of the girl in question shading imperceptibly from kinsman into servant. Skeldon states that the recruitment of servants from peasant communities via *compadrazgo* relations between peasants and local notables was the crucial mechanism that set in motion a complex process of migration via kinship networks (Skeldon 1974: 215).

Within the kinship system, gender and seniority were the main principles of differentiation. At the ideological level, there was a stress on complementarity and parallelism between the sexes which goes back to Inca times (Burkett 1977, 1978, Silverblatt 1978, 1980). Complementarity was manifested in a bilateral system of descent and inheritance which gave women independent access to property, prior to and throughout marriage; a segregation between male and female roles that attributed equal value to each; and a cosmology that legitimized this complementarity and expressed it symbolically (Nuñez del Prado 1975a, 1975b, Bolton and Mayer 1977, Isbell 1978, Skar 1979, 1981). The family was viewed as a solitary unit, with a functional division of labour and a dual structure of decision-making. However, there was inequality within the family with respect to power and authority, as we shall see below.

There was a marked segregation between men's and women's activities in the home and on the farm (Nuñez del Prado 1975a, 1975b, 1982, Skar 1979, Bourque and Warren 1981, Deere 1982, Radcliffe 1986a, 1986b).[20] Children were assigned economic roles at an early age[21] and thereafter men were responsible for sons and the women for daughters (Nuñez del Prado 1982, Isbell 1978). The segregation between male and female activities was not confined to the home and farm; it extended to the wider network of kinship relationships. Men were involved in reciprocity with male kin and women with female kin (Bourque and Warren 1981: 144–9). The same appears to be true of fictive kinship (*compadrazgo*).[22] Thus the forms of reciprocity, the composition of the networks and the content of the exchanges tended to reflect the gender-segregated nature of men's and women's activities.[23]

With the incorporation of the peasantry into the wider society it appears that gender became increasingly unequal within the family. In many areas, peasant women tended to stay at home to mind the farm while the men went off to work for wages (Laite 1981, Campaña 1982, Villalobos 1978, Deere 1982).[24] However, the peasant economy was becoming unprofitable compared with the higher wages commanded by men. Education became a better investment for boys than for girls, producing a large sex-differential in educational levels in the countryside (Campaña 1982, Babb 1985, Radcliffe 1986b). This gave men greater familiarity with the Spanish language (see Villalobos 1975: 19–27), increasing their status within the community.

It is difficult to obtain a clear picture of the distribution of power within the peasant family because it has been ignored in many kinship studies, or else an equality of power has been inferred (but not demonstrated) from the structure of the division of labour and the ideology of complementarity. However, it seems that men had more power within the home and community. Women had long been marginalized from community institutions;[25] although they might be present at assemblies they were not consulted directly and rarely spoke (Bourque and Warren 1981: chapter 7, Sarávia 1982, Radcliffe 1986b). Although they participated in such activities as land invasions, they were not usually involved in the leadership of peasant organizations.

Within the family, authority rested on gender and seniority. There was an emphasis on obedience and 'respect' and physical coercion played an integral part in the socialization and disciplinary process (Caravedo *et al.* 1963: 237, 251, Bolton 1972: 96, Escobar 1973: 86–7, La Jara 1983: 14). There is some evidence of violence against wives (Bolton 1974: 48–52, Caravedo *et al.* 1963: 250, Sindicato de Trabajadores del Hogar 1982, Stein 1974, Bourque and Warren 1981: 108–9, Nuñez del Prado 1982), especially linked to men's drinking and disputes over property (Boyden 1983). It would appear that physical violence was practised at many levels: by parents against children, husbands against wives, and by older siblings against younger ones (Sindicato de Trabajadores del Hogar 1982: 36–9).[26] The large number of children who came to Lima in order to escape from their homes bears witness to this (see Caravedo *et al.* 1963: 254).[27]

Various writers have maintained that *machismo* was traditionally absent from peasant society (e.g. Skar 1979, Wilson 1983, Bolton 1972: 211), arguing that there was little emphasis on men's sexual prowess and little control over women's sexuality.[28] Femininity was defined by fecundity and industry rather than physical beauty or sexual virtue, and masculinity by bravery and aggressiveness rather than sexual conquest. However, control over the sexuality of *married* women does figure in some monographs, and jealousy is often cited as the cause of violence against them (e.g. Bourque and Warren 1981). There was also some concubinage, particularly amongst rich peasants (Bolton 1972: 65–6, Boyden, personal communication). Various studies report that the conception of virility amongst peasant men was changing (Babb 1985), with an increase in predatory attitudes towards women and the frequenting of brothels in nearby rural towns (Escobar 1973: 88). There is scattered evidence of abandonment of wives, failure to marry pregnant girls and the development of bigamous relationships with women in the city.[29] Many urban workers reported experience of family break-up in their communities of origin. Of my case studies, 29 per cent had been abandoned or orphaned when they were children. In Mercado's study of women street sellers, most of whom were from the *sierra*, 22 per cent had never known their father (Mercado 1978: 24, see also Caravedo *et al.* 1963: 252).

There is a clear ambiguity between the egalitarian division of labour and its accompanying ideology of gender complementarity on the one hand, and the authoritarian power structure and the declining status of women, on the other. This ambiguity was the product of the interaction between class and gender in peasants' relations with the wider society and, as they became more differentiated socio-economically, within their own communities too (Mallon 1986). Despite its internal contradictions, however, rural women had more autonomy and economic participation than their sisters in the city, even if more hardship.

THE LABOURING-CLASS FAMILY[30]

Much of the literature on family structure amongst the urban poor paints a picture of instability, magnifying the plight of female-headed households and deploring high fertility rates and illegitimacy. In Lima during the period under review, the picture was very different. The labouring-class family showed surprising strength and stability, legal marriage was the norm rather than the exception, there was a relatively low proportion of female-headed households, and falling fertility rates. Extended kinship networks were the basis for widespread cooperation in the community and labour market.

The labouring-class family was influenced by both the peasant and the bourgeois family. Rural principles of kinship solidarity and cooperation had been transplanted into the urban environment and provided a major basis for social and economic organization. Aspects of gender and age differentiation were also transferred including the expectation that women and children should contribute to the household income. However, many labouring-class men had begun to absorb the *machista* attitudes of the middle class, with the accompanying expectation that their wives should stay at home while they enjoyed sexual freedom. The combination of traditional rural authoritarianism and *machista* attitudes of male dominance resulted in violence against many women.

Kinship, reciprocity and the labouring class

Kinship networks played an important role in structuring neighbourhoods, labour markets and formal organizations in Lima. This was particularly true of first generation migrants, but it was also generalized amongst the labouring class as a whole. People from the *sierra* were referred to as sheep because they 'moved together in herds' (Caravedo *et al.* 1963: 231, Lobo 1982: 73). Kinship was a major mechanism of formal and informal resource allocation, it was a basis for day-to-day interaction and it provided a defence against hostility from other urban groups.

As Skeldon (1974, 1977a) and others have noted, kinship networks provided crucial information about jobs and housing, and the mechanism for obtaining both. Many studies have shown migrants usually had a job lined up for them on arrival in the city, or spent very little time getting one (Martinez *et al.* 1973). Since kinship overlapped with locality in the country-side, these networks were as much about common birthplace (*paisanía*) as family, and incurred similar norms of reciprocity.

The gradual build-up of these networks could lead to the invasion of whole occupations and parts of an enterprise by kinsmen from a particular community (*paisanos*). These jobs were never advertised and there were never any vacancies. Jobs were passed on from one worker to another and the length of employment and the time of transfer were arranged by the workers themselves (Skeldon 1974). Chaplin (1967) wrote that this practice was fostered by textile companies as a way of obtaining 'green' (i.e. docile) labour, but it had to be discontinued because kinship was providing too firm a basis for worker solidarity.

Extended kinship networks were strong in the neighbourhood as well as the labour market, where they were an important basis for the allocation of consumption goods. Kinship provided a residential base for migrants on first arrival and often led to the establishment of permanent houses nearby. It also played a role in the organization of squatters' land invasions (Isbell 1978: 180–4, Raffo 1985: 34–6). Whole neighbourhoods came to consist of extended kin and *paisanos* (Lobo 1976: 115, Isbell 1978: 184). Lobo (1982: 136–7) mentions a deliberate preference for marriage to *paisanos* because they were more 'reliable' and gave access to networks of reciprocity (see also Altamirano 1984: 108).

The build-up of kinship networks in the neighbourhood through migration and intermarriage formed the basis for most labouring-class social interaction. In Mendocita, an inner-city slum, 76 per cent of women's visiting patterns were with kinsmen and *compadres*. Most of these contacts were within Mendocita itself. Women in particular had very few contacts outside the neighbourhood (Caravedo *et al.* 1963: 113–15). Kinship was the basis for informal recreational activity in the neighbourhood (e.g. gangs, football teams); it played a role in formal organizations such as the provincial clubs

(Lobo 1982: 82, Altamirano 1984: 108–9) and in the ritual and ceremonial life of the community (Lobo 1982: chapter 9).

Within the extended kinship network, the sibling group was particularly important. There was a hierarchy of authority amongst adult siblings based on birth order, which mirrored that in the nuclear family. This ensured the cohesion of the extended family.

> 'It is important for brothers and sisters to stick together, mainly so that there will be mutual aid.' ... 'We could not survive here in the city were it not for the aid of our siblings at those times when we really need it.'
>
> (Lobo 1982: 92–3)

Because of the close links between siblings, nephews and nieces were treated as one's own children. This provided a framework for fostering when families split up or fell on hard times. *Compadrazgo* also played an important role amongst the labouring class, providing a fictive kin link with upwardly mobile kinsmen, employers, members of a political party and so on. These links were useful for getting jobs and dealing with the pervasive urban bureaucracy e.g. hospitals, social security offices, schools and colleges, the law courts, and so on (Anderson Velasco 1982).

As in the countryside, kinship networks were gender segregated. As far as employment was concerned, they reflected the general pattern of occupational segregation. Thus women were recruited into outwork and street selling through their female kinsmen, while the men were recruited into construction sites and factories through their male kin. Within the neighbourhood, there was segregation in the sphere of consumption. Amongst women the networks consisted of childcare, food provisioning, washing of clothes, cash loans, borrowing of utensils etc., whilst for men they had to do with house construction and repair, loaning of tools, a bicycle or cash, or drinking together (Lobo 1982: 98). Because of women's limited participation in the formal economy and the sphere of politics, their capacity for creating *compadrazgo* networks was much more limited than men's. They were confined to existing kinsmen or middle-class families for whom they worked in domestic service, whereas men had a greater range of employers, workmates and intermediaries to whom they could turn.

The nuclear family/household

The nuclear family was the predominant household unit in the labouring class. Between a half to three-quarters of all households were of this type (Caravedo *et al.* 1963: 24, Matos Mar 1966: 72–3, Raffo 1985: 21), most of the rest being multi-family households. There was a strong affective identi-

fication with the nuclear family, and children played an important role as the
focus for family solidarity.

The majority of labouring-class couples were legally married[31] and about
a third were *convivientes* (living together).[32] Whether formally married or
not, the conjugal unit showed great stability. Of Fernández's shanty town
sample, 83 per cent had only ever lived with one partner and almost all the
rest had only had one previous union. Two-thirds of all couples had been
together for more than ten years (Fernández 1983: 9–10, see also ONE 1979,
cited by Barrig 1982). The data were similar amongst recent migrants as well
as those with longer residence in Lima, and amongst the poorest as well as
less poor families.

Fertility amongst labouring-class families was higher than amongst the
middle class, but lower than in the provinces, and falling (Stycos 1968: 148,
Sara-Lafosse 1978: 16, Anderson *et al.* 1979: 16, 21). In Sara-Lafosse's study
the average number of children in the labouring-class sample was 4.3, while
in the middle-class sample it was 2.6. On the whole, children were not seen
as a source of potential income but rather as an economic cost, and most
labouring-class mothers desired smaller families. Undoubtedly there were
still many families with very large numbers of children (e.g. seven or more)
but statistically they were the minority within the labouring class as a whole.[33]

It is extremely difficult to obtain data on the abandonment of wives and
family break-up, but the little there is suggests low separation rates. Fernández's survey, mentioned above, showed that 17 per cent of women and 16
per cent of men had been in more than one union (Fernández 1983: 9). Matos
Mar (1966: 70–2) reported that 15 per cent of nuclear families in Ciudad de
Dios had stepchildren. Census data for 1972 show that in seven labouring-
class districts of Lima the proportion of single women who were separated,
divorced or widowed was between 14 and 16 per cent (Census vol. I pp.
60–7), and most of these were widows.[34] Similar proportions were found
amongst a group that is often thought of as attracting abandoned women:
street sellers (Mercado 1978: 14). Matos Mar's study reported that female-
headed households were 19 per cent of the total; of these almost two-thirds
were mothers living alone with their children and a third were composite
families headed by women (Matos Mar 1966: 70).[35] A citywide survey in
1967 found that female-headed households were 11 per cent of the total in
shanty towns and 18 per cent in inner-city slums (cited in Collier 1976b, see
also CISM 1967: 42).

The nuclear family had a capacity to absorb additional kin on a short- or
long-term basis. Some of these may have been unmarried or abandoned
mothers and their children,[36] others were nephews, nieces, grandchildren or
godchildren being raised on a semi-permanent basis. Still others were migrants temporarily visiting Lima to finish their schooling, or to look for a job.

According to surveys, these extended households were between 16 and 23 per cent of the total (Caravedo *et al.* 1963: 24, Matos Mar 1966: 72–3, Raffo 1985: 21–3). However, it should be noted that household size and structure was fluid, and could vary over quite short periods. This was an effect of the close links between the nuclear and extended families, particularly the strength of sibling bonds.

GENDER INEQUALITY IN THE LABOURING-CLASS FAMILY

In general, there was substantial gender inequality within the labouring-class family, manifested in a segregated domestic division of labour and a male-dominated structure of authority. Despite this, there was a strong ideology of family solidarity.

The domestic division of labour and distribution of resources

Whatever the expectations about married women working, the reality was that men were the main breadwinners and women were primarily responsible for consumption. In Sara-Lafosse's study (1978: 21), men were the sole source of income in 68 per cent of families. In my household sample, reconstructed from the 1974 employment survey, the average number of income earners per family was 1.6, and 20 per cent of labouring-class wives were in paid work. The extra income earners apart from the head of household were more likely to be sons or daughters than wives (see chapter 8, table 8.5).

Shanty-town studies confirm the low participation rates of labouring-class wives. In Villa El Salvador, while 72 per cent of women had worked prior to starting a family, only 40 per cent continued afterwards (Chueca 1982: 15). In Pamplona only 32 per cent of the wives worked (Ortiz 1983: 15) and in Huascar only 34 per cent did (Raffo 1985: 47–50). Women were involved in some informal income-generating activities in the local neighbourhood, which would have escaped inclusion in official statistics, but the level of income was very low and would not have assuaged women's prime economic dependence on the male breadwinner.[37] Yet most women believed that it was a woman's obligation to work just as it was a man's and many studies report that more women would have liked to work than were able to (Anderson *et al.* 1979: 31, Chueca 1982: 28).

Within the home, there was a marked segregation between male and female roles. Women had exclusive responsibility for the day-to-day running of the home: cleaning, laundering, shopping, food preparation, mending, getting the children to school, dealing with health problems etc. (Sara-Lafosse 1978: 19, Chueca 1982: 27). Men had prime responsibility for house construction and maintenance and for the representation of the household in the community. The only spheres of joint responsibility related to residential moves and the education of the children (Chueca 1982: 27, Sara-Lafosse 1978: 19, 30–4).

There were various systems for dealing with the organization of the domestic budget. In many families the husband gave his wife a *diario* (housekeeping allowance), retaining an unspecified amount for himself for his 'personal expenses'. According to Lobo (1982: 103–4) this system was less common amongst the *serranos* who preferred a pooling system. Whatever the system, it appears that men had responsibility for certain parts of the domestic budget, usually the larger items of expenditure, and women controlled the day-to-day expenses (Sara-Lafosse 1978: 31–2, Anderson *et al.* 1979: 28).

The socialization of girls and boys was differentiated at an early age. All children were expected to help with domestic chores, especially with childcare. With the onset of puberty girls were increasingly confined to the house (Boggio 1970: 103, Caravedo *et al.* 1963: 70), therefore the burden of domestic work fell disproportionately on them (Chueca 1982: 25, Anderson *et al.* 1979: 53–4, Bunster and Chaney 1985: 184, Ennew 1986). In cases of dire economic need, children would be sent out to work, rather than the mother (Boyden 1985: 53–5). Child labour, whether paid or unpaid, interfered with education. During the 1970s, education was highly valued amongst labouring-class families, as a mechanism for mobility, therefore child labour was avoided if at all possible. Surveys show that most child labourers came from very poor families with a higher than average number of children.[38]

The structure of power and authority

Within the labouring-class family there were two systems of power: one based on gender and the other on seniority. Both were highly authoritarian, with a strong emphasis on respect and obedience. Males had power over females at all levels: husbands over wives, fathers over daughters and brothers over sisters. Seniority also involved a similar hierarchy of power relations.

Despite the functional division of responsibility between spouses, the male head of household had ultimate power and authority in the labouring-class family. This was justified by his role as progenitor and breadwinner. Some women said he had a 'natural' right to command (Bunster and Chaney 1985: 140). In the absence of a male head of household, power often devolved to the eldest son rather than to the wife. Men's power was reflected not just in the division of labour in the family, but in their influence over women's sphere. Women might run the home and look after the children, but ultimately they were accountable to their husbands. Men's views on the way the children were brought up were to be respected, and they held their wives responsible for the children's progress at school (Raffo 1985: 52).

Male power over women existed at other levels within the family. Brothers had power over sisters from an early age right into adulthood. Even after the sibling group had dispersed and formed separate nuclear families, male siblings could exert an influence over their sisters and their sisters' children (especially if there was no male head of household).

'All my uncles watched over me, I had to obey them all, they had me on a short rein' ... 'My uncle is very strict, he was the same with my mother, the same with me and with a cousin of mine.'

(Barrig 1982: 75)

The seniority system partly compensated for women's subordination in the gender system. The principles of seniority were expressed in parental power over children and older siblings over younger ones (Lobo 1982: 128–31). This was a source of power for mothers and elder sisters. Even in adulthood, the eldest female sibling retained authority and influence within the extended family group, which explains the tales of 'wicked aunts' who took young boys and girls to the city to be retained as servants (see e.g. Barrig 1982: 174–5).

There was a strong emphasis on obedience and discipline within the labouring-class family. In Sara-Lafosse's sample (1983: 4–5), 71 per cent of fathers and 88 per cent of mothers stated that they expected blind obedience from their children. The inculcation of obedience was via verbal abuse (shouting, swearing and humiliation) or physical aggression. In Sara-Lafosse's study (1983: 28) over half of labouring-class families used physical punishment as a form of 'correction' and the vast majority of these used a whip (see also Lobo 1982: 125). According to Pimentel (1983: 22), labouring-class parents maintained that this was necessary to give their children a 'good upbringing'. School teachers were expected to mete out the same treatment to their children, since this is how they 'learned'.[39]

Verbal and physical aggression was not just a part of child socialization; it was a general manifestation of power. Men were aggressive towards their wives, brothers towards their sisters, elder siblings towards younger ones, and so on:

'I don't love my father because he beats us, he beats us all.... I have my sisters, they are good-natured, at times they hit me but not hard, but my elder brothers do hit me because I don't pay attention when they tell me to do things for them. I have another little brother of a year old, he doesn't hit me, I hit him.'

(Pimentel 1983: 61)

Rotondo's study of police records between 1955 and 1957 in Mendocita showed that family violence accounted for about a third of all reported crime. Of these the single biggest category was aggression against the wife or *conviviente* (Caravedo *et al.* 1963: 78–9). Barrig (1982: 35) mentions that the vast majority of complaints of marital violence made to the Palace of Justice in Lima came from the shanty towns. Some commentators have pointed to the stress of unemployment and alcoholism as a factor in family violence (Caravedo *et al.* 1963: 235–7, Barrig 1982).[40] Others have linked it to family and gender ideologies.

Legitimating ideologies

Gender inequality within the labouring-class family reflected elements of the bourgeois and peasant families, and the combination of these different traditions produced variations and contradictions at the ideological level. The peasant ideal of a 'complementary unity' between men and women coexisted with *machista* notions of inequality and domesticity. In some families, women expected to contribute to the family income, and they did so despite bearing and rearing several children (see chapter 6). Many studies report that more women would have liked to work than were able to (Chueca 1982: 28):

> 'It is a woman's obligation to work just as it is a man's.'
>
> (Anderson *et al.* 1979: 31)

> 'All my life I've worked, it seems strange to be without a job.'
>
> (case studies)

In others the men subscribed to the *machista* notion that a man's worth was demonstrated by his ability to keep a wife at home, or simply would not trust her to work outside the home.

> 'He's very bitter because I've had to go out to work, according to my husband, I shouldn't work.'
>
> (Pimentel 1983: 53)

In some cases, peasant traditions of authoritarianism merged with male supremacist notions of *machismo*, accentuating power and violence; in others there was a more egalitarian trend, influenced by middle-class liberalism and feminism. Various sources suggest that family violence was linked to rural origins. La Jara shows that whereas 61 per cent of mothers from the country-side and 60 per cent of those from the *sierra* were likely to use physical punishment with their children, only 47 per cent from the coast and 35 per cent of those from urban areas were. Similar differences existed amongst fathers (La Jara 1983: 12–13).[41] Pimentel (1983: 37) maintains that although the rural family was authoritarian, it was less prone to extreme violence, and that migrants from rural origins were less violent than those from urban backgrounds, although they chastized more frequently. However, she found a high correlation between experiences of violence as a child and the use of violence as a parent, and many of these childhood experiences took place in rural areas.[42]

Most authors have linked domestic violence to *machismo* (Pimentel 1983: 32, Sara-Lafosse 1978, Fernández 1983, Castillo Rios 1985: 118). There were various examples of *machista* attitudes amongst the labouring class. Many women complained that jealousy from their husbands was a major reason for family quarrels and limited their ability to make friendships outside the home (Caravedo *et al.* 1963: 237, Barrig 1982: 37–8). Boggio (1970: 107) noted that some labouring-class families subscribed to the idea that girls' virginity should be preserved until marriage. Prostitution was condoned by a small minority of fathers (Sara-Lafosse 1983).

Few studies show exactly how widespread *machismo* was. According to Fernández, only about half of labouring-class men exhibited *machista* attitudes. Her collapsed dichotomous variable gave 60 per cent in the non-*machista* category and 40 per cent in the *machista* category. Her measures of authoritarianism were much greater than this. Moreover, she found no significant statistical association between the two in the case of labouring-class men (Fernández 1983: 27).

The above evidence suggests that within a common pattern of male dominance, there were different and even conflicting ideologies of gender which could be traced ultimately to the bourgeois and peasant families. However, despite these structures of power and inequality, there was also a strong ideology of gender complementarity and family solidarity. The family was seen as something sacred, the source of comfort and support in a hostile world. In Mendocita, over half of the surveyed population said that their greatest happiness was the family, the children and the home (Caravedo *et al.* 1963: 174). Women showed great loyalty to their spouses and kinsmen, stressing mutual tolerance and understanding (*comprensión*) between couples.

> 'Family is community, you work, I work, I do my job and we make something together.'
>
> (Barrig 1982: 158)

As we saw earlier, there was also strong affective and normative solidarity within the extended kin group, and this was the basis for reciprocal exchanges of resources.

'I must keep the family together. We are all the same.... I would do anything for my brothers and sisters.'

(Lobo 1982: 29)

CONCLUSION

Throughout its history, family, kinship and gender had interacted with class to accentuate and polarize social and ethnic divisions. Undoubtedly, the strength of the family and the family–class interaction was due to its ability to mobilize strategic resources for the groups concerned. The labouring class was caught between two different family traditions, which although sharing some common features such as a segregated division of labour and male authority, differed substantially in terms of gender ideology.

This class was strongly influenced by its rural origins, three-quarters of them being migrants. Many aspects of rural kinship institutions, such as the stress on extended networks of reciprocity had been incorporated into urban labour markets and community life. However, the labouring class faced an urban society that was structured by bourgeois family patterns, particularly the *machista* ideology which assumed greater domesticity for women. They confronted these values in schools, public sector bureaucracies, workplaces, charity organizations, and the courts. Urban culture too (particularly the media), was deeply penetrated by these values. Not surprisingly then, we find a contradictory combination of different gender ideologies within the labouring class. One important lesson to be drawn here is that patterns of labour force participation that were apparently similar to that of the middle class had different ideological roots, and should not be explained in terms of a simplistic stereotyped representation of *machismo*.

In the face of substantial poverty, gender inequality and domestic violence, we might ask why women showed such support for the family? Three points are relevant here: women's economic dependence on men and children's dependence on their mothers, the institutionalization of male power in the wider kinship system, and the ideology of reciprocity and solidarity. The high degree of gender segregation in the labour market and the home made it difficult for women to survive on their own economically, and this was accentuated by their children's dependence on them. Many women declared that they were bound to their husbands by their children (e.g. Pimentel 1983: 64). However, as we have seen, women were subject to the authority of other male relatives as well as their husbands' and a woman without a spouse came under the jurisdiction of these other males (brothers, uncles) who could exert as much control as a spouse. Thus the structure of segregation and subordination within the nuclear and extended families coupled with the

pervasiveness of kinship in all spheres of labouring-class life made it well
nigh impossible for women to 'go it alone'.

However, it would be a mistake to interpret the strength of the labouring-
class family solely in terms of dependency or coercion. Just as it did in the
countryside, segregation and inequality within the family coexisted with an
ideology of reciprocity and solidarity. These notions of mutuality and cooperation played a crucial role in legitimizing internal differences within the
family and in promoting its stability. The next three chapters will examine
the economic divisions that were produced by differentiation and mobility in
the manual labour market, and the way they interacted with gender. Chapter
8 returns to the analysis of the labouring-class family and the interplay
between divisions and solidarities within it.

5 Divisions amongst the labouring class

The process of economic growth between 1940 and 1972 produced an enormous numerical expansion in the labouring class of Lima, as well as increasing internal heterogeneity. One measure of this was the polarization between formal and informal sectors: 60 per cent of manual workers were employed in small informal enterprises and only 19 per cent in ones with more than a hundred workers. However, the formal/informal dichotomy was not the sole or even the major source of segmentation amongst these workers. It was certainly not a sufficient basis for identifying a separate 'class' division such as a 'labour aristocracy' and a 'lumpenproletariat' or a 'formal proletariat' and an 'informal petty bourgeoisie' (Portes 1985). Skill and gender were two further divisions, just as important for earnings as enterprise size.

The debate about the informal sector originally intended to address the question of the relationship between growth and inequality, not class structure. Yet it has been used to indicate differences in relations of exploitation and market advantage which are important elements of a class analysis (see chapter 2). Earnings are used as a proxy indicator of class position, and segmentation (i.e. consistent differences in earnings) as a measure of class division. However, we must not forget that class is also about the experience of work, i.e. the degree of autonomy, pace of work, forms of authority between supervisors and supervised, the quality of the working environment, etc. Although our data is fragmentary in this respect, it suggests that the formal/informal sector division was even less relevant for this aspect of class. The experience of work did differ between some formal and informal enterprises, but there were many similarities between them and some important internal variations.

On both counts, however, the most enduring division was between men and women: profound gender segregation in the workplace meant that women's earnings, skills and their experience of work were very different from men's whichever sector they were in. Thus, if there were any grounds for the identification of separate fractions within the labouring class, it would be on the basis of gender.

A METHODOLOGICAL NOTE

The data in the next two chapters come from the manual sample of the 1973 Ministry of Labour employment survey and my own 192 case studies. These sources are described in the Appendix. The collection of employment data with survey methods is perilous amongst a group where informal employment is so prevalent. Definitions of 'work' and 'job' are fuzzy round the edges and shade easily into odd jobs, casual work and forms of unpaid labour. This can lead to some underestimation of certain types of work, particularly those done by women in the home. A full discussion of these problems is provided in Scott (1988) and the Appendix; suffice it to say here that, after a careful review of the Ministry of Labour fieldwork methods and data, I came to the conclusion that the degree of underestimation was probably less than 5 per cent.

Since the formal/informal division is subject to much scrutiny in this chapter, it may be useful to remind readers that it is defined here in terms of enterprise size, using less than five workers and five+ workers as the cut-off point. In some part of the analysis, however, the five+ group will be sub-divided into medium and large enterprises (5–99 and 100+ workers).

GENERAL CHARACTERISTICS OF THE MANUAL WORKFORCE IN LIMA, 1973

The Ministry of Labour sample of manual workers had a total of 2,377 employed persons,[1] of whom a third were women. Nearly three-quarters were migrants, but less than 10 per cent had arrived in the last year and almost two-thirds had been in Lima for ten years or more. Migrants were a similar proportion of both men and women workers, and there was very little difference between male and female migrants as to the type of place of origin.[2] This workforce was not especially young: nearly 60 per cent of them were between the ages of 20 and 40. However, there were slightly more women in the 10–19 age group (see table 5.1, p. 100).

There were marked differences in the marital status of the manual workforce: a considerably higher proportion of the women were single (51 per cent as against 35 per cent). Nearly two-thirds of the men were self-declared household heads and the rest were sons, siblings or other relatives of the household head. In contrast, 28 per cent of the women were domestic servants living with their employers and 17 per cent were female heads of household; only a third were wives and the remaining fifth were daughters or siblings of the household head. As a result of these differences in marital status, there were only 250 wives compared with 1,026 husbands in the sample of 2,377 workers. These data confirm the low labour force participation rates of labouring-class wives, mentioned in the previous chapter.

There were very few illiterates (5 per cent); over half the workforce had some primary education and a third had some secondary education. There were sharp discontinuities within these levels because of dropout rates. Of those who had attended primary school, 45 per cent had failed to complete the full five years and at secondary school level, 64 per cent had dropped out before the cycle was complete. The aggregate figures show that women had slightly less education than men; more of them were illiterate and fewer had secondary education. There were also higher dropout rates within each educational level (see table 5.2, p. 100).

These characteristics give a picture of a stable workforce, primarily of migrant origin but with a long period of residence in the city, some formal education and living in established family groups. Differences between men and women were slight, and mainly related to age and marital status.

INCOME DISTRIBUTION AMONGST MANUAL WORKERS IN LIMA

There was substantial differentiation in earnings amongst the labouring class, and particularly marked differences between men and women. Whereas the Gini coefficient for labour incomes was 0.476 for Lima as a whole, it was 0.417 for manual workers. The distribution of monthly earnings was highly skewed. The majority had very low incomes, with 43 per cent below the minimum wage. On the other hand, there was also a long tail, with some very high earnings. We shall find this occurring within almost every category analysed below and it contributes to the high coefficients of variation there. The distribution of female earnings was even more skewed and the proportion below the minimum wage was almost double that of the men. The median monthly earnings was 2,556 soles, just above the minimum wage of 2,400 soles,[3] but while the male median was 3,010 soles, the female one was 1,289 soles – about half the minimum wage level.

Table 5.1 gives the age–earnings profile of the manual workforce. It shows that earnings rose rapidly in the early part of a man's career, then peaking at 40–49 years and subsequently declining. Women's profile was much shallower; earnings started lower, rose much more gradually, peaked at a much lower level and then reverted to that of women in their twenties. This age–earnings profile has implications for men's and women's career patterns, analysed in chapters 6 and 7. Table 5.2 shows that earnings rose with education amongst both men and women, but at each level of education men were earning much more. There was a considerable earnings premium to be had for those who finished each cycle, and the numbers bunched noticeably at this level.

One explanation of the low level of female earnings was the large number of domestic servants, who received part of their income in kind (food and lodgings). However, they were only a third of the female manual workforce.

Table 5.1   Average monthly earnings of the manual workforce by age and sex, Lima 1973

	% distribution			x̄ monthly earnings	
Age	*Men*	*Women*	*Total*	*Men*	*Women*
10–19 years	11	22	15	1,835	1,049
20–29	33	34	34	3,145	1,634
30–39	25	22	24	4,212	1,937
40–49	16	14	15	4,526	2,152
50–59	9	5	8	4,120	1,619
60+	5	2	4	3,455	1,951*
Total	99	99	100		
N	1,566	784	2,350		

Source: Ministry of Labour employment survey 1973
* Only 17 cases. Minimum wage = 2,400 soles in 1973
x̄ = arithmetic mean

Table 5.2   Level of education of the manual workforce, Lima 1973

Level of education	% distribution			x̄ monthly earnings	
	Men	*Women*	*Total*	*Men*	*Women*
None*	2	11	5	3,066	1,369
Incomplete primary	21	34	25	3,162	1,365
Complete primary	32	30	31	3,657	1,812
Incomplete secondary	27	16	23	3,552	1,879
Complete secondary	16	8	13	4,210	2,768
Higher	3	1	2	3,995	**
Total	101	100	99		
N	1,581	796	2,377		

Source: Ministry of Labour employment survey 1973
* Includes pre-school ** Only 4 cases

Hours of work was another factor; however, only 30 per cent of the women were working less than forty hours per week, while about a quarter were working more than sixty hours.[4] Table 5.3 shows that women's earnings were significantly below men's however many hours they worked, and that low earnings were associated with very long hours as well as short hours.

Table 5.3   Weekly hours worked and monthly earnings by sex, Lima 1973

Hours worked per week	Men		Women	
	%	x̄ earnings	%	x̄ earnings
1–19	4	2,295	7	1,466
20–39	14	2,908	22	1,627
40–59	65	3,831	46	1,912
60–79	13	3,692	19	1,425
80+	4	3,855	5	1,683
Total	100	3,609	99	1,703

Source: Ministry of Labour employment survey 1973

We can see then, that the very considerable variation in earnings within the labouring class was strongly associated with gender, and that although education, age and hours worked contributed to this association, strong sex differentials in earnings remained. Let us now examine the contribution of the formal and informal sectors to this picture.

LABOUR MARKET DIVISIONS AND THE FORMAL/INFORMAL SECTORS

The data below show that the formal/informal sector division was an important source of variance in earnings and welfare entitlements amongst manual workers. However, gender was another major division in this labour market, producing differentials in earnings that were actually greater than those associated with the type of sector. These two sources of segmentation crosscut each other, so that the formal sector was not exclusively 'male' nor the informal sector exclusively 'female'. The overlapping of the formal/informal division with gender meant that there were gender divisions within different sized enterprises and a formal/informal division within the male and female workforces. This introduced earnings variance into each sector: low-paid women in the formal sector and relatively prosperous self-employed men in the informal sector. Thus the formal/informal dichotomy could not be equated with a division between a high-paid labour aristocracy and a low-income lumpenproletariat. These groups did exist within the manual labour market, but there were a lot more in between – and some of them were in the formal sector and some in the informal.

General structure of the formal/informal division

Overall, the proportions of formal to informal employment were 40:60, but the figures for men and women were very different – 51:49 for men and 16:84 for women. Because of the different male and female distributions, the formal sector was much more male (86 per cent), and in the informal sector men also predominated because they were such a large proportion of the total manual workforce.[5]

The distribution of manual employment by economic sector was skewed towards commerce and services: a third of the sample was in manufacturing, 15 per cent in construction and transport and the remaining 52 per cent in commerce and services. However, almost two-thirds of the men were in the first three sectors whereas four-fifths of the women were in the last two (see table 5.4).

Within each economic sector there was a polarization between formal and informal enterprises, although it was variable; commerce stands out as the sector with the greatest proportion of informal workers, while manufacturing, construction and transport had the highest proportions of formal workers. The vast majority of the workforce in the very largest enterprises (100+) were in the manufacturing sector; on the other hand, most informal sector workers (<5 group) were in commerce and services. Thus there is some justification

Table 5.4   Distribution of the manual workforce by enterprise size and sex within economic sectors, Lima 1973

Economic sector	Ent. size		Sex		% in <5 group		
	<5 %	5+ %	M %	F %	Men	Women	Total
Manufacturing	20	50	40	18	36	46	38
Construction	5	9	11	*	49	—	49
Transport	7	9	12	—	51	—	51
Commerce	33	10	21	29	77	92	83
Services	35	21	16	53	36	91	71
Total	100	99	100	100	48	84	60

Source: Ministry of Labour employment survey 1973
* = less than 0.5%

for the notion that manual workers were polarized between factory jobs and petty commerce and services. However, this was a tendency rather than a rigid dichotomy. We should note the importance of informal production in the first three sectors and that there were some large establishments in commerce and services.

The internal composition of the informal sector was slightly different for men and women. Self-employment was the most predominant category for both, but much more so for men than for women (68 per cent and 48 per cent respectively). Wage work was also more prevalent amongst the men, who were probably apprentices. These two categories were almost 90 per cent of male informal employment. Amongst the women, the next most important category after self-employment was domestic service (38 per cent), and these two amounted to 86 per cent of female informal work. The rest were unpaid family workers and salaried workers who would have been shop assistants in very small stores.[6]

Earnings

The earnings data show a consistent segmentation by enterprise size and sex, but the sex differentials were larger than the enterprise ones. Overall, manual women's earnings were 43 per cent of men's, while informal earnings were 65 per cent of formal earnings. The data below show these two variables continually crosscutting each other, so that enterprise size was an important source of earnings variance for both sexes, but within each enterprise size group, there were significant sex differentials. Note that the formal/informal differential was greater amongst women and the sex differential was wider in the informal sector.[7] Therefore women were doubly penalized by their concentration in the informal sector.

Table 5.5 presents the average monthly earnings and the coefficients of variation for each enterprise size group by sex. Mean earnings rose progressively, if modestly, in each size group, although there was a noticeable leap in the largest one (100+).[8] (This confirms the advantage of a tripartite division in enterprise size, as was suggested in chapter 3.) There were significant differences between men's and women's average earnings within each size group, especially at the lower end of the spectrum, where most women were concentrated. Men's average earnings never fell below the minimum wage, whereas women had to work in establishments with over fifty workers before they could reach this level. The coefficients of variation were high in all groups, but especially amongst the smaller enterprises and amongst women.

There was some variation in earnings levels between economic sectors. The highest paying sector by far was transport, with an average of 4,749 soles; followed by construction and manufacturing with 3,784 and 3,463 soles respectively. Commerce and services had the lowest earnings; in services the average (2,061 soles) was below the minimum wage and in commerce, only just above it (2,555 soles). Within economic sectors there were significant earnings differentials according to size of enterprise and sex. Table 5.6 gives the figures for the two extreme groups (<5 and 100+) and shows that once

Table 5.5   Distribution of employment and monthly earnings by size of enterprise and sex, Lima 1973

Enterprise size	Men		Women		M %	F %	Women's earnings as % of men's
	x̄	V	x̄	V			
1–4 workers	3,252	0.75	1,494	0.95	48	84	46
5–9	3,237	0.61	1,878	0.76	9	5	58
10–19	3,331	0.57	2,386	0.24	7	2	71
20–49	3,498	0.44	2,361	0.49	6	2	66
50–99	3,587	0.46	2,811	0.24	5	2	78
100+	4,570	0.51	3,465	0.50	25	6	76
total	3,609	0.64	1,703	0.88	100	100	47

Source: Ministry of Labour employment survey 1973
x̄ = mean monthly earnings (excluding earnings over 14,999 soles)
V = coefficient of variation (standard deviation divided by x̄)

Table 5.6   Distribution of the manual workforce by enterprise size* and sex within economic sectors, Lima 1973

Economic sector	D	F%	Men		D	Women		D
			x̄ earnings			x̄ earnings		
			<5	100+		<5	100+	
Manufacturing	75	18	3,445	4,565	75	1,710	3,119	55
Construction	76	—	3,437	4,298	80	—	—	—
Transport	85	—	4,652	5,502	84	—	—	—
Commerce	57	41	3,052	3,163	96	1,779	5,000	35
Services	51	62	1,788	4,365	41	1,315	3,620	36
Total	57	33	3,252	4,570	71	1,494	3,465	43

Source: Ministry of Labour employment survey 1973
* For simplicity only the extreme poles are represented here; workers in enterprises with 5–99 employees are omitted
D = earnings differential: earnings in <5 as proportion of 100+
F% = percentage of women within each sector

again, the sex differentials were wider than the enterprise size ones, and the enterprise differentials were smaller amongst men than amongst women.

In each economic sector, men's average earnings were well above women's in both large and small enterprises, and in all cases except services[9] they were above the minimum wage level. In contrast, women's average earnings in all the sectors in which they predominated were below the minimum wage; and even in the large enterprises, they were only just above it. The problem for women then was that they were concentrated in the economic sectors with the lowest average level of earnings (commerce and services), and within those sectors, in informal activities which were amongst the lowest paid of all.

We have seen that income variance was extremely high within the informal sector. This was largely because of the variety of employment conditions there and high male–female differentials. Table 5.7 shows wide variations in earnings between employment statuses, and once again these were crosscut by gender.

There were large differences between the earnings of the self-employed, wage workers and domestic servants, and between men and women in each of these categories (even in domestic service). Self-employment is a particularly interesting case, not only because self-employed men earned so much

Table 5.7 Employment status of the manual labour force, by formal/informal sector and sex, Lima 1973

Employment status	$\bar{x}$ earnings		F earnings
	Men	Women	as % M's
Informal enterprises (<5)			
self-employed	3,781	1,918	51
unpaid family labour	*	*	*
domestic servants	1,462	1,017	69
wage workers	2,732	1,443	53
salaried workers**	2,991	1,628	54
Formal enterprises (5+)			
wage workers	3,761	2,674	71
salaried workers**	4,394	3,382	77
N	1,431	749	

Source: Ministry of Labour employment survey 1973
*   Figures meaningless because of zero earnings
** Manual workers paid by the month (see Appendix and note 6)

more than self-employed women, but because the former's earnings were marginally higher than those of male wage workers in the formal sector. Thus for men, the informal sector offered an attractive alternative to the formal sector, whereas for women this was not the case.

Fringe benefits and unionization

The data presented below confirm the suggestions made in chapter 3 that fringe benefits and welfare entitlements were fairly widely distributed amongst manual workers, even in some informal enterprises, although the quality and quantity was variable. Unionization rates were low and generally confined to the largest enterprises.

Unfortunately, the Ministry of Labour survey did not have much information on fringe benefits, therefore I have to rely on the case study data. These data cover two types of benefit: 'fringe benefits' are work-related benefits provided by employers, and 'welfare benefits' are non-employment benefits, partly funded by workers themselves. The analysis here is based on wage earners only, although this includes some informal sector workers such as domestic servants and apprentices.

Fringe benefits were widely prevalent amongst manual wage earners and not confined to formal enterprises. In the <5 group, only 28 per cent of workers had no benefits at all, and in the 100+ group, only 14 per cent.

Table 5.8   Fringe benefits at work provided by employer (proportion of the workforce in each size group with access to benefits), Lima 1974

Type of benefit	Enterprise size		
	<5	5–99	100+
Transport	—	13	43
Clothing and equipment	24	48	62
Factory products	5	3	19
Cooperatives	—	5	19
Paid holidays	35	78	57
Free meals	54	33	29
Lodging	45	5	—
Other	14	3	—
No facilities	28	18	14
N	58	40	21

Source: Author's case studies (weighted), wage earners only

However, it is important to distinguish between types and quality of benefit. Large enterprises were more likely to provide facilities such as transport to work, protective clothing and equipment, products from the factory, paid holidays and cooperatives, but small enterprises were more likely to provide food and lodgings (table 5.8). Most of these were domestic servants or apprentices living with their employers.

Since welfare benefits required a contribution from employees, a good way to assess coverage was to ask whether a deduction had been made from the worker's pay packet. Table 5.9 shows that such deductions were widespread in both large and intermediate enterprises. In fact, on this measure, only 10 per cent of the workforce in these two groups were without any coverage. Workers in the <5 group were much less well covered, although even here a third had social security. The most significant benefits were those relating to social security, unemployment and pensions, and here there was a more marked association with enterprise size.

Note the low proportion of workers, even in large enterprises, who were paying union dues. In the larger Ministry sample, only 21 per cent of all those who were eligible for membership (i.e. who worked in enterprises with over twenty workers) were unionized. However, the figure was substantially higher in the 100+ group, where 61 per cent of workers were unionized. This still left 39 per cent of workers non-unionized, underlining the point that unionization was uneven, even in large enterprises.

Two-thirds of the men and over half of the women had had deductions made for social security. However, only a quarter of the women had access to pensions or unemployment funds, compared with 43 per cent of the men.

Table 5.9   Deductions from workers' pay packets for welfare benefits (proportion in each size group with a deduction made), Lima 1974

	Enterprise size		
Benefit	*<5*	*5–99*	*100+*
Social security	36	88	81
Pension fund	5	65	81
Unemployment fund	7	65	67
Union dues	2	23	33
Savings fund (*mutual*)	2	5	10
Other	—	8	19
No deductions	62	10	10
N	58	40	21

Source: Author's case studies (weighted), wage earners only

Women were much more likely to have access to benefits if they worked in the largest enterprises, and there was no difference in the degree of coverage of men and women in this size group.[10] Interestingly, there was no difference in the union membership of men and women in this group either. Institutional protection may thus have had an important role in reducing sex inequalities in this subsector.

We must remember that these data exclude the self-employed who were about a third of the manual workforce and a slightly larger proportion of the women (37 per cent). They had negligible access to fringe benefits or unions, although some – mainly men – had private insurance schemes and were members of producer or vendor associations. Therefore the degree of institutional protection of the labouring class as a whole was much less than these figures suggest.

LABOUR MARKET DIVISIONS AND SKILL[11]

The analysis so far shows that while the formal/informal division within the manual workforce was a major source of earnings variance, it was crosscut by a source of even larger differentials, gender. However, even after enterprise size and gender had been taken into account, there was still a large amount of variation to be accounted for. This section will consider the third major division amongst manual workers – skill. In chapter 3 it was suggested that the formal sector was less homogeneous in terms of skill than is normally assumed; this section will provide further evidence of this point. It will also show that the informal sector had a wide range of skills too; indeed in some industries, the ratio of skilled to unskilled was higher than in the formal sector. However, men and women were not equally distributed between skill levels; in both sectors men were generally in the most skilled jobs and women in the least skilled.

There was wide recognition of the importance of skill amongst the labouring class. There were two aspects to this: the notion of a trade, involving specialized technical competences (e.g. plumber, electrician, carpenter), and the internal skill statuses within a trade (e.g. apprentice, journeyman, master). Many trades had historical origins in the artisanal guilds, which flourished in Lima at the turn of the century (Blanchard 1982, Sulmont 1977). Others were associated with modern technology. Skills differed qualitatively and quantitatively between trades: for example, jewellers and electricians were considered to be highly skilled, but cooks and barbers less so.

Having a trade meant having a training, a 'specialization', a profession, a craft. It was associated with technical expertise, experience and knowledge. It was considered to be crucial for the acquisition of high incomes, successful self-employment, pride in work and social esteem. The following statements from the case studies are illustrative:

'conocer el oficio es básico' (knowing a trade is basic)
'me gusta este trabajo, es mi especialidad' (I like this work, it's my speciality)
'se gana más especializándose' (you earn more if you specialize)

The acquisition of a trade was through on-the-job training. This was based on an internal hierarchy of skill statuses through which workers had to pass in order to profess the trade. There were three broad levels: (a) *aprendiz* or *ayudante* – trainee, apprentice or builder's mate, (b) *oficial* or *operario* – semi-skilled journeyman, and (c) *maestro* – fully skilled master craftsman. Beneath these three levels was the unskilled category of *peon* (labourer), but this did not usually form part of the trade structure.

In informal enterprises, it was common for young children to start off as *ayudantes*, although they were often used as a source of cheap unskilled labour, fetching and carrying, acting as watchdogs and so on. This status merged with that of apprentice, where they became attached to a particular *maestro*, and were given some cash (a *propina* or tip) and/or food and lodgings. Gradually they would reach the stage when they could carry out tasks without supervision, at which point they became *oficiales* and were paid the going wage for the job. They might then continue to work for the same *maestro* or might seek work in another establishment. Some crucial expertise had usually to be acquired before they could pass to the status of a *maestro*, such as reading plans (builders) or cutting cloth (tailors). It would then become possible to set themselves up on their own, or to move to a highly skilled job within a large enterprise. Even there, a *maestro* usually had a high degree of responsibility and autonomy. The passage from one level to another did not appear to be formalized by certification and the length of training was indeterminate. The case study data show that it took about three years to become a *maestro*, on average. However, some individuals had taken as long as seven years. Promotion was often dependent on the personal whim of the *maestro* himself, and he might delay transmitting a particular skill in order to keep a good man at *operario* level.[12]

The same skill classification (but including the unskilled category) was used in formal enterprises and was a basis for pay determination and collective bargaining. Training was provided on the job in this sector also, although with some minor differences. Traineeships or apprenticeships were more clearly defined and the training period was shorter and more specific (1.9 years on average, according to case study data). However, large firms recognized the skills practised in small enterprises, especially in those industries where technology did not differ greatly between different sized firms (e.g. footwear and clothing). This facilitated movement between the two sectors at the higher skill levels, as we shall see in chapters 6 and 7.

Trade skills did not correlate well with formal education. They pre-dated the expansion of formal education and there were still some old *maestros* with only a few years of schooling. According to the case study data, 70 per cent of those with *maestro* status had only primary education. Secondary schooling conflicted directly with the apprenticeship system, which usually started at the age of 12. Although there had been some attempts by the government to organize formal apprenticeship schemes, these were not attended by large numbers of workers. Amongst the case studies, very few workers indeed had attended any vocational courses, only thirty out of 192. According to the Ministry of Labour, only 5 per cent of those who had learnt a trade had done their training through formal vocational courses. The vast majority (80 per cent) had acquired their skills on the job.

Trade skills tended to predominate in the manufacturing and construction sectors, where they were prevalent in both formal and informal sectors. As already mentioned in chapter 3, large manufacturing firms varied greatly in the skill composition of their workforce and if anything, the proportion of unskilled labour actually *rose* with enterprise size (SERH 1970). According to this source, industries with the highest proportions of skilled manual labour were the metal-working and engineering industries, printing, wood products and furniture. Industries such as food products, footwear and clothing, paper, leather goods, rubber and chemical products had greater concentrations of unskilled and semi-skilled workers, possibly because of a greater reliance on assembly and packaging work. On the other hand, most of the small manufacturing establishments were headed by skilled *maestros*, and because of their small workforce size, the proportion of skilled labour was high. Within the construction industry, skill distinctions were virtually identical in large and small firms alike, and many of them were linked directly through the practice of subcontracting. On the whole these two sectors had the highest proportion of skilled trades.

In transport, driving was the crucial skill and some training was required to obtain the professional driving licence, although this was usually acquired informally. Moreover, for self-employed drivers, mechanical skills were often necessary. In commerce, although sales skills were unquestionably crucial to the success of an enterprise, they were not formally recognized and there was no specific training. In the services sector, hairdressers, barbers and restaurant cooks were virtually the only trades to have a *maestro* status, but the apprenticeship system was weak and the perceived skill level low. It seems then, that commodity production and transport provided greater possibilities for skill differentiation than services.[13] It is no accident that these were the sectors with the highest earnings.

It is difficult to assess the skill distribution of the manual workforce overall, since the Ministry of Labour question on this was ambiguous.[14] The case study data gave figures of 38 per cent skilled, 29 per cent semi-skilled and 33 per cent unskilled. However, there may be an overestimation of skilled workers here because the data set was biased towards older age groups (see Appendix). The differences for men and women were staggering: only 12 per cent of the women had *maestro* status compared with 52 per cent of the men, and conversely, 68 per cent of the women were unskilled compared with only 15 per cent of the men. The only skilled trade open to women was dressmaking, and significantly, this trade had a weak apprenticeship system. Many women 'picked it up' from their mothers or attended short vocational courses. The same went for cookery and hairdressing.

Table 5.10 shows the very different male and female distributions of skill. Within informal enterprises, 53 per cent of the men were skilled but only 9 per cent of the women were. There were so few case study women in large enterprises that the figures on skill are not worth noting, but other research has shown that women were mostly concentrated in unskilled or semi-skilled jobs such as sewing machinists, assemblers or packers (cf. Guzman and Portocarrero 1985). This means that most of the skilled jobs in large enterprises went to men, although we should also note the existence of semi-skilled

Table 5.10   Distribution of skill by enterprise size and sex, Lima 1974

| | Enterprise size | | | | |
	<5	5–99	100+	*Total*	*N*
Men					
Skilled (*maestro*)	53	60	33	52	62
Semi-skilled	31	28	50	33	40
Unskilled	16	12	17	15	18
Total	100	100	100	100	
N	65	37	18		120
Women					
Skilled (*maestro*)	9	*	*	2	7
Semi-skilled	13	*	*	20	12
Unskilled	78	—	—	68	41
Total	100	*	*	100	
N	53	5	2		60

Source: Author's case studies, weighted
* Too few cases for meaningful statistics

and unskilled male jobs in these enterprises. In summary, men had much greater access to skilled jobs than women and they were by no means penalized by being in informal enterprises; on the contrary, that is where most of them exercised their skill. Women, on the other hand, were confined not only to the informal sector, but to unskilled jobs there.

These data show that the formal/informal sector division did not map on to skill divisions, the former being skilled and the latter unskilled, as suggested by some authors. The manual workforce was indeed stratified by skill, but these divisions were crosscut by the formal/informal division rather than running parallel to it. This is illustrated in stylized form by figure 5.1.[15] The symbols represent the two sectors and the horizontal lines, different levels of skill. The shaded areas indicate the typical location of women.

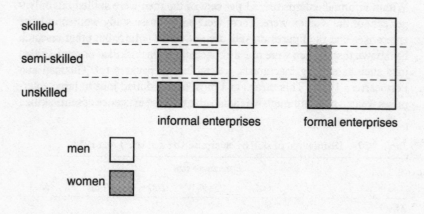

Figure 5.1   Job differentiation according to formal/informal sectors, skill and gender, Lima 1974

The internal hierarchy of skills within the formal and informal sectors was reflected in earnings. Table 5.11 gives cross-sectional data from the case studies, which despite the small numbers, especially at the lower skill levels, suggests a strong association between earnings and skill. Note that the range of variation between skilled and unskilled earnings was widest in small enterprises and amongst the self-employed, and narrower in the larger enterprises. In comparison, the earnings levels of *skilled* workers in different sized enterprises did not vary so much. Thus skilled artisans could earn as much in self-employment as in the formal sector. Once again, however, earnings differentials existed between men and women within each category; thus

Table 5.11 Average daily wage* of manual workers by enterprise size, skill and sex, Lima 1974

Level of skill	Men			Women			Total			
	SE	WW<5	WW 5+	SE	WW<5	WW 5+	SE	WW<5	WW 5+	N
Skilled	248	200	236	99**	—	141**	221	200	230	66
Semi-skilled	126**	125	179	96**	83**	127**	113	120	168	51
Unskilled	109***	40**	127**	81	50	—	88	48	127**	59
Total	203	133	199	89	52	131	155	94	190	176
N	33	31	52	24	28	8	57	59	60	

Source: Author's case studies (weighted) published in Scott (1991)
Notes
* Minimum daily wage in 1974 was 100 Peruvian soles
** Note very small numbers in these cells (<10)
SE = self-employed
WW<5 = wage workers in establishments with less than five workers
WW 5+ = wage workers in establishments with five workers and over

women earned less than men however much skill they had. This hierarchy of skills and its association with earnings had important implications for patterns of job movement and career formation within the working class, as we shall see in the next chapter. The work history data show that upward moves in skill level were directly associated with increases in earnings.

In summary, within the *formal* sector there was considerable skill hete-rogeneity, with large quantities of unskilled and semi-skilled labour as well as skilled. Men had almost exclusive access to the skilled jobs, although they were also hired at lower levels. Women, on the other hand, were largely confined to these lower levels. In the *informal* sector, there was also a range of skill levels and a similar distribution of men and women between them. Women's exclusion from skilled artisanal-type trades (with the exception of dressmaking) was a major reason for their confinement to low-skilled infor-mal work.

OCCUPATIONAL SEGREGATION, FEMINIZATION AND INFORMALITY

Since occupations are strongly related to trades and skills, we must now consider the role of occupational sex segregation in this picture. To what extent was women's concentration in low-skilled, informal jobs due to their confinement to certain 'female' occupations? We have already seen in chapter 3 (especially table 3.9) that there was a high degree of occupational sex segregation in Lima, and that it was especially pronounced amongst manual workers. Let us now examine how this factor interacted with the formal/informal sector division and what implications it had for women. The detailed analysis of this issue has already been published in Scott (1991), so only the summary findings are reported here.

Manual occupations were highly gender segregated: three-quarters of the men were working in male-dominated occupations and a similar proportion of the women were working in female-dominated ones (Scott 1991: table 6). This intense segregation applied to occupations in both formal and informal sectors, although there was a positive association between feminization and informality. Most occupations straddled the two sectors, but some were more confined to one or the other. There were three groups: one where they were concentrated in the informal sector, an intermediate one where they were distributed almost equally between both sectors, and one with greater con-centration in the formal sector. Nearly half the workforce was in the first group, about a third in the intermediate group and less than a fifth in the last one.

The distribution of men and women between these groups was quite different. Nearly half the men were in the intermediate group, with a quarter

Table 5.12 Manual occupations by degree of informal sector concentration and female concentration, Lima, 1973

Degrees of concentration in informal sector	Degrees of female concentration in occupation				
	Almost exclusively male (0–10%F)	Below average female share (11–32%F)	Above average female share but absolute minority (33–49%F)	Absolute majority of women (50–89%F)	Almost exclusively female (90–100%F)
Above average concentration in IS (61%+)	Jewellers		Street pedlars Shop assistants Barbers & hairdressers*	Retail stores Laundry workers* Garment workers*	Boardinghouse-keepers Domestic servants
Half to average concentration in IS (30–60%)	Carpenters Drivers Painters Metal workers Bricklayers Shoemakers Electricians Apprentices Other operatives	Butchers, bakers Waiters & waitresses*	Cooks*		
Less than half average IS concentration (<30%)	Caretakers Cleaners Mechanics Stevedores Printers Potters & glass workers Postmen & messengers	Textile workers Packers & labellers			

Source: Ministry of Labour employment survey 1973 (published in Scott 1991)
* These occupations are internally segregated but cannot be disaggregated because already coded

in each of the others, whereas the overwhelming majority of women (89 per cent) were concentrated in the first group. Domestic servants, boardinghouse-keepers, laundresses and dressmakers, which alone accounted for over half of the entire female manual workforce, were concentrated in the informal sector and were over two-thirds 'female'. Table 5.12 shows the association between the sectoral location and sex specificity of these occupations.

One outstanding characteristic of 'male' occupations compared with 'female' ones was that the former had a greater range of skill than the latter. Almost all women's occupations with the exception of garment workers were unskilled, while men's were mainly skilled trades of the type mentioned in the previous section. Most of the latter fell into the intermediate group that were in both formal and informal sectors. In general, earnings tended to be highest in occupations that had the highest skill levels and the greatest possibilities for bridging the two sectors. Thus the combination of skill hierarchy and sector overlap promoted opportunities for men and accentuated women's disadvantage. As we shall see in chapters 6 and 7, it provided the basis for greater career mobility amongst men enabling them to improve their position as they moved up the skill hierarchy and between formal and informal sectors. Women had few such possibilities; their occupations did not form part of a skill hierarchy and did not straddle the formal/informal divide. The one exception to this was dressmaking, but only 13 per cent of women fell into this category.

Note that a number of occupations in the third group (concentration in the formal sector) were unskilled: caretakers, office cleaners and packers and labellers. This is further evidence of the fact that not all workers in formal enterprises were skilled. All these occupations, except packers and labellers, were dominated by men; they had low earnings in comparison with the more highly skilled jobs in the same sector, but most were covered by minimum wage legislation which put them well above the earnings of similar occupations in the informal sector. Male office cleaners and laundry workers, for example, had more than double the earnings of domestic servants and laundresses in the informal sector.

It would appear then, that much of the inequality between men and women was occupationally based. To the extent that occupations acted as a vehicle for training, recruitment and career formation, the segregation of occupations by gender meant a channelling of men and women into very different labour markets. Explanations of this segregation are discussed in chapter 8 (pp. 168–75).

SELF-EMPLOYMENT

We come now to a more detailed analysis of the self-employed, in particular their relations with the wider economy and the reasons for their internal diversity. Self-employment was an important category within the labouring class, accounting for a third of the manual workforce and about half of informal manual employment. In fact, if family labour and wage workers in small enterprises are included in the figures, both of whom were probably working for the self-employed, almost all of informal employment except domestic service was in some way contingent on self-employment. In this section, I shall take up some of the points made in chapter 3, about the overemphasis in the informal sector literature on subcontracting, exploitation and depressed markets for the self-employed.

As we have seen, self-employment was a highly differentiated category, with large variations in skill levels and earnings. The situations of men and women within this category were very different. However, not all of the variation here could be explained by skill and gender. The key factor was unequal access to crucial productive resources, such as capital, clients and locations. Barriers to entry were a crucial determinant of variation in earnings and a major factor in explaining the poor position of self-employed women.

Self-employment is a problematic category for analysis, because it refers to a range of different employment situations and the income derived from it is not easy to measure precisely. Definitions of self-employment are unclear and subjective perceptions sometimes do not correspond with objective reality. The common terms used to define self-employment were 'trabajo por mi cuenta' (I work for myself), 'soy independiente' (I'm my own boss, I'm independent), 'no me manda nadie' (I don't take orders from anyone) etc. What is alluded to here is some concept of economic independence, a normal condition of which would be ownership of the means of production and control over the decision-making processes involved in production. Theoretically, the autonomous self-employed person owns his or her tools and equipment, purchases inputs, hires labour as necessary, and determines the price of the final product (subject to competition). The income is a return to all factors of production, not just labour, and therefore is not strictly comparable to a wage.

However, many producers who would classify themselves as self-employed did not enjoy the full degree of autonomy outlined above. In both manufacturing and construction there were complex chains of subcontracting which produced various combinations of autonomy and dependence. Some producers would run small workshops on the basis of subcontracts from large firms and at the same time they employed outworkers. Outworkers had contracts with factories, shops or even small workshops, which provided them with raw materials although they worked with their own tools or machinery and paid for running costs (e.g. electricity). Some artisans combined working autonomously for the market with outwork, others would hire their services out to large employers, on a self-employed basis. There were self-employed owners of taxis, lorries and microbuses who would work a shift each day themselves, and then lend the vehicle to others (*palancas*) in return for a percentage of the fare takings. In commerce, there were many who worked on a commission basis for other sales establishments. Young boys selling magazines at traffic lights would be working for newspaper vendors and street sellers plying their wares on the pavement were employed by nearby shops (cf. Bromley 1982). These ambiguities are analysed more fully in Scott (1979).

These situations were intermediate between true self-employment and wage labour, and some writers have interpreted them as 'disguised' wage labour subject to indirect exploitation by capital (Bernstein 1979, Gerry and Birkbeck 1981). However, they can also be seen as a form of shared self-employment: workers were sharing the costs (and risks) of setting up an enterprise; chipping in different factors of production – a vehicle, tools, expertise or labour – under a variety of arrangements too complex and fluid to permit easy classification. Calculating the size of this semi-independent group is hazardous, but detailed analysis of the case studies put them at 14 per cent of the sample; if amalgamated with the true self-employed, they would have represented 29 per cent of that category; when placed with wage workers – as they were in this study – they were 21 per cent there. They were around a quarter of informal sector employment, when defined by enterprise size. On any definition, therefore, they were a minority of informal sector employment.

It is difficult to establish whether such workers were more disadvantaged in income terms than the true self-employed; in the case study data, average weekly earnings were actually higher amongst this intermediate group than amongst the self-employed, although there were very small numbers here.[16] However, the essence of a piece rate system is that you can push earnings up by working long hours. The question is whether there was sufficient demand to permit this. The fragmentary evidence from the case studies suggests that, in the early 1970s, there was.

As indicated earlier, self-employment was differentiated by skill. There were skilled *maestros* running their own businesses with a high degree of autonomy, and unskilled service workers taking in laundry, bootblacking, car washing etc. Outwork was semi-skilled, consisting of simple assembly functions. Examples from the case studies consisted of one man who sewed soles of shoes on to uppers, another who sewed up pre-cut pieces of material into suits, a woman who assembled egg boxes, and another who folded and stuck envelopes.

The majority of the self-employed were fully autonomous, producing directly for the market with their own means of production. However, the degree of success was very variable. Apart from skill, it depended on access to crucial economic resources, particularly to working capital and markets (a good network of clients, a strategic location for his or her stall etc.). It was crucial to have a good clientele of regular customers, and/or a strategic location for access to casual trade. Almost all self-employed workers mentioned competition as a problem. Many of them were reliant on custom markets – networks of regular clients who stuck faithfully to them despite competition. Usually this was because of the quality of their work (e.g. their skill, quality of service, reliability etc.), a kin link or the availability of credit:

> 'Ya me conocen', 'ya me buscan', 'ya tengo mis clientes'
> (I'm well known now, people look for me now, I have my (regular) clients now).

A strategic location might provide access to more customers or better-paying ones. A shop in the downtown area of Lima would provide more custom than one out in the shanty towns where people were poorer, a stall in the centre of the market would have bigger takings than one on the margins, and a bus or *colectivo*[17] line with a heavy flow of traffic would be more lucrative than a less crowded one. As might be expected, the more strategic locations had their price: higher rents, mafia-like rings controlling the best *puestos* (stalls) in the markets, and transport cooperatives controlling the number of buses and *colectivos* allowed on the 'line'.

De Soto (1986) argues that many producers confined themselves to the informal sector in order to avoid institutional intervention. However, my data show that the self-employed did not escape bureaucratic control. Almost all small-scale businesses had a licence or permit of some sort, and some required several different types. Only 17 per cent of the men and 22 per cent of the women in self-employment were working without any documents. Despite grumbling about it, very few of them mentioned documentation as a major obstacle to entry or expansion.

Some of the self-employed were able to set themselves up in business at relatively little cost, but these were the least lucrative situations (cf. Moser 1977). The better positions almost always involved an investment cost, either in locale and installations, a vehicle or merchandise. A tailor would need a sewing machine, tools and basic inputs; a car mechanic would need a garage, tools and machinery; a store keeper would need a refrigerator, sales counter and stock; a bus or cab driver would need a vehicle; jewellers needed a downtown site and expensive tools; street traders needed enough working capital to buy stock and transport from the wholesale markets to their stalls; even little food stalls required cooking equipment, plates and cutlery. Only construction workers were able to ply their trade on the basis of skills and simple tools alone.

All the high-income earners amongst the self-employed had made substantial investments, often running into 50–100,000 soles, i.e. thirty to forty
times the minimum wage. Many of these workers had built up their businesses
gradually from their own savings, had loans from their kinsmen, or would
club together to buy crucial equipment; others used their redundancy or
separation payments when they left formal employment. Only one of the case
studies, out of a total of ninety-six, had used a bank loan. Access to capital
was the most commonly cited factor determining the success or failure of the
self-employed and their possibilities for expansion.

Mobility and flexibility were another ingredient of success, particularly
in commerce and services. As opportunities declined in one line and opened
up in another, they would shift their activities, moving to different parts of
the city or even travelling to the interior, and bringing in friends and relatives
on a commission basis as necessary. Here the lack of fixed capital and formal
contracts was an advantage, although a cushion of savings was usually
necessary. Some of the career patterns described in chapter 7 provide
examples of this extraordinary versatility and flexibility.

Women were the real losers on all counts. They were confined to the least
lucrative markets, they had least access to crucial economic resources and
were the most inflexible and immobile. Two-thirds were working from home,
mostly in dressmaking, small shops, laundry work or meals. Although many
had regular customers, they were limited by the purchasing power of neighbours who like themselves were very poor. Some, such as the dressmakers,
might have invested in a sewing machine, and they were usually better off
than the others. The rest made do with very small amounts of capital and were
thus limited to a small scale of operations.[18] Women's low earnings in
self-employment were therefore due to a lack of access to skill, capital and
lucrative markets and the fact that many of them were tied to the home.

This analysis of self-employment shows a high degree of linkage with the
wider economy, be it in terms of purchased inputs, markets supplied, or
chains of subcontracting which ultimately led to large firms. Indeed, the
higher the degree of linkage (i.e. supplying a larger market, higher income
customers, or purchasing higher cost inputs), the higher the earnings. Thus,
contrary to some interpretations, integration with the capitalist sector of the
economy did not bring greater exploitation and poverty. On the contrary,
those who suffered most in this situation were those who were excluded from
such linkages, such as women.

Underpinning this situation was the general buoyancy in the economy.
This was creating short-term shortages in supply that informal producers
were able to meet. Even subcontracting was a response to this situation, so
that although outworkers lacked the stability of permanent wage earners,
there was enough work for them to be able to achieve comparable earnings.

However, we must remember that self-employment was deeply stratified by skill, gender and unequal access to resources and markets. These were important barriers to entry which meant that even in an expanding situation, not everyone was able to participate equally in the growth process.

LABOUR MARKET DIVISIONS AND THE EXPERIENCE OF WORK

We have seen that the manual labour market was deeply segmented by enterprise size, skill and gender. But what does this tell us about that other aspect of class relations, the experience of work itself? How diverse were the physical conditions of work, its pace and intensity, the structure of work groups, the degree of autonomy, forms of authority, the quality of relationships within the workplace etc.? Work attitude data show that manual workers gave considerable importance to these aspects of work. They were strong influences on the development of work identities, forms of solidarity, and attitudes towards other classes (see chapter 9).

The case studies indicate that work experiences did not differ between formal and informal sectors as dramatically as labour market variables, and there were important differences within both sectors. Amongst those working for large firms, there were major differences in the situation of construction and transport workers, compared with factory workers, while commercial and service establishments were different again. Within the informal sector, there were variations between those who worked in the busy downtown markets, those who worked at home in the distant shanty towns, and domestic servants working in other people's homes all over the city. Against this, the high degree of personalism throughout the labour market meant that social relations in the workplace had a similar quality in many different types of enterprise.

Qualitative differences in the experience of work between different sized establishments were most pronounced in the manufacturing sector. The large capital-intensive firms had mass production techniques, machine-pacing of work, large work groups performing specialized tasks, close supervision, and depersonalized incentives to increase productivity, such as piece rates. They had shorter hours and a better quality working environment. The pay and conditions of the work were superior to those in smaller enterprises, but the pace and intensity of work was greater. Many of the foreign firms imported their own management style along with the technology, implanting a workplace culture that was more impersonal and less authoritarian than the Peruvian tradition.

Medium-sized factories and large workshops were more labour intensive and had longer hours of work. Many of them were sweatshops, with poor, cramped working conditions and very intense direct control over labour, backed up by a policy of rapid hire and fire. Some workshops had a paternalistic style, with the *patrón* (boss) working alongside his employees and adopting a quasi-kinship relationship with his employees. Others were more authoritarian; many workers complained of 'despotism' at work (Briones and Mejía 1964: 47). At the informal end of the continuum, there were independent artisans working in the downtown areas, close to the markets, or else in their own homes, scattered about in the slums and shanty towns. These workers enjoyed a slower pace of work, independence from bosses and supervisors, and more direct contact with their customers; but they were isolated from other producers and lacked the companionship of the industrial work group.

In construction and transport there were few differences between formal and informal enterprises. In construction, the small workgroup was the norm whatever the size of the firm, and its membership was transient. In transport, the work of drivers and conductors was by its very nature solitary, mobile and fraught with the pressure of too many passengers and chaotic traffic. Working for a bus company rather than oneself mainly meant more regular hours and perhaps better maintained vehicles, otherwise the work was the same.

In commerce and services, there was great heterogeneity in working conditions. Shop work in large downtown stores meant a relatively clean environment, low-intensity work, and small fragmented workgroups; small shops had more direct personal relations with the boss and other employees. Hotels and restaurants were similarly differentiated: a better working environment and slower pace of work in the larger places; inferior conditions, a busier pace and more personalistic work relations in the smaller ones. Informal sector work in the markets and on the streets was very different; the high competition between traders made for an intense pressure of work. The hours were very long and the working facilities minimal. Traders often had to rise before dawn and travel long distances to collect their produce. Others would have to sit for hours in isolated sites on street corners. Those with small shops appended to their homes had the benefit of proximity to the family and a slower pace of work, but they had to put in extremely long hours to make a living.

Domestic service was an occupation with very specific characteristics. Most servants lived in and were subject to the most direct forms of subordination of all. Some employers treated their maids well, others subjected them to verbal, physical or even sexual abuse, exhibiting substantial class and racial prejudice towards them (Rutté Garcia 1973, Sindicato de Trabajadores del Hogar 1982, Bunster and Chaney 1985). The inferior status of the maid within the household was signalled in a myriad of ways: the curtailment of their personal space, their inferior living quarters,[19] being restricted to the kitchen at all times except when cleaning, not being able to eat at the same time as the family, nor the same foods, having to wear a uniform at all times, not being able to leave the house except for very specific tasks etc. They were at the beck and call of their employers at any hour and most days, with very little time off. Maids used to have trouble getting their pay regularly, and this was often a deliberate device used by employers to stop them leaving. One informant told me that upon starting work with one family, the *patrona* took all her clothes and possessions from her and held them as a ransom to stop her from running away. Small wonder that for many of these maids, marriage was an escape.

Domestic service was considered menial, not so much because of the physical work but because it involved daily humiliations by another social class. In days gone by, wealthy households used to have large retinues of servants, including butlers, housekeepers, cooks, nannies and maids, who could keep each other company. By the mid-1960s, however, these domestic retinues were shrinking and many maids found themselves on their own with their employers. They lived in almost continual isolation from other similar workers and from their own families.

Most formal and informal enterprises had a high degree of personalism in workplace interactions because of the presence of kinsmen or direct control by those in authority. This personalism straddled vertical relations between bosses, supervisors and employees as well as horizontal relations between workmates. It was an important element in adding to or subtracting from the quality of life at work. Working in close proximity to the boss was fine if he had good working relations with his employees, but if he was authoritarian or moody, it could make trouble. The work history data showed that many workers left their jobs because of 'problems' at work.

Similarly, the all-pervasive kinship networks had advantages and disadvantages. Within the largest enterprises, the presence of kinsmen and neighbours was a source of informal interaction that to some extent offset the dominance of the machine and formal supervision. When asked how they got on with their supervisors, many workers replied that they got on well because he was a relative. In small enterprises, the presence of relatives gave a familial quality to workplace interaction which many workers preferred. However, as we saw in chapter 4, the labouring-class family was highly authoritarian. Young children and wives often had a raw deal working for their relatives.

There were great differences between men's and women's experience of work. The striking characteristic of men's work was its mobility and independence. The vast majority of men were on the move – in construction gangs, transport, ambulatory sales and services. Many of those in more static occupations, such as storekeepers, travelled about to obtain their merchandise, or if they worked in the wholesale market, they were surrounded by movement and variety. In manufacturing, work was more sedentary and subject to supervision. However, the division of labour within factories and workshops meant that many wage workers were in control of others, e.g. *ayudantes* or apprentices, and this somewhat diluted their own sense of subordination. Moreover, the overlay of kinship on to the authority structure masked the experience of being ordered about by and dependent on another class.

Almost a third of the men were self-employed, but this was self-employment that involved a pride in craftsmanship, the ability to mobilize capital and resources and to command the labour of family helpers or other occasional helpers. Men had to suffer the insecurity of poverty and the pressure of having to maintain their wives and families but their sense of personal freedom was not generally threatened by the world of work. As we saw in chapter 4, the *machista* concept of masculinity emphasized men's ability to subordinate others rather than to be subordinated, their freedom of movement rather than being hemmed in and tied down, and their sense of personal pride and dignity. The world of work did not threaten these notions, on the contrary it supported and reinforced them. Many men described their work using the language of *machismo*, hard physical labour and 'possession of the street' being equated with manliness.

Women's experience of work was the complete opposite of this. Their occupations offered few possibilities for pride in work, self-fulfilment or personal prestige. On the whole, they were immobile, confined to their own or other people's homes. When they worked for others, they were subjected to harsh discipline, especially in domestic service. Women who worked in medium- and large-scale factories were confined to a very sex-segregated environment. They were subjected to much greater routine and discipline than the men. Most of them worked in clothing sweatshops where subordination to the machine and production targets was intense. Others worked in assembly and packaging functions, where again their work was highly regimented and controlled. Few of these jobs involved training other workers or the exercise of skill and discretion that could offset the feeling of total control by employers and supervisors. Small wonder then, that women preferred working for themselves at home, at their own pace, even if it involved lower earnings and low status work.

We can find parallels between conceptions of femininity and the world of women's work. Bourgeois conceptions of *machismo* considered that unmarried girls had to be monitored, controlled and supervised. This suited employers well, since it legitimated the close control of factory girls and domestic servants. Such employers would legitimize their practices with a paternalistic ideology that it was 'for the girls' own good'. Self-employment for women meant immobility, confinement to the home and dependence on the male wage. Family and gender thus not only conditioned men's and women's participation in the labour market, it also differentiated their personal experience of work; and the world of work in turn confirmed and supported the structure of gender inequality within labouring families. We shall return to the relationship between gender divisions in employment and the family in chapter 8.

LABOUR MARKET DIVISIONS AND CLASS

This chapter has shown that there was considerable diversity within the labouring class in terms of both labour market positions and work experiences. This diversity could not be subsumed by a single formal–informal polarity but consisted of various cross-cutting axes of segmentation. In terms of specific job preferences, the case study data show that manual workers were well aware of the advantages and disadvantages of different types of employment. Asked whether it was better to work in a small enterprise or a large one, 59 per cent said the latter was preferable because of the higher incomes, greater job security and better access to social security benefits. However, when asked whether it was better to be a wage worker or self-employed, two-thirds (and 60 per cent of those currently employed in large enterprises) said the latter. Mostly this was because of the greater independence, but some said they could earn more in self-employment.

The recurrent criteria for evaluating different jobs were income, skill, independence and working conditions. However, people were also concerned with the intrinsic satisfactions of work; whether they found it interesting, whether it involved effort or discomfort, and whether they were treated well by their employers. Pride in work and self-respect were important to manual workers; maximizing incomes was only one part of the picture for them. There was also a stress on petty entrepreneurship, freedom from routines and supervision, and pride in craftsmanship and hard work. They realized that there were trade-offs involved in choosing different elements, and that both formal and informal sectors could offer different combinations. We shall see in the next chapter that there was considerable movement between different types of employment; therefore these preferences were well informed. There was considerable fine tuning within the range of options available, but also a general resignation to the fact that none of them was wonderful.

The analysis of internal heterogeneity can easily lose sight of the broader criteria which separate manual workers as a whole from other classes. Even though the boundary between them and the middle class was fuzzy, it did exist. Non-manual work was considered to be lighter, better paid and more respected. Yet, when asked whether they would prefer office work to manual work, only a fifth said they would prefer the former. Statements such as 'I was born a worker, I'll always be one' and 'this is my station in life' together with a certain disparagement of office work suggest that there was a cultural gap between these classes as well as an economic one. Therefore, even if they wanted professional jobs for their children, their own aspirations were oriented towards the best jobs within the labouring class. Chapter 9 will show that the manual/non-manual boundary was more important for the determination of labouring-class identity than divisions between skill levels, genders or formal and informal sectors. In order to understand how this generalized class identity was forged, and came to be shared by both men and women, it is necessary to look at people's accumulated experiences over their lifetimes and the way in which these experiences were brought together within the family. The following chapters take up these issues.

6 Mobility within the labouring class I: aggregate patterns

The previous chapter documented the remarkable diversity in the manual labour market produced by the growth process. This diversity was structured by three major divisions: enterprise size (the formal/informal sectors), skill and gender. This chapter and the next examine the pattern of mobility across these divisions. Here we shall analyse the volume of movement between formal and informal sectors and between skill levels, in the course of workers' lifetimes, and the degree to which these patterns differed between men and women. We also look at the pace of mobility, i.e. the frequency of job changing, the length of time spent in different jobs, and whether or not women were a more unstable workforce than men. The next chapter describes the career paths which underlay these aggregate patterns. There we shall see how movement towards the highly skilled and better self-employed jobs was achieved and how some workers – particularly women – were trapped in a series of dead-end jobs.

Informal sector theory contains many assumptions about the mobility and stability of labour which will be contradicted in these chapters. It assumes that there is little movement between the formal and informal sectors because of barriers to entry in the former sector and ease of access in the latter. Labour stability is thought to be high in the formal sector because the jobs are better and there are less voluntary quits, while it is low in the informal sector because of the volatility of incomes, job sharing and moonlighting. These assumptions have found their way into class theory, thus the 'formal proletariat' is assumed to be a stable group, while the 'informal proletariat' or the 'marginal mass' is transient and unstable. We shall see, however, that there was much more mobility between sectors and fewer differences in labour stability than is assumed by the theory.

There were major differences between the mobility patterns of men and women, with women more confined to informal sector jobs and less upwardly mobile. This kind of situation is often explained with reference to labour stability. Men are assumed to be a more stable and committed workforce because of their role as family breadwinners, while women are transient and unstable because they drop out of the labour market to have children. This notion parallels assumptions about the varying degree of stability in the formal and informal sectors; thus men's concentration in the former is related to their higher labour force commitment and women's concentration in the latter is linked to their transience as a workforce. However, the data presented here show that women's average job durations were actually the same as men's, once age had been taken into account. Women's breaks from employment for full-time housework produced a shorter working life than men's, but *when* they were at work, they were as stable as men. Their career patterns differed from men's because of confinement to a narrow range of jobs, not because they were a transient workforce.

Diversity within the labouring class would make it possible for subgroups to emerge that were identified with particular parts of the manual labour market, and this has implications for class formation. For example, the 'labour aristocracy' is a group that holds a monopoly over skilled and highly paid jobs, while the lumpenproletariat is one that becomes trapped within a series of dead-end jobs. If these groups coalesce over time and the boundaries between them rigidify, status distinctions, group subcultures and a sense of common interests and identity may grow and find expression in political action (cf. Goldthorpe 1983b).

On the other hand, a high degree of movement between groups or labour market segments makes the boundaries between them more fluid, with a disintegrating effect on group solidarities. If workers move in and out of wage labour, for example, they are unlikely to identify with political movements aimed at defending the interests of the industrial working class, or to think of themselves as part of an elite. However, it could also be argued that the diversity of experience produced by mobility creates a more general sense of identity, one that *encompasses* the different types of jobs which workers typically move between, rather than differentiating between them. Moreover, if the mobility process is very widespread, it may itself be viewed as a collective interest to be defended politically. I believe this was the case in Lima during the early 1970s.

The questions to be addressed in this chapter are whether the formal/informal division produced 'cores' with continuous employment in one or other sector and a distinctive pattern of job stability, whether the skill divisions produced elites, and how far men's and women's mobility processes differed. We shall find that there was extensive movement between the formal and informal sectors, and that the 'core' within each sector was very small indeed. There was relatively open access to skilled positions and little evidence of a craft or technological elite. Formal sector jobs were not more stable than informal ones; if anything the reverse was the case. Within *both* sectors there were stable and casual groups, and a process of upward mobility towards higher skilled, more stable and better paid jobs, together with entrapment in dead-end jobs. On the whole, men were associated with the first of these and women with the second.

METHODOLOGICAL NOTE

The analysis of mobility in these two chapters is mainly based on work history data from the case studies. A special life history technique was used to collect these data and covered every job ever held, up to the point of interview (see Balan *et al.* 1973 and Appendix). The Ministry of Labour 1973 survey had some work history data, but it contained less precise information and a narrower range of variables.[1] Nevertheless it provides a useful complement to the case study data because of its larger size and better coverage of workers in large enterprises. These data will be referred to in the section on job changing and job duration.

The life history technique permits a relatively precise calculation of job change, job duration and total working life. However, the measurement of mobility depends crucially on how 'job' and 'job change' are defined (see Appendix). In brief, a 'job change' was considered to have occurred whenever there was a change in (a) the trade or occupation, (b) the skill level of a job, (c) the employment status, or (d) the enterprise. Changes in labour force status, such as unemployment, withdrawal for full-time housework, military service, illness etc., were also regarded as breaks in employment. This definition tends to produce a higher number of changes than many datasets which only record occupational or employer changes.

Mobility variables are also affected by how first entry into the labour market is defined. This is problematic in Peru because of the prevalence of child labour. As indicated in previous chapters, many children, especially migrants, started work at an early age. Therefore the practice in Peruvian official statistics of defining entry at the age of 14 years was inappropriate in my view. In this study, child labour was coded as a job and incorporated into the mobility analysis.[2]

FIRST ENTRY INTO THE LABOUR MARKET

Informal sector theory assumes that migrants are engaged in agricultural work prior to migration and enter the tertiary sector immediately after their arrival in the city. Access to manufacturing jobs is only possible after a period of time there. The Lima data show that this picture was true for women but not men. Although most migrants came from an agricultural background, migrant men had experience of manufacturing and formal sector employment both prior to migration and on arrival in the city, in fact more so than the Lima-born. Migrant women, on the other hand, were more likely to go straight into domestic service in the city.

As chapter 4 showed, the labouring class had a strong migrant/agricultural background. About three-quarters of them were migrants and nearly half were from peasant families. Just over a third of informants' fathers and over half of their mothers were in agriculture at the point when they entered the labour force.[3] Child labour was important amongst most of the migrants, especially boys,[4] but much less so amongst the Lima-born. Of the male migrants, 18 per cent had started work before they were 10, and two-thirds were in work by the time they were 15. In contrast, only 39 per cent of Lima-born men had started work before the age of 15. Even when child labour is excluded, the tendency remains for migrants to start earlier than the Lima-born and for men to start earlier than women.

Most migrants had arrived in Lima in their teen years or early 20s: 28 per cent were under 15 years, 31 per cent were between 15 and 19, 21 per cent between 20 and 24, and the remaining 20 per cent were over 25 years. The degree of experience of work outside Lima was very variable: some had had a considerable number of jobs in both the countryside and provincial towns, others knew very little of the world of work outside the capital. Nearly two-thirds of the men had started their working lives outside Lima, mostly in the *sierra*,[5] but only a third of the women had done so.

When child labour is included, half the male migrants had started off in agriculture, and two-thirds in informal enterprises. If child labour is excluded, these figures fall to 23 per cent and 31 per cent respectively. On the latter figures, slightly *more* migrants started off in manufacturing and in formal enterprises than the Lima-born. Migrant men were more likely to have worked as labourers in formal establishments outside Lima, whereas local men started off in apprenticeships in small enterprises in Lima. The reverse was the case for women: migrant women entered informal employment, mainly in domestic service and to a lesser extent petty manufacturing, but Lima-born women had gone into small factories and shops.

Interestingly, these patterns remained very similar after arrival in Lima; only 37 per cent of migrant men took their first job in the informal sector, whereas just over half of local men did. Migrant men were only marginally more likely to have gone into commerce and services than local men, and slightly more went into manufacturing. However, 72 per cent of migrant women went straight into the informal sector in Lima, but only 42 per cent of local women did so.

In summary, with the exception of child labour on the family farm, entry into the labour market was not as different for migrants and the Lima-born as assumed by informal sector models. The major differences were between men and women, and only the latter conformed to the informal sector stereotype.

MOBILITY ACROSS LABOUR MARKET DIVISIONS

This section looks at the extent of movement between labour market segments. For this purpose, the total sequence of job changes in each individual's work history was classified according to the degree of mobility between economic sectors, enterprise size groups, employment statuses and skill levels. Table 6.1 provides data for the sample as a whole and then for the over-30s only. The data show a high degree of movement overall, but much more for men than for women.

Taking economic sectors[6] first, and ignoring jobs in agriculture for the moment, we find a high degree of intersectoral movement.[7] In total, only 37 per cent of all cases had been confined to the tertiary sector (commerce, transport and services); less than a quarter had spent all their time in secondary sector jobs (manufacturing and construction) and the remaining 40 per cent had held jobs in both secondary and tertiary sectors. Amongst over-30-year-olds there were slightly higher proportions with all-secondary sector jobs and less with all-tertiary jobs, but the same proportion with experience of both sectors. A five-sector classification reveals even more intersectoral movement: less than 10 per cent of cases had been confined to any one sector and just over half the cases had moved between three sectors or more.

However, there was much more intersectoral movement amongst men and more tertiary confinement amongst women. Almost two-thirds of women had only ever had tertiary jobs compared with a quarter of men, less than 10 per cent had only had secondary sector jobs compared with 31 per cent of men and just over a quarter had moved between secondary and tertiary sectors compared with 46 per cent of men. Excluding the under-30s reduced this sectoral confinement somewhat, but women were still much more concentrated in the 'tertiary sector only' category than men.

Disaggregating intersectoral movement by current employment reveals lower rates. Sixty per cent of men *currently* employed in manufacturing and construction had always had secondary sector jobs while 46 per cent of those in commerce and services had always had tertiary sector jobs. Still, this should not overshadow the fact that 40 per cent of those currently in secondary sector jobs had been in commerce and services at some time and that the *majority* in the latter sectors had some manufacturing or construction experience. The picture for women was different; those currently employed in manufacturing were more likely than men to have had experience of other sectors (mainly in domestic service), while those currently in commerce and services were *much* more likely to have only ever been in those sectors. In summary,

Table 6.1 Individual cumulative work history transitions, by sector, employment status, enterprise size, skill and sex, Lima 1974

| | Total sample | | 30+ years only | |
	Men	Women	Men	Women
Economic sector				
all tertiary	23	65	20	57
all secondary	31	8	37	11
secondary & tertiary	46	27	43	32
Formal/informal sectors				
all informal	16	56	7	54
all formal	11	11	11	8
mixed starting informal	49	24	52	28
mixed starting formal	24	9	29	10
Employment status				
all self-employed	4	10	3	20
all waged	45	48	35	24
wage & self-employed	51	42	62	57
Skill				
immobile	28	74	19	61
mobile	49	10	60	14
semi-mobile	19	13	17	22
downwardly mobile	4	3	3	3
Total	100	100	100	100
N	(128)	(64)	(95)	(33)

Source: Author's case studies (weighted)

amongst men there was a small group with exclusively secondary sector experience but for the majority there was a great deal of movement between sectors; amongst women there was much more tertiary sector concentration.

Movement between formal and informal sectors reveals a similar picture – a diversity of experience for men, but restriction for women. There is little evidence of barriers to entry in the formal sector or confinement to the informal sector. Sixty per cent of the sample had been in both sectors, only

29 per cent had remained within the informal sector all their working lives and 11 per cent had stayed in the formal sector. The majority of cases (70 per cent) had started out in enterprises with less than five workers, but well over half of these had subsequently moved into large ones. Similarly, of the 30 per cent who had started out in large enterprises, nearly two-thirds had subsequently moved into small ones. However, women were much more confined to small enterprises than men. Dividing the cases by age shows that confinement to small enterprises remained virtually unchanged for women over their working lives but it dropped sharply amongst men; thus over half the women over 30 had always been working in informal enterprises compared with only 7 per cent of men, while the vast majority of men (81 per cent) had been in both formal and informal ones.

Comparing past trajectories with current employment shows that at the time of interview, the majority of men in both sectors had experience of working in the other: 70 per cent of men currently in informal enterprises had worked in formal ones and 75 per cent of those currently in formal enterprises had worked in informal ones. Most of this latter group had started out in small enterprises, gradually making their way up into large ones. However, only a third of women currently in the informal sector had ever worked in formal enterprises,[8] and those currently working in formal enterprises were much less likely to have worked in informal ones. Women tended to enter the formal sector directly, rather than through lateral movement from the informal sector, like men did.

Regarding employment status, once again the data show little evidence of enduring reliance on either self-employment or wage labour, but rather of extensive movement between the two. The case studies were almost equally divided between those with sole experience of wage work and those with a mixture of wage work and self-employment. *Only a tiny minority had only ever worked on an exclusively self-employed basis.* Since self-employment was strongly associated with age, the figures for the over-30s are particularly revealing. They show even less with 'all waged' experience and more with a combination of wage work and self-employment. The main trend was of movement between the two categories of employment. Thus of men over 30 years currently in wage work, 47 per cent had at some time been self-employed and of those currently self-employed, 91 per cent had experienced wage work.

However, there was less movement between these categories amongst women. Of women over 30 who were still wage workers, 39 per cent had been self-employed, and of those currently self-employed, 68 per cent had been in wage work. A much greater proportion of women had only ever been self-employed compared to men (20 per cent as against 3 per cent).

Note that many in the 'all waged' category had spent their time as wage labourers in informal enterprises. This was especially the case with women;

63 per cent of them had only worked in small enterprises compared with 25 per cent of men. The high figure for women is largely due to the inclusion of domestic service in wage work. In fact, two-thirds of women in the 'all waged' category had done some domestic service and over half (55 per cent) of all women had done it at some time or other. Only a quarter of men and as many women had done their wage work exclusively in formal enterprises. This confirms the existence of a 'core' industrial proletariat but it was small and mainly male. In comparison, the informal 'core' was slightly bigger (29 per cent) and was mainly female.

Finally, let us turn to skill. The transition categories were defined thus: the 'immobile' were those whose jobs had all been unskilled or semi-skilled; the 'mobile' had reached *maestro* status and stayed there; the 'semi-mobile' had progressed upwards from unskilled jobs through apprenticeships and into semi-skilled work, but had gone no further; and the 'downwardly mobile' had once been in skilled jobs but had subsequently fallen to lower positions. The differences between men and women were more marked here than on any other variable, with a concentration of women in the 'immobile' category and of men amongst the 'mobile'. *Excluding the under-30s, 60 per cent of men were 'mobile' compared with only 14 per cent of the women, and 61 per cent of the women were 'immobile' compared with 19 per cent of the men.*

In sum, these data show that there was much more movement between labour market segments than has been assumed by the informal sector literature; there was movement between secondary and tertiary sectors, between formal and informal enterprises, between wage labour and self-employment and between different levels of skill. However, most of this movement was of men; women were concentrated in the tertiary sector, in small enterprises and in unskilled jobs.

MOBILITY AND OUTCOMES

Let us now look at the outcomes of these different patterns of mobility, restricting the analysis to mid- or end-career people (over-30s only). We know from the previous chapter that the best manual jobs were those with high skill (*maestro* status) and high earnings, the two being closely related. I shall now examine how the different patterns of movement were related to skill mobility and current income. A high proportion of the men were mobile in skill terms and of these over half had earnings that were three times the minimum wage. In comparison, only 14 per cent of the women were in the mobile group and none of them were in the high income group;[9] 61 per cent were immobile and most were earning less than the minimum wage. The data were thus very polarized between mobile men and immobile women; table 6.2 presents the data on mobility profiles for these two contrasting groups.

Table 6.2 Skill mobility and income outcomes of career patterns, two major groups only, over 30s only (frequencies), Lima 1974

	Mobile men	Immobile women	High income men	Low income women
Economic sector				
all secondary	23	1	10	2
all tertiary	9	14	6	12
secondary & tertiary	24	5	18	7
Formal/informal sectors				
all informal	6	13	1	12
mixed	44	6	24	9
all formal	6	1	8	—
Employment status				
all waged	17	4	15	3
all self-employed	3	4	1	3
waged & self-employed	36	12	18	14
N	56	20	56	20
percentage of all men	60	—	36	—
percentage of all women	—	61	—	66

Source: Author's case studies (weighted)

Taking the probability of achieving skill mobility first, it is clear that success was associated with some experience of secondary sector employment and movement between formal and informal sectors. Immobility was linked to confinement within the tertiary sector and small enterprises. Most of the men who had reached *maestro* level had done so within manufacturing or construction or a combination of these two with the tertiary sector; in contrast, three-quarters of the immobile women had only ever worked in commerce and services. Of mobile men, 80 per cent had moved between formal and informal sectors while 73 per cent of immobile women had been confined to informal ones. The effect of employment status appears contradictory; for men the greatest chance of mobility was to combine wage labour with self-employment. Sixty-one per cent of mobile men had done this and 64 per cent of men who had combined these two statuses had achieved mobility. However, amongst immobile women, the largest group also had this combination, reflecting the fact that much of the wage labour was domestic service and did not contribute to a mobile career.

The analysis thus far has concentrated on patterns of movement between the various segments of the labour market. But how fast was the rate of movement? Did people change jobs more frequently in the informal sector than the formal, as posited by the theory? To what extent did it differ between men and women? Could women's confinement to the disadvantaged parts of the labour market be explained by their instability in the labour market, as implied by their status as secondary wage earners?

JOB CHANGING AND JOB DURATION[10]

The analysis below shows that (a) there was a generally low movement in the manual labour market, as manifested by the number of jobs held and the length of job duration, (b) the rates of movement were *not* noticeably higher in the informal sector than the formal; on the contrary, the reverse was the case, and (c) although women were in the labour force for a shorter period than men, there were no significant differences between men and women in terms of job duration. These findings contradict the usual assumption that high rates of job changing are characteristic of the weaker groups in the labour market, such as informal sector workers and women. Apart from a very small group of casual workers, job changing was associated with upward mobility, while long job durations reflected entrapment in bad jobs.

Low rates of job change amongst manual workers were commented on by various authors writing in the 1960s (Briones and Mejía 1964, Chaplin 1967: 133).[11] The Ministry of Labour 1973 data gave an average of 1.8 jobs per manual worker during the decade 1963–73, over half the workforce having had less than two jobs during the period. These rates are low according to international mobility studies at the time.[12] The job duration data give an overall average of 6.3 years in current job and 4.4 years in the penultimate job. The main factor affecting current job duration was age,[13] and there were some very long durations amongst men in their 30s and 40s (average 7.2 years and 12.7 years respectively). There was a J-shaped trend in the relationship between enterprise size and job duration; the longest durations were in the largest *and* smallest enterprises, and the shorter durations were in the 5–99 group. The job durations of the self-employed were longer than that of wage workers – the gross means were 8.0 and 5.5 years, with 8.9 and 6.2 for men and 6.5 and 3.9 for women. However, there was a strong association between age and self-employment; controlling for age sharply reduced the differential but durations were still longer amongst the self-employed.

Average job duration was longer for men than women, although less in the penultimate job than current job. Current job durations had an overall mean of 6.3 years, with 7.0 for men and 4.9 for women. However, on penultimate jobs, the means were much closer – 4.4, 4.5 and 4.0 respectively. The differential on current jobs was mainly due to the different age structure of the two workforces, women being much younger. An equation regressing enterprise size, self-employment (dummy), age, income and sex on job duration produced an r^2 of 0.30. Of the variance, 28 per cent was explained by age; sex contributed only 0.06 per cent and was not statistically significant.

As mentioned, the case study data permit us to measure job change more precisely and to distinguish different types of job change, e.g. changes in occupation, sector, enterprise type and skill level. These data show a low rate of occupation change and slightly higher rates of enterprise and job change (table 6.3). On average, manual workers had 2.5 occupation changes during their working lives, 4.3 enterprise changes and 5.0 job changes. In general, a higher number of job moves was associated with being in the advantaged rather than the disadvantaged parts of the labour market. Skilled workers had

Table 6.3 Average job changes, different measures, by sex and age, Lima 1974

| | Average number of jobs | | | |
| | Age groups | | | |
	<30	*30–39*	*40+*	*Total*
Occupations				
men	2.8	2.6	3.1	2.9
women	1.7	2.2	2.1	1.9
Economic sectors				
men	2.8	3.3	3.9	3.4
women	1.9	2.2	2.3	2.1
Enterprises				
men	3.6	5.1	5.9	5.1
women	2.1	2.8	3.3	2.6
Jobs				
men	4.0	5.6	6.9	5.8
women	3.1	3.6	3.8	3.4
N	64	56	72	192

Source: Author's case studies (weighted)

had more jobs than the unskilled, formal sector workers more than informal workers, and men more than women.[14] Thus job stability was a symptom of entrapment rather than advantage.

These trends are confirmed by the job duration data.[15] Average duration figures were: 5.8 years per occupation, 5.7 years per enterprise, and 4.6 years per job. Average occupation duration was 5.8 years, but in many cases it was considerably longer. *Maestros* for example had an average occupation duration of 11.5 years; tailors, shoemakers and dressmakers 9.0 years; skilled construction workers 7.2 years; retail salesworkers and street pedlars 7.7 and 7.0 years respectively, and bus drivers 6.8 years. There were also some extremely long durations amongst female unskilled work such as boarding-house-keepers (7.1) and washerwomen (7.2 years). Many, if not most of these, were in the informal sector. The most casual occupations were apprenticeships (2.8), loaders and porters (3.7) and bootblacks (2.9). In the middle were a number of occupations that were more associated with the formal sector (e.g. packers and labellers 5.3, mechanics 4.4, sales representatives and shop assistants 5.1) and others were in the informal sector (cooks and domestic servants 5.2).

Because of the association between occupations and economic sectors, job stability figures for economic sectors were also relatively high, although internal diversity indicates these figures should be disaggregated. There is little indication of high rates of instability in the sectors normally associated with the informal sector, i.e. commerce and services. There was only a narrow range of variation between sectors, and in fact, commerce had the longest average duration. The average job durations were: manufacturing 4.8 years, construction 4.0, transport 4.8, commerce 5.1, services 4.1.

As with the Ministry of Labour survey, the work history data show that the strongest effect on job duration was age, with average duration rising from 3.4 years amongst the under-20s to 5.9 years amongst 30-year-olds and 7.7 years amongst the over-40s. In this data set, average job duration was *longer* in informal enterprises (5.3 years) than in medium or large formal enterprises (3.6 and 4.8 years respectively).[16] The short job durations in medium-sized formal enterprises, already noted above, are consistent with the findings in the previous chapter that working conditions there were inferior to those in the largest firms. If there was any sector of the labour market to be characterized by cheap labour and rapid turnover, it was these 'sweatshop' (formal) establishments.

Here too there was a J-shaped association between job duration and skill, being moderately high amongst unskilled jobs, falling at apprenticeship level, then rising through the skilled levels. Amongst men, average durations for unskilled work were 4.2 years, 2.8 years for apprenticeships, 5.3 years for semi-skilled work and 5.7 years for skilled work. The pattern was very similar for women. However, there was an interaction between skill and age, with some of the longest job durations amongst the older age groups being amongst the unskilled as well as the highly skilled. This pattern was again true for women as well as men, but the paucity of women in skilled jobs meant that amongst older women, long job durations were mainly at the unskilled level.

The Ministry of Labour data suggested a relationship between employment status and job duration; in the case histories too, jobs were held longer in self-employment than in wage work. Average job duration in the latter category was 3.9 years, whereas in self-employment it was 6.6 years. The job duration figures for the self-employed were higher than for wage workers within every age group and amongst women and men. However, a long job duration in self-employment meant very different things for men and women: for the latter it was entrapment at low levels of skill and income whereas for men it was the culmination of a successful career.

There was little to distinguish the average job durations of men and women; overall, women had the same average job duration as men (4.6 years). Such differences as existed were due to their different ages and locations in different sectors rather than gender itself. In the case study data too, regression analysis shows that once these were controlled for, sex had an insignificant effect on job duration.[17] It appears then that while women might have been a younger and less experienced workforce they were not a more unstable one.

THE ISSUE OF FEMALE LABOUR FORCE COMMITMENT

The above data suggest that women were not a more unstable workforce than men; if anything, the contrary was the case. How does this square with their low rates of labour force participation after marriage? The life histories permit us to examine the past pattern of labour force participation for those who were in paid work at the time of interview. These data reveal that (a) the largest group of women workers were single and childless, (b) women who did withdraw from work to look after their families had usually done so only once; they did not move in and out of employment frequently, and (c) there was a significant group of women who had worked continuously throughout their lives, despite having a family. As a result of these three factors, there was a significant number of working women with long and stable work histories. Nearly half the women in their 30s had worked for over twenty years and just over half of the over-40s had worked for more than thirty years.

As noted in the previous chapter, the female workforce was very skewed towards young single women because of the low participation rates of married women. This, plus the long breaks taken for full-time housework before returning to work, meant that as a group, they had less aggregate work experience than men. On average, they had only spent fourteen years in work compared with men's twenty-seven years.[18] A third of the women had been working for less than ten years compared with only 9 per cent of the men, and less than 1 per cent of them had worked for more than forty years, compared with nearly a fifth of the men.

It might be thought that women's lack of success in achieving high-income jobs and a mobile career pattern was due to their more restricted labour force participation. However, this was not the case. Analysis of men and women over 30 showed that there was little relationship between a person's career pattern, the length of their working life, the length of their breaks from employment or their total number of job changes. Controlling for age and sex, there was little difference between those who were mobile or immobile with respect to these participatory variables, and it was not statistically significant.[19]

In any case, women's tendency to withdraw from work after marriage and childrearing cannot be equated with transience as a workforce. Of the women who had returned to work, 89 per cent had only taken one break from employment and had a very stable working life thereafter. Moreover, there was a significant group of women who had continued to work despite having children. The female labour force was therefore divided between three relatively stable groups: first, young single workers, many of whom started work at a very early age (40 per cent of the case studies), second, stable returners, most of whom had only taken one break from employment (32 per cent) and third, permanent workers who remained in work even while they had families (28 per cent). Amongst the last two groups, no doubt many were working out of economic necessity, but according to interview statements, many had a positive commitment to work, as well. Therefore the confinement of these women to marginal areas of the labour market cannot be explained in terms of low work commitment.

CONCLUSION

The above analysis has shown that there was considerable movement across labour market divisions, although the *rate* of movement was slow. The 1960s and 1970s had produced rapid growth in the labour market but not volatility. It was possible to achieve success within the manual labour market, but it was painfully slow, built up after years of patiently putting money aside, creating the right contacts and waiting for the right moment to change jobs or go self-employed. Immobility was characterized by entrapment in bad jobs rather than by 'here-today, gone-tomorrow' types.

The data present little evidence to support the notion that the formal sector was characterized by high job stability and the informal with instability. The formal sector had both short- and long-tenure jobs, the former being concentrated at the lower skill levels and amongst the young and the latter being reserved for highly skilled, older and more experienced workers. The informal sector had predominantly long duration jobs, although there were a variety of reasons for this. First, apprenticeships were longer than in the formal sector because of the idiosyncratic nature of the *maestro–aprendiz* relationship; second, skilled self-employment was considered a desirable end in itself; and third, there was a pool of people trapped in refuge jobs at the low-skilled level, with extremely long job durations (these points are illustrated in the next chapter).

The major differences in mobility patterns were not between formal and informal sectors, but between men and women. Women were less upwardly mobile than men, they were more confined to the informal sector and to employment in commerce and services. In terms of job duration, they were as stable a workforce as men, but their long duration jobs were associated with confinement to low-skilled and low-income jobs, rather than the culmination of an upwardly mobile manual career. For men, working in unskilled and poorly paid jobs was only a temporary stage in their working life, but for women it was a permanent state. The implications for women were clear: progress depended on getting an upwardly mobile husband and educating their daughters so they would get white collar jobs.

At the personal level, most workers experienced labour market diversity directly, and their perceptions and attitudes about the benefits and drawbacks of different types of job were well informed. The prevalence of an upwardly mobile career pattern strongly influenced their aspirations for the future and the development of their labour market strategies. At the structural level, the high degree of movement between different labour market segments meant that the labouring class was not polarized between a labour aristocracy and a lumpenproletariat. These groups did exist, but they were very small. Moreover, both groups were highly gender specific: the formal proletarian 'core' was 79 per cent male and the informal 'core' was 72 per cent female. Given their small size and the high permeability of the boundaries around these groups, it is unlikely that they could have formed the basis of a distinctive set of traditions and solidarities based on the workplace. On the contrary, what most of these workers had in common was the experience of mobility itself, especially considering that many – even women – had already experienced upward mobility through the migration process. This was what most of their institutions and solidarities were oriented towards.

7 Mobility within the labouring class II: career paths

The previous chapter documented extensive mobility between different labour market divisions. But how was this mobility achieved? What were the career paths that carried people towards highly skilled factory jobs rather than unskilled street peddling? What were the mechanisms through which people charted these trajectories? This chapter provides an analysis of these patterns of movement, based on the case studies. The objective is to indicate how these careers were structured, how the passage from one job to another was achieved and in what ways they differed for men and women. We are also interested in the extent of diversity experienced personally by individuals, because of its implications for the development of class consciousness.

Work histories are analysed here in terms of 'careers'. These are patterned sequences of job holding, built up over people's lifetimes as they moved about in the labour market. No assumption is made about upward progression, although as we shall see, men's trajectories often were 'careers' in this sense. In the following pages a number of the typical career paths are identified. These are illustrated with vignettes describing actual cases.

GENERAL PATTERN OF MANUAL CAREERS

The differentiation between formal and informal sectors and between different levels of skill, outlined in chapter 5, created the possibility for upward movement within each sector as well as lateral movement between them. Figure 7.1 gives a graphic representation of the main trajectories. Path A represents upward movement from unskilled and apprenticeship levels to that of *maestro* within informal enterprises. Path B shows a similar upward movement within formal ones. Path C represents lateral movement between informal and formal enterprises which went on at unskilled and semi-skilled levels. Path D indicates that some of those who reached skilled positions within formal enterprises moved across into self-employment (but rarely vice versa). Path E shows that there was some direct entry into semi-skilled jobs in formal enterprises, while paths F and G show movement from informal wage labour into self-employment at low levels of skill. These are sometimes referred to as 'refuge' careers.

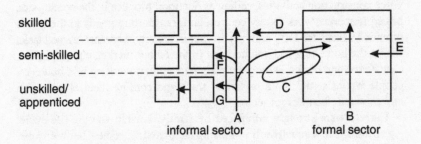

Figure 7.1 Career paths and employment divisions in Lima

Men and women had very different paths: most of the men could be found on the trajectories in the centre of the figure (A, B, C and D), while the women predominated on the edges, in E, F and G. For men, the starting point of the work history was usually in an informal enterprise, although some would also take casual jobs in formal ones; however, the port of entry into an upwardly mobile career was almost always through an informal sector apprenticeship. This would be followed by upward movement through skill levels within informal or formal enterprises. Most men reached *maestro* level within small enterprises and many of those who did so within large ones eventually moved back into skilled self-employment. However, despite extensive lateral movement between sectors and types of enterprise, the overall trend for men was vertical.

In contrast, amongst women the trend was lateral. For most, especially those with little education, the starting point was domestic service. After this they might try other types of wage work or move directly into unskilled self-employment (e.g. petty trade or laundry work). Others, especially the better educated ones, would go directly into semi-skilled factory jobs or shop work and after marriage would set themselves up as self-employed seamstresses or outworkers. Women did not usually pass through the workshop training process that men did, and few reached *maestro* status.

Sectoral specificities were important in structuring manual careers. The strong trade allegiances mentioned in chapter 5 meant that the vertical mobility process tended to be contained within economic sectors. Intersectoral movement mainly occurred at the unskilled level while workers 'shopped around' different jobs; this took place during times of transition, such as at the beginning of an occupational career, just after migration, on finishing military service or at the end of a person's working life. Each sector had its 'refuge' careers at this level. Functional linkages between jobs facilitated migration and intersectoral movement. For example, farm work could involve construction activities, selling agricultural produce in the countryside linked to market work in city centres, and transporting goods to the towns provided a basis for lorry and bus driving in the city. Servants learned tasks within the home that had counterparts in the labour market, e.g. gardeners, chauffeurs, and cooks. During the main part of their working life, however, people would settle into a particular trade and confine themselves to job moves within the relevant sector.

Careers were strongly influenced by family, kinship and the life cycle. Again and again we shall see how kinship facilitated movement between jobs. It could also constrain movement: several informants mentioned that they could not get a particular job because they had not got a kin contact there or that they were working with relatives and could not get away. People's first introduction to the world of work was within the family, as children in unpaid family labour on the family farm, shop or workshop, or as *ayudantes* to their parents in mines and on plantations. Apprenticeships provided the first attenuation of links with parents, although they could be living and working with *maestro* kinsmen. Girls were sent to work in private homes as live-in maids. Casual workers in larger enterprises had more autonomy, although they would often be residing with relatives and money would still have to be sent home. However, some children had a more abrupt entry into the labour market, occasioned by the death or desertion of a parent.[1]

After the first job there would follow a period of relative freedom when workers could change jobs at will, according to their individual preferences and aspirations. Military service (obligatory for men aged 18–20) was an important stage in the male life cycle. It was a major stimulus to migration (many conscripts were sent to Lima), and it provided an opportunity for learning new skills. Women enjoyed less freedom than men at this stage, and could be recalled from the labour market to help out at home, possibly even returning to their village (cf. Radcliffe 1986a). Marriage and the birth of the first child brought a period of stabilization for men as well as women; wage workers would often move into self-employment at this point, while women took up jobs that were compatible with their domestic duties or moved out of the labour market altogether.

The more mature stage of the life cycle would see a period of rising prosperity for some families, particularly those running small enterprises, as the cost of raising children began to diminish and they could benefit from family labour. For others, it meant declining fortunes, with increasing vulnerability to illness and failing physical powers. In the absence of adequate sickness benefits or pensions, such workers would have to shift into 'refuge' jobs. Old age thus saw a polarization between the successful and the unsuccessful, the former gradually easing themselves into retirement and the latter taking up casual jobs such as caretaking. Migration compounded life cycle effects; the ones who migrated early in their lives benefited more since they could take advantage of apprenticeships and casual unskilled jobs that provided entry to subsequent careers. Those who migrated late were too old to embark on such trajectories and were confined to dead-end jobs. Here we find men joining the same 'refuge' trajectories as unskilled women.

These structural variables – enterprise structure, labour market divisions, life cycle and kinship – played an important part in the shaping of careers, but individual characteristics played a role too and there was also an element of chance. Some people were more aggressive than others in creating opportunities for themselves, and some had more bad luck. Manual workers were very vulnerable to chance since they had little economic security and were unable to insure themselves against it. A fire might destroy a business that had taken years to build up; illness could undermine the ability to continue working. Desertion by a husband or death of a wife might suddenly alter economic circumstances. Reading through the life histories, one is struck by the rich variety of experiences – fortunate and unfortunate – and the tenacity with which these men and women strove to improve their individual and family circumstances.

MANUFACTURING CAREERS

There was a greater variety of career paths within this sector than in any other and they were more gender differentiated too. The whole process of mobility was structured by the internal training and promotion systems within formal and informal enterprises. Careers could be formed entirely within the informal sector (an 'artisanal' career), within the formal sector (a 'factory' career) or through a combination of the two ('mixed' career). The port of entry was usually at the level of *aprendiz* or *ayudante*, despite the relatively high educational levels in this sector.[2] There was a noticeable male artisanal tradition with sons following into their father's or uncle's occupation and inheriting a trade-based network of kinsmen that was crucial for access to resources. A high proportion of those who reached the position of self-employed *maestro* had this background. On the other hand, there were a number of unskilled jobs within this sector, mostly in outwork or repairs. These jobs offered a source of 'refuge' employment to those who had come into manufacturing late, or had fallen on hard times for some reason.

Career patterns within manufacturing were very different for men and women because of the types of industries to which women were restricted and the limited training and promotion in these industries. Women did not follow the 'male' pattern of vertical mobility but entered factories or self-employment directly at the semi-skilled level and remained there.

Men in manufacturing careers

There were two routes into manufacturing for men: via informal apprenticeships or via casual unskilled factory work. Sooner or later, however, the latter would join the former. Thereafter the route to skilled work was either within the informal sector or by combining formal and informal employment. Most of the workers who ended up in skilled self-employment had done so via the 'artisanal' route A (fig. 7.1), i.e. becoming apprenticed to a self-employed *maestro*, then working as an *oficial*, and finally setting themselves up on their own.

Gonzalo was a jeweller. He came from Huancayo, a large provincial town where his father was a printer. After completing his primary school education, he came to visit some relatives in Lima, and became apprenticed to his uncle in the jewellery trade. His apprenticeship lasted three years, after which he continued to work with the uncle on a wage labour/commission basis. At the age of 34 he got married and shortly after set up his own business. The following year he acquired a locale next door (in the downtown area of Lima). By 1970 he had seven assistants, but later had to reduce the number because the rise in taxes and the price of gold was cutting into profits. The key to his success was access to a central location and the network of clients he had established while working with the uncle. He was earning three times the minimum wage.

Rigoberto was a tailor. He came from a jeweller's family in Lima. When he was 13 his father died so he had to go into an apprenticeship with his brother-in-law who was a tailor. One year later he was working as an *oficial pantalonero* (trouser maker) with the same brother-in-law on subcontracts from shops. He remained in this job for twenty-two years, mainly because he had not had the opportunity to learn other aspects of the tailoring trade. However, he eventually made friends with a *saquero* (jacket maker) and they swapped skills, thus enabling him to go self-employed. Five years later he had a flourishing business, built up on the basis of subcontracts with clothing shops. Now with the status of *maestro* he employed six other workers and had a shop fronting on to the street in the central business district. However, four years later he had a break-in and was robbed of all his machinery. He had debts that took years to pay off. Since then he has worked alone from home, relying on the neighbours for custom. He was earning the equivalent of a minimum wage.

Some workers entered this trajectory at a later period, after trying their hand at jobs in the formal sector. However, whatever the prior experience, the port of entry was always through the post of *ayudante*. Hermías and Benin provide examples of 'mixed' careers, C and D.

Hermías was another tailor. He was the son of a greengrocer from Chancay valley near Lima. After completing primary school he worked for five years in his father's shop. He used to accompany his father bringing produce to Lima and eventually he decided to move there to continue his secondary education. At the age of 20 he obtained a cleaning job in a bookshop where a neighbour worked. This shop was one of a chain in Lima and he ascended to counter assistant, cashier and then to the accounts department; but then the shop had a fire and went bankrupt. At the age of 27, and with a wife and child, he decided he must learn another trade and started work with a tailor friend. He then got a job as *pantalonero* in a tailor's workshop and stayed there for ten years, later working as *saquero* as well. At the age of 36 he decided to set up a workshop with a friend, but it failed when the friend went off with the money. The next year he decided to go it alone, working with his son. At the time of interview he was earning three times the minimum wage.

Benin was a small manufacturer of paintbrushes. He was born in a village in Huanuco. His mother had been abandoned by his father, and she struggled to work the farm on her own. He spent most of his teen years helping her and working as a wage labourer on neighbouring farms. When he was 20, his mother took the family to Lima, and he obtained a job there selling bread. The following year he was called up for military service and during this time he worked as a mechanic's assistant in the armoured car division. On leaving, an uncle got him a job in a small factory that made paintbrushes. After he had worked there for a time (three years as an *ayudante* and four as a machinist) he decided to set up his own workshop. He went to work in a fishmeal factory to save some money (the wage was double that in the paintbrush factory), and a year later he had set up on his own. At the time of interview he had been going for five years, was employing four assistants (nephews) and had earnings that were twice the minimum wage (and probably more).

The length of time taken before passing into skilled self-employment is striking, the major reason being the lack of a crucial skill or capital. For some workers, an alternative to staying indefinitely with a *maestro* was to take up outwork contracts with shops or factories (i.e. path F).

Hernan was a tailor-outworker. He was relatively highly educated. He had completed secondary schooling and did two years at the Topographical Institute in Arequipa, Peru's second city. He worked as a clerk on construction sites and came to Lima with one of the biggest construction companies there. However, when his contract finished he had difficulty finding another job. His cousins were already in Lima, mostly in the tailoring trade. So he joined a cousin in his workshop and within a year started working on outwork contracts. He was working at home, with his own sewing machine and tools, making up jackets and school uniforms for a shop in the city centre. He said that the main obstacle to setting up his own workshop was the cost of renting an adequate locale and purchasing a stock of material – but also that he did not know how to cut cloth to fit clients. He was earning 1.5 times the minimum wage.

A number of workers remained at the unskilled level, either because they had entered the trade too late, or because they did not stick at it long enough and went off into other unskilled jobs such as street sales, construction etc. For these men the only option was to set themselves up in unskilled self-employment doing small repairs (path G).

Raul was a shoe-repairer. He was born in a village in Ancash. Between the ages of 9 and 15 he was looking after the animals on his parents' farm. Then he joined the stream of labour from the area towards the sugar plantations, getting work as a cane cutter. He stayed there until the age of 26 and then moved to Lima, getting work on a cotton plantation on the outskirts of the city. Six years later he moved into the wholesale market of *La Parada*, where he worked as a porter and street pedlar. Subsequently he got work in construction, where there was much demand for labour during the 1950s. However, his age was against him, and this option began to close off as he was approaching the age of 50. In between construction jobs he worked as a bottle seller and learned to repair shoes. One day, a friend told him there were stalls available in one of the markets where he could work as a shoe repairer. At the time of interview he was 64 years old and was working with nothing more than a bench, a sewing machine and a stool. He was earning three-quarters of a minimum wage.

Turning now to formal sector workers, there were a variety of moves between different sized enterprises, facilitated by the transitional position of *ayudante* (assistant). However, all my informants who were currently employed in large factories had been through small enterprises. They had subsequently been taken on as assistants in the larger establishments and had then ascended to *maestro* status through internal promotion. Several had changed to other firms after reaching this level, perhaps being head-hunted by their next employer.

Juan was a solderer. His father was a blacksmith on one of the largest sugar plantations in Peru. At the age of 13 he was working unofficially as his father's assistant and after two years he obtained a position as a cleaner in the forge. At 18, an uncle got him a job in a foundry in Lima as assistant boilermaker; shortly he rose to the status of master boilermaker. Six years later he got a job in an engineering plant that made racing cars, where another uncle worked. Initially taken on as an assistant, within the year he was a master fitter. At the age of 27 he was offered a job by the manager of a new Electrolux plant. Once again he reverted to the status of *ayudante*, although his wage was higher than before. One year later he was a master solderer, mending articles that had been broken in transit from abroad. Some years later the firm started assembling the same articles in Peru, and he had one of the most highly skilled jobs in the plant. At the time of interview he had been with this firm for twenty-one years and was earning two and a half times the minimum wage.

Women in manufacturing careers

The trajectories of women in manufacturing differed from the men's in several important ways. The majority of female employment in this sector had to do with clothing, and the basic skills were usually learnt outside the labour market, either at home or in vocational courses. Therefore women were much less dependent on apprenticeships in small workshops for induction into the trade, and clothing factories could recruit directly at the semi-skilled level.[3] As a result, there was a much greater convergence on medium- and large-scale enterprises than small ones (path E), and more job changing at the semi-skilled level. Outside the garment trade, there was some direct recruitment into unskilled factory jobs, such as packing and labelling. These did not involve any training and did not form part of an internal career structure. Finally, in contrast to the men, recruitment to most factory jobs, especially in the clothing trade, did not depend on word-of-mouth recruitment. Most were obtained via notices in the window or in the newspaper.

Women's trajectories were more affected by the domestic cycle in this sector than others. There was a pattern of high mobility through semi-skilled factory jobs prior to childbirth, and self-employed dressmaking and outwork afterwards. Outwork was particularly important for women, and was often a continuation of employment with their previous full-time employer. There was also some unskilled outwork such as assembling egg boxes and folding envelopes, usually obtained through neighbourhood contacts. Note, however, that some factory workers held on to their jobs throughout the period of family formation. The following provide examples of women in 'factory careers'.

Gladis was a button sewer from Lima. She completed her primary schooling and then helped at home for two years. Between the ages of 15 and 21 she had a series of factory jobs, one in textiles, two in laboratories bottling perfumes and one sewing buttons on sweaters in a small knitting factory. All these jobs were obtained through the newspapers. At 24 she got another job, this time through a friend, as button sewer in *Inca Textil*, a factory with fifty workers and a reputation for good working conditions. At the time of interview she had remained with this employer in the same semi-skilled job for twenty years, despite marrying, having five children and then being widowed. After all those years she was still earning only 5 soles more than the daily minimum wage although she was entitled to a number of fringe benefits.

Domitila was a packer at a candle factory. She was born in a village in the central *sierra*. Her father was a miner and died when she was 8. She came with her mother to Lima and they worked together on a vegetable stall in downtown Lima. At 10 her mother placed her in domestic service because 'there wasn't enough money to buy clothes'. The people she worked for allowed her to go to school and she did three years of primary school. She married at 14 and had her first child at 17. The following year she decided to get work because she had to maintain her mother and didn't want to be dependent on her husband. So she got a job corking bottles in a factory. She stayed in this job for four years, having three further children at the same time. Then her mother went blind and was no longer able to look after the children while she worked; so she left the factory and started taking in washing. When she was 29, and by now with eight children, she got a job packing candles in a factory. At the time of interview she had been in this job for seven years, had had two more children and was still on the minimum wage.

Several women had followed the 'artisanal route' within informal enterprises (path A), but acquiring their skill through vocational courses rather than working with a *maestra*:

> *Matilde* was a seamstress from Chincha, a coastal town. After completing her primary schooling she came to Lima with her family and did a course in dressmaking at an academy there. She set herself up as a dressmaker at the age of 16, working from home. She established a home with her boyfriend and had two children by him, maintaining the dressmaking work throughout. At the time of interview she had been working for twenty-four years and was earning just above the minimum wage.

Some women came into manufacturing late in life from economic necessity, e.g. death of or desertion by the husband. The main options here were outwork, sewing for neighbours or manufacturing small items for sale in the market.

> *Teresa* was a mechanic's daughter from a northern coastal town (Ferreñafe). The whole family came to Lima when she was 8 and she went to school there. When she was 13, her mother fell ill and Teresa had to look after the nine brothers and sisters. She married at 17 and had five children of her own. When she was 29 her husband abandoned her so she learned to sew 'out of necessity'. Two years later she started sewing shirts on an outwork basis for a factory, but the factory went bankrupt. She then learned raffia work at a mother's club and started making hats, bags etc. which her children sold in the market. She was earning barely a quarter of a minimum wage.

Most women's work in manufacturing was focused on one activity: dressmaking. This was a unique occupation for women; it was the only one with a high level of skill (comparable at least to that of a tailor); it straddled formal and informal sectors and it could be carried out at home. However, sewing jobs in factories were highly routinized and concentrated at the semi-skilled level, with few possibilities for promotion. For self-employed dressmakers, the market conditions were not usually auspicious: hampered by their confinement to low-income clients (neighbours), they were doomed to low levels of earnings despite their skill. In contrast to the men, whose trades could lead them towards skilled factory jobs or relatively prosperous self-employment, dressmaking offered neither for women. However, in comparison with the alternatives open to women in other sectors, dressmakers were in a better situation than most.

CAREERS IN CONSTRUCTION

Career trajectories in the construction sector were very like those in manu-facturing: they were heavily structured by the process of skill acquisition, the first stage of which involved working as an *ayudante* with a *maestro*, and career formation depended on movement between different employers and between wage labour and self-employment. However, there were some differences. First, there was much greater use of subcontracting by large firms and hence a blurring of the distinction between formal and informal sectors and between employment statuses. Second, the temporary nature of construc-tion contracts meant that workers moved more frequently between different employment conditions. Thus the most common career paths were those that crossed sectors, i.e. C and D. Third, although there was great trade allegiance and occupational stability at the skilled levels, there was a large pool of unskilled casual labour which facilitated lateral movement for people in 'refuge' careers.

Most workers were initially recruited as *ayudantes* by informal employers although there were also some unskilled labouring jobs (*peones*). A distinc-tion should be made between those in general building activities (e.g. bricklaying) who worked in small gangs that operated like mini-enterprises, and specialists such as plumbers, electricians, carpenters, painters etc. who usually worked alone or with a mate. Few large enterprises contracted labour directly or had workers on the permanent payroll; they usually operated through a site manager who subcontracted work to the *maestros*. The latter therefore played a key role in the hiring, training and promotion of less skilled workers.

The entire industry ran on very personalistic relationships. Knowing the right person and having the right recommendation were crucial for finding jobs and gaining skills. Once workers had become known to the large construction companies, they would be 'called for' when new contracts came up, and they thus could rely on more or less permanent work. Similarly, the self-employed would build up networks of clients who maintained a regular demand for work. Work sharing was common; when one person had more than enough work he would call on his friend or relative to help out, and the latter would return the favour when he was in a similar situation. Entry into self-employment in this sector depended not on capital or workshop location, but on reputation and an efficient network of friends who would recommend clients and subcontract work.

The pool of unskilled labouring jobs permitted easy access for recent migrants and facilitated movement into this sector from unskilled work in other sectors, particularly agriculture, commerce and services. Therefore there were lower levels of education than in other sectors,[4] and age at entry varied enormously. However, those entering later were unlikely to reach the level of *maestro*.

Humberto was a *maestro* bricklayer. He was born in Ayacucho of a peasant family. At the age of 10 his aunt brought him to Lima, promising that he could continue his education while staying with her. However, he was put to work in her boardinghouse for the next eight years and then placed in a chalk factory nearby (the aunt taking his wages). He escaped from this place and found work on a *hacienda* just outside Lima. While there he did some construction work, building silos. He made friends with the other workmen, who soon got him a job as watchman on a construction site. From here he worked as a *peon* on a number of different sites. At the age of 30 he was taken on as an *oficial* in a construction gang led by a *maestro* and this continued for the next five years. Six years later, he set himself up as a self-employed *maestro* and has been working ever since on small contracts with two assistants. At the time of interview he was earning roughly twice the minimum wage, depending on the contract.

Guillermo was a semi-skilled bricklayer, born in Ancash. He spent his early years helping on the farm and did only one year of primary school. At the age of 11 he travelled to the coast (Chimbote) with an uncle to work as a labourer in construction. He worked there for seven years and then did three years on a farm, three in a charcoal factory, one in a chalk factory and another two on a sugar plantation. He returned to Chimbote and became a lorry driver's mate, and later a porter in the market. 'I was changing jobs to earn more and because I was an adventurer.' He then returned to agriculture for the next eleven years, three of which were back on his parents' farm. At the age of 42, he travelled to Lima to stay with his brothers and worked with his brother-in-law in construction. At the time of interview he was working as an *oficial* in a small construction gang of eight people and earning 1.5 times the minimum wage.

In contrast to these complex work histories, most of the specialists who had reached the level of *maestro*, whether self-employed or wage-earning, had relatively shallow occupational careers – they had entered apprenticeships early in their lives, had passed directly to the status of *maestro* and had remained in the trade for the rest of their working life.

Lucho was a specialist floor layer. He was born in a northern coastal town and spent his early childhood helping his parents in agriculture. He did three years of primary school and then at the age of 16 joined a *maestro* friend of the family, as a builder's labourer and worked with him for six years. At the age of 22 he was called up for military service, and when he came out a banker brought him to Lima to help build his house. Subsequently he obtained a job with a big construction company making special floors for bakeries. Two years later he was taken on by Graña y Montero, one of the biggest construction companies in Peru, and was still working with them twenty-four years later. He was earning the state regulated wage for skilled construction workers but was receiving as much again in overtime payments and bonuses (more than three times the minimum wage).

In summary, the construction sector had both vertical careers leading towards *maestro* level and lateral movement within a pool of casual unskilled labour. The latter appears in cross-sectoral trajectories as a source of temporary employment or as 'refuge' jobs for the unemployed. It was not, however, a job for the old or infirm because of the heavy physical demands on workers.

TRANSPORT CAREERS

Jobs in this sector differed markedly according to whether the job involved vehicles or not. On the one hand there were drivers of buses, lorries, taxis and private cars, whose incomes were amongst the highest of any manual workers, and on the other there were loaders, porters and messengers whose earnings were amongst the lowest. However, the numbers in the second group were very small.

As an occupation, driving contrasts with the other trades considered so far in two ways. First, there was no internal skill hierarchy; the main requirement for driving was a professional driver's licence, which could be obtained outside the labour market. Therefore recruitment was relatively open; workers could come into the occupation through a variety of routes and did not have to spend time in lengthy apprenticeships. On the other hand, a large proportion of drivers were self-employed and had to purchase costly vehicles. Therefore recruitment favoured those in high-income jobs, which in turn meant persons with a higher than average level of education and good formal sector jobs. Only two workers in this sector had not completed primary school and almost half had some secondary schooling. Three quarters of the case studies had worked in large firms, and had used separation or redundancy pay to purchase the vehicles.

Second, there was a high degree of lateral movement between wage labour and self-employment and between formal and informal enterprises. One reason for this was the rapid depreciation of the vehicles, no doubt due to their intensive use, which would force the self-employed back into wage employment. As a source of upward mobility therefore, driving was a high-income occupation that workers arrived at *through other occupations* rather than within the trade itself. The rate of inflow from other sectors was therefore high, and, since vehicles depreciated in the long term, there was also some outflow to other occupations. This contrasts noticeably with other trades which had little intersectoral movement once workers had reached the top of the hierarchy within the occupation.

There were a number of routes into driving jobs. Some workers became driver's mates as young boys, either because they had a driver in the family or knew one in the village. Others had come into the job through working as mechanics. Many had been employed in delivery services run by shops and factories. Two had worked in the USA as truckers. A few had been drivers within domestic service. One national service recruit became the private chauffeur of an army general. Finally, a few adventurers had raised the money for an old second-hand car and were prepared to try their luck.

Edelberto was a self-employed microbus driver from Nazca, on the coast. He came to Lima aged 11, with the rest of the family. He and his brother worked as street pedlars while continuing their secondary education. After leaving school, he worked as a building labourer and at 23 was called up for military service. On being demobbed he found a job as a storekeeper in the big mining company, Cerro de Pasco. After three years there he left and bought a taxi in Lima with his savings. This worked well for a year or two, but the car was old and began to need a lot of repairs. He sold it and got a job as a driver on a new hydro-electric project in the Mantaro valley behind Lima, and soon became one of the transport overseers. Seven years later when the project finished, he was made redundant. He returned to Lima with his redundancy pay and bought a microbus. At the time of interview he was working the vehicle on a self-employed basis earning four times the minimum wage.

Rodrigo was a mechanic-cum-taxi driver. Born in the northern *sierra* (Cajamarca) he worked on the family farm until he was 25, when his sister, who was married to a policeman in Lima, sent word that a big import–export company was looking for staff. He immediately got a job there as a packer. While in this job he completed his primary education at night school and did a course in car mechanics. Then he took a job in a similar company, with responsibility for organizing the stores. All the while he was practising as a mechanic at the weekends, on contracts with a motor company. At 41, a *compadre* got him a travelling sales job with a toy factory. He had always wanted to have his own car, and soon he bought one and joined a line of *colectivos*. However, after a time it began to break down a lot, so he spent more of his time repairing vehicles on the line and only used his car occasionally. He was earning twice the minimum wage.

Now let us turn to porters, dockers and loaders; dockers were the exception within this group, since they had a closed shop cooperative and relatively high earnings. Entry into this occupation was extremely difficult (there was a waiting list), and depended entirely on kinship links. There were two categories of job, casual and permanent, the first serving as the port of entry to the latter, and consisting mainly of dockers' sons. Porters and loaders worked in very large formal enterprises, e.g. the airport, or were self-employed in areas such as markets and stations. Both of these jobs were filled by people at the end of a long history of unskilled work.

Joaquin was a porter in the central market and 67 years old at the time of interview. He was born in the mountains in Huanuco and spent his youth working on the family farm. He never went to school. When he was 28 his parents died in an accident and he started drinking. His family were always accusing him of being a good-for-nothing and told him to look for a job. At 30 he started living with a woman who had her own farm. Three years later, they went to Lima to join some relatives and Joaquin worked in construction for seven years. Then they went back to the village and worked on the farm again. Four years later he returned to Lima alone, working in construction again and sending money back to his wife. This continued for many years, until he could no longer stand the arduous work in building. Aged 56, he turned to some of his countrymen who were bringing tomatoes into Lima from Huanuco, and worked for them carrying boxes and sacks. At the time of interview he had been doing this for eleven years and was also looking after a relative's smallholding on the outskirts of Lima. His total earnings from the two jobs barely amounted to a minimum wage.

Non-vehicular transport jobs were typical 'refuge' jobs, poorly paid, labour intensive and involving some of the worst physical drudgery. They usually formed only a small part of a person's working life, either at the beginning or the end. Only a few, such as drunks and dropouts lived off these jobs for any sustained period of time. Careers in driving were the total opposite of this. They had a speculative nature, with easy entry and high earnings but substantial installation costs, hard work and high risks. Those who were successful became the aristocrats of the labouring class, rich, flamboyant (shiny new buses) and entrepreneurial, but those who failed had to return to wage employment and/or work in other sectors.

CAREERS IN COMMERCE

Commercial jobs were very heterogeneous; they included shop assistants working for large modern establishments, market traders, street pedlars, front-room shops attached to people's homes and travelling salespersons. There was a variety of employment situations, besides wage labour and self-employment, including work on commission, co-partnerships and family labour. Unlike other sectors, there was a unique opportunity here to run enterprises involving the whole family (see Herminio, below).

Despite the popular image of commerce as a source of 'refuge' employment, sustaining the flotsam and jetsam of the urban labour market, there were clearly identifiable career structures within this sector that could lead to incomes comparable with the highest paid factory jobs or a departure from manual employment altogether. Commercial activity was perceived by many as intrinsically rewarding, with socially recognized entrepreneurial skills and a community of interest. Trading was viewed as a respectable occupation in its own right and not just as a refuge activity.

There were a number of different career paths in commerce, each attracting very different types of person. Shop assistants were likely to be young, Lima-born, relatively highly educated (most had some secondary schooling) with aspirations to rising into white collar management. Street peddling was more likely to be taken up by migrants with few trade skills and little experience of formal sector employment, while owners of small stores had often been highly skilled factory workers. Sales work provided temporary employment for those intending to get other jobs in the near future, or for students trying to support themselves while completing their studies, but it was also a longstanding principal occupation for many workers. Becoming the owner of a market stall or a small shop could be the culmination of a gradual process of accumulation within self-employed commerce, or a desperate last ditch attempt to generate earnings by those on the breadline.

There were three types of trajectory: the 'shop work' career (B), the 'petty merchant' career (A), and the 'refuge career'(G). Men and women both participated in the first of these, although women often dropped out after marriage; men predominated in the second, sometimes with women as partners, and women predominated in the third. The 'shop work' career was mostly in the formal sector and hardly qualifies as a manual career.[5] However, since many manual workers moved on and off the bottom rungs of this career and the earnings were similar to those in other manual jobs, I shall briefly mention it for purposes of comparison. Initial entry was dependent on formal education, some secondary education being required as a minimum. First jobs would consist of counter assistant, followed by cashier, supervisor, administrator etc. Sometimes it was possible for manual workers with less education to obtain entry into these careers, particularly if they had personal contacts or if the shop was very small, e.g. a boutique or *bazar*.[6] Boys could gain entry by doing cleaning jobs initially. However, the small size of these establishments usually meant that career opportunities there were limited.

> ***Osvaldo*** worked in a shoe shop. He was born in Lima, his father being an administrator on the guano islands. He was in his second year of secondary school when his father died, so he had to go out to work. He got a job through a relative, cleaning a small *bazar* (four employees) that was part of a chain selling variety goods. He stayed in this job for seven years, but the company was not doing well and eventually went bankrupt. He then got a job in a larger store (ten employees) selling groceries in the central market (his cousin was married to the owner). Five years later there was family trouble which made it necessary to change jobs, and he got one in a shoe shop through his brother-in-law. At the time of interview, he was 36 and earning the minimum wage, plus commission.

'Petty merchant careers' were built up within informal establishments and led ultimately to relatively prosperous self-employment, compared with other manual jobs. These careers often started with activities such as deliveries, loading, and street vending, followed by a period as a waged salesman on a stall or a commissioned salesperson for a company. A few had had good factory jobs. The crucial steps in getting established involved access to a good location and enough accumulated working capital to be able to sell the more profitable commodities. Personal contacts were crucial in securing these resources.

> ***Tomás*** was a butcher. He was born on the northern coast and spent his early years working on the family farm and in casual agricultural work on nearby *haciendas*. He attended school for only three years. At 18 he married and rented a relative's farm for five years. Then he got entangled with other women and had to leave the village. He volunteered for the Civil Guard in Lima and moved there with the family. He worked in this job for four years, but was dismissed when he fell ill and turned to taxi driving in a rented car. After four years of this he became an itinerant meat seller in one of the markets. This job proved more to his liking since it was both profitable and less dangerous than taxi driving. Several years later he was able to rent a locale to expand his butchery business and supplemented this by selling fruit and flowers outside the hospital at the weekends. Nine years later he won some money on the lottery and was able to buy one of the butchery businesses owned by his landlord. At the time of interview the Ministry of Agriculture had rationed meat so that it could only be sold for a fortnight each month. The other weeks Tomás

was working his car as a taxi. With the two activities, he was making more than double the minimum wage.

Herminio was a newspaper seller. He started out, aged 8, as a stevedore in the port of Huacho near Lima. He barely attended school and only completed the first grade. At 15 he was helping on his father's fishing boat, but two years later he had an accident at sea and didn't want to return. He then became a lorry driver's mate, helping to deliver goods to the market in Lima. A year later he decided to stay there, working as a loader in the market. He remained in this job for the next four years, until he married a vegetable seller there. After his marriage he worked on her stall and remained in this job for twelve years. At the age of 37 he inherited his mother-in-law's newspaper stall and moved into that line of business, working with his sons. His wife, meantime, was selling breakfasts from a small stall in the market as well. At the time of interview her earnings were marginally below the minimum wage and his were about 30 per cent above it.

'Refuge careers' were concentrated in the unprofitable sales lines such as vegetables, or the small front-room shops attached to the home (*tiendita*) that relied on sporadic custom from impoverished neighbours. These jobs were usually taken up by people who were in dire economic need, who had few skills or qualifications to do anything else, or who needed to be able to look after children while they worked. There were some men in this situation, such as Evaristo, who had failed to save enough to switch into the more profitable lines.

Evaristo was a street vendor of biros. He was born in Ancash and spent his early youth helping on his parents' farm. He did three years of primary school and then at 17 travelled to the coast to work in the cotton harvests. At 20 he was called up for military service which he did in Trujillo, one of the big coastal cities. When he was demobbed he travelled to Lima to see his brother, married and decided to stay. He worked for a time on the guano islands but returned to Lima when his wife became ill. He then took up selling biros with a loan from his brother. He claimed that at that time (1960) he was making as much money as a factory worker, but subsequently the trade had declined because of competition. He had stayed with this job ever since (fourteen years), but from time to time had done casual jobs in construction as well. At the time of interview he was earning only marginally above the minimum wage, but claimed he could not expand for lack of capital and a locale.

The majority in these 'refuge careers' were women. Most had only a few years of education and several were illiterate. Many had worked in domestic service. Only one had ever worked in manufacturing and even that was only unskilled outwork. None of the women had ever worked in the formal sector. Many of them were widowed or deserted, or were married to men with low or unstable incomes.

Lucia was a vegetable seller. She was born on a peasant farm in Apurimac, and came to Lima with her parents, aged 8. She did three years of primary school, then went into domestic service at the age of 11. She worked in various houses for eight years, finally leaving when she became pregnant to set up house with a bricklayer. After the birth of her child she set up a small stall in the wholesale market *La Parada*, and had worked there selling vegetables ever since (eight years). At the time of interview she was earning roughly the minimum wage.

Juana had a *tiendita* in her house out in the shanty towns. She was born in Lima, the daughter of a bricklayer. She completed her primary school and then spent six years helping various members of the family, especially an aunt who had many children. When she was 19 a relative introduced her to the owner of a small shop and she worked there along with five others. Her pay must have been very low, because two years later she became a servant in a private house (non-resident) and her salary doubled! At 23 she started to work for a family of foreigners and her salary rose again. When she was 26 she left this job because she had met her husband and had a child. Her husband, who was a printer, did not want her to work as a servant any more, so they started to save to set up their own shop at home. She was running it during the week and he would take over at weekends. At the time of interview she had had five children and was attending the shop for about twelve hours a day. Despite these long hours, her earnings were about half the minimum wage.

Ana was a lottery ticket seller. She was born in Chile and came to Lima with her family, aged 8. She went up to second year at secondary school but then got pregnant at 15 and left. The following year she started selling lottery tickets in the Union and San Martin squares in downtown Lima. She had three more children and was abandoned by her partner. At the time of interview she had been in the same job for thirty-two years and was earning barely a third of the minimum wage.

In summary, some careers in commerce would lead eventually into middle-class employment within the formal sector, others led to good positions at the head of informal enterprises and yet others were impoverished culs-de-sac. The first trajectory acted as a channel for upward mobility for young men and women with education. The second offered the possibility of mobility within the labouring class, but required investments and contacts that only men could mobilize. The third was the option more usually taken up by women and old men.

CAREERS IN SERVICES

Some jobs in the services sector were similar to those in manufacturing in that they had an institutionalized skill with an apprenticeship structure (e.g. hairdressing, photography). Others were more like commercial enterprises but selling a service rather than a product (e.g. restaurants, bars), with similar opportunities for family collaboration and relatively lucrative self-employment. Both of these provided possibilities for upward mobility depending on the acquisition of skill, capital and clients (path A), and both were dominated by men. A third category of jobs were similar to shop work in that they provided the bottom rungs of a career that could lead into non-manual employment (B). Nursing was the example here: a number of men and women from labouring-class backgrounds could get jobs as auxiliaries in local clinics and hospitals, with a view to ascending later. As in the case of shop work they only entered my sample as young men and women, and would later disappear from view as they moved into white collar work.

However, the vast majority of jobs in this sector consisted of unskilled personal services such as domestic service, laundering, shoeshining and caretaking. Such jobs could not form part of an upward mobility process; they were a source of temporary employment for recent migrants and for those in between jobs. They also provided supplementary earnings for wives wishing to add to the family income, or for the ill and the old who were not capable of doing more demanding work. They were classic 'refuge jobs', jobs of last resort or a temporary expedient while waiting for something better to turn up. There were many whose entire working lives had been spent in these jobs (path G). Such workers usually had little education and a background of unskilled work in other sectors, and they were primarily women.

Skilled jobs in services (barbers, hairdressers, chefs, photographers) were not considered of such high status as those in manufacturing or construction, nor did they generate comparable earnings. Nevertheless there was a similar hierarchy of *ayudantes*, *officiales* and *maestros*, a similar trade allegiance, and considerable costs involved in setting up an independent business.

Pablo was a barber. He was born in a small town on the northern coast and his father worked on nearby *haciendas*. He was in the process of acquiring his primary education when his father died, so he started doing casual agricultural labouring jobs while he finished at school. At 14 he was cane-cutting on one of the big sugar plantations, and for the next eight years, he did casual work in the local area. At 22 he was called up for military service and became an army barber. When he was demobbed, he became an apprentice barber in Chiclayo. The next year he came to Lima and got another job as a barber. Six years later, when he was 30, he set up his own barber's shop in a shanty town and worked there on his own for several years. However, trade was poor and he was forced to give up. His wife had a small shop selling fizzy drinks and he worked with her for a year. Then he went back into wage employment working as *maestro* barber in a shop in the centre of Lima. Even there, however, the earnings were still very low, marginally below the minimum wage at the time of interview.

Food sales could vary from selling a ready-made meal in a large saucepan on street corners to installing a small bar or restaurant in a room of one's own house or running a separate restaurant. In most cases, access to a locale and some use of family labour were necessary. Such establishments were usually run by men, with their wives and daughters as helpers.

Ignacio had a small bar-restaurant. He was born of a peasant family in Chanchamayo and did four years of primary schooling. At 12 he was helping on the farm and at 14 looking after a fruit warehouse nearby. At 16 he was a trucker's assistant transporting fruit to the nearby town of Tarma. At 19 he got married to a woman in Tarma whose parents had a fruit store in the market, and he worked with her there for four years. When he was 24 they decided to establish a fruit shop and restaurant in La Oroya, a large mining town, where a relative had obtained a locale for them. However, two years later he and his wife split up and she kept the business. He went to Lima and set up a small restaurant there with one of his own family. A few years later he obtained another locale in one of the shanty towns and transferred his business there. It was a good location, near one of the main highways. His second wife was helping with the cooking and two cousins were working as waiters. He was earning double the minimum wage.

Amongst the men, 'refuge' jobs were only taken up at the end of their working lives. For example, one man had spent most of his life as a master baker, but after retiring from this decided to install a small café, where he was still working at the age of 71. Another had been a miner all his life, but contracted pneumonia at the age of 60 and was brought to Lima by his family for medical treatment. He got bored sitting at home and went out to shine shoes in the local market. A third man had been an itinerant fruit seller all his life and at 58 became a caretaker at the local market. Women would take up refuge jobs (making dinners, taking in washing) at times of crisis – if their husband became unable to work, died or left them. One woman started selling meals outside the cinemas after twenty years in full-time housework, because her husband had become a drunkard and had stopped working. Another set up a small restaurant in her home after twelve years of full-time housework because her husband had died. Many women took in washing when their husbands took off.

'Refuge careers' amongst women usually started with a period in domestic service, which prevented them from getting a good education, followed by marriage to an unreliable breadwinner and/or abandonment. Sending girls into domestic service was a way of reducing consumption in very poor families and was often linked to the death or departure of the father.

Damiana was a maid from Ancash, where her father was a farm worker. She went to school for only one year because she had to look after her brothers and sisters while her parents went to work in the fields. At 19 her parents told her to look for work because they could not maintain her any more. The local schoolteacher got her a job as a maid in the town nearby, but this was badly paid so she decided to try her luck in Lima. On arrival she answered an advertisement in the window of a private house but they treated her very badly so she only lasted a month there. This experience was repeated in a series of domestic jobs where she stayed between six to nine months, either because they treated her badly, made her work very hard, or would not let her go to school. Finally at the age of 23 she found a family where she was happy, was earning a reasonable wage and was able to continue with her primary schooling.

Justina was a washerwoman. She was born in the northern *sierra* where her mother had a farm (she never knew her father). She did three years of primary school, while helping on the farm. At the age of 12 she was sent to Lima into domestic service, 'there was no other alternative'. She then worked in different houses until she was 21, when she married a bricklayer. While she was having children she tried different jobs, food selling, outwork etc. At the time of interview she had been working as a washerwoman for three years, 'from necessity'. She would sometimes work every day, sometimes every three days, and was earning about half the minimum wage, on average.

Eugenia was a caretaker. She was from the central *sierra* and was brought up by foster parents. She never went to school, but spent her time looking after the animals and helping in the house. At 15 she was sent to Lima to work as a maid for a relative, but they treated her badly, keeping her in and not letting her go to school. Three years later she was befriended by another woman who offered her a job and treated her much better. At 22 she married and had two children, but the husband left her. She started to provide meals for the men working on a building nearby, and subsequently got the job of caretaker and cleaner in the building. At 28 she married again and had another child, but kept her job as caretaker. At 31 she was asked to look after the next-door building as well. When she was 37 her second husband left her. At the time of interview she was still caretaking, as well as cleaning and taking in washing. Her gross earnings were still below the minimum wage, although her lodgings were provided as part of the job.

CONCLUSION

We already know from chapter 5 that the manual labour market was deeply segmented by enterprise size, skill and gender, and chapter 6 showed that there was extensive movement across these divisions. This chapter has traced the career paths which carried people to different destinations and the mechanisms which facilitated it. These mobility processes can be likened to a railway system: the production and employment structures provided the basic network through which routes were charted, family and kinship influenced the entry points and the transit stops, and the life cycle determined the types of routes chosen and the speed of movement.

There were many career paths through the manual labour market, but overall, there were two general patterns. One was vertical, involving a slow process of upward mobility towards *maestro* status. The other was lateral, consisting of horizontal movement between low-skilled 'refuge' jobs. The upward movement sometimes involved lateral movement between formal and informal sectors, but 'refuge' careers at the bottom were largely confined to the latter. There were major differences in the career trajectories of men and women, men predominating in the vertical mobility process and women in the lateral one. Men's upward mobility was built up through apprenticeships, wage work in establishments that had promotion systems, and the accumulation of resources through savings and kinship networks. Women's immobility was the result of a lack of access to appropriate training, confinement to low paying jobs that did not have promotion systems, or consumer markets that permitted little accumulation. Gender segregation in employment was thus an enduring lifetime experience, whereas the other divisions corresponded only to particular phases which individuals passed through in the course of their work histories.

Two major questions will be addressed in the chapters that follow: first, what was the role of the family in producing these enduring forms of segmentation and what was their impact on the occupational composition of the family, and second, what was the effect of this cross-sectional and longitudinal diversity on class consciousness?

8   Employment, family and class

So far, this book has been concerned with individual positions in the labour market and individual career patterns, and with the pattern of gender segregation in both. This chapter looks at the relationship between labour market divisions and the family. There are three main issues: first, what was the role of the family in promoting and reproducing gender divisions in employment? Second, what were the effects of these divisions on the household economy, and third, what were its implications for class?

In looking at the role of the family in fostering gender divisions in the labour market, we have to consider the structure and ideology of the family and the various ways in which it influenced supply, demand and mechanisms of recruitment in the labour market. Were the low participation rates of women the product of *machista* gender ideologies which thought married women should stay at home, or were they an effect of the limited range of options open to women? How far was gender segregation the product of differences in endowments (education and training), and how far that of occupational sex-typing in the workplace? How do we explain gender segregation within the informal sector, much of which would have been compatible with women's domestic constraints and required little in the way of formal credentials? What role did the all-pervasive kinship networks play in promoting gender segregation?

The second part of this chapter looks at the contribution made by women's work to the household, the way that labour market divisions were reflected in its occupational composition and the implications of these factors for the relationship between gender and class. The question that arises here is how gender divisions in the family and the labour market related to the common class position of the family as a whole.

As mentioned in chapter 2, different class theories have different approaches to this issue. Marxist analysis, which focuses exclusively on individual relations of production, would attribute different class positions to the men and women analysed in this book, given their very different labour market positions and career patterns. Weberian theory, which emphasizes life styles and status, might focus on the implications of their different productive roles for the consumption patterns of the family/household. Some Marxist–feminist positions, which have tried to incorporate the family into the analysis of class, would focus on the way in which women's domestic roles contributed to class reproduction. However, there is a problem here: for the family is simultaneously a site for *different gender interests* but *complementary class interests*. We therefore need to know how this contradiction was played out in this empirical case, and whether one took priority over the other.

Debates about the relationship between class and the family are strongly linked to a conceptual separation between production and consumption as bases of class position. In my view, this separation only has heuristic value and is not useful for analysing consciousness and action. In a situation of poverty and hardship, work is indissolubly linked to consumption, and the two play an integral role in the formation of class identities. Moreover, these two spheres of social activity are brought together in the family. However, this mediating role cannot be understood by the simple assumption of a common interest in a particular life style. We need to investigate how productive roles are incorporated into the household economy, how the relationship between income earners and dependants is structured, and what role consumption plays in collective struggles.

It could be argued that women's dependency on the male breadwinners gave them a common interest with men, despite their different occupational experiences, and that the focus on long-term mobility for the family as a whole reinforced this common interest. Another argument is that occupational diversity in the household played an indirect part in the shaping of class identities and interests; close kin relations with people in different jobs produced an identification with a variety of work situations. Thus economically inactive women or those in different jobs could identify with the positions of their husbands and brothers, and engage in common political action. A third approach considers the contribution of women's domestic activities to processes of class reproduction, and how these activities have spilled over into community management and local level politics (e.g. Moser 1987). Much of this discussion has been conducted within a debate about women's different *gender* needs and interests, and does not look at its relationship with *class* (Molyneux 1985, Moser 1987, 1989). However, as Molyneux has pointed out, at the practical level, gender and class interests are conflated.

Below I shall show that wives' contribution to the household economy was relatively minor in comparison with the wider pattern of dependence on a male breadwinner. However, women played a major role as defenders of the life chances of the family. In the next chapter, we shall see that men and women shared a common class consciousness and were involved in political actions in the workplace and the community. Therefore, despite profound gender divisions within the family and the labour market, women tended to support the common class interests of the family rather than the gender-based interests of feminism.

EXPLAINING GENDER SEGREGATION IN THE MANUAL LABOUR MARKET

Before analysing the role of the family in explaining women's (and men's) position in the labour market, we have to think more generally about the nature of the process of labour allocation in Lima. Economic theory tends to see labour allocation as an individualistic decision-making process controlled by market forces on which the family only exerts an indirect influence from the supply side, i.e. by influencing women's availability for work, their investment in education and training, and their preferences for certain types of work rather than others. Recent work has also shown that gender influences the demand for labour because of its influence on work roles, workplace interaction and the sex-typing of work.

However, this presupposes an economy in which workplaces are separated from the home and employers from producers, i.e. the *formal* wage labour market. In a country like Peru, we have to consider that labour allocation in the informal sector had a slightly different structure, in which the family had a more direct role. As on peasant farms, where the family was the unit of production and resources were allocated on the basis of kinship statuses, access to resources in informal enterprises (such as apprenticeships, tools, credit, and clients) were confined to the kin group. Moreover, as previous chapters have shown, even within the formal labour market, kinship networks had a capacity to influence recruitment processes. However, I shall argue below that these kinship networks acted as a mechanism of discrimination against women and thereby perpetuated gender segregation. First then, let us briefly review the structure of recruitment in Lima, and the role of family and kinship in it.

Kinship networks and the labour market

Chapter 4 showed how closely family and economy were intertwined, not only in rural areas, but in the city too. Kinship networks had facilitated the migration process, leading to the colonization of areas of the city and particular niches in the labour market by groups of relatives. Smith has described how the strawberry sellers in Lima all came from a particular village in the Mantaro valley (Smith 1984). In the wholesale market, kin networks linked growers in the countryside, truckers, loaders, wholesale merchants and even street traders. I found a colony of kinsmen from Huancayo who seemed to have all the skilled jobs in the textile industry sewn up. The cases described in the previous chapter provide countless examples of how kinship channelled movement between jobs.

For manual workers, few jobs were available on the open market. Success depended as much on who you knew as what you knew. The Ministry of Labour survey shows that very few workers obtained their jobs through impersonal means such as employment agencies or newspapers. Over half got them through relatives and friends, and a fifth, through personal contacts with employers (see table 8.1). The case studies showed similar results: 70 per cent got their jobs through personal contacts.

Table 8.1   Mechanisms of recruitment amongst manual workers, Lima 1973

Mode of recruitment	Men	Women	Total
Employment agencies	2	6	3
Newspapers	4	3	4
Unions and associations	1	—	1
Employers	20	15	18
Relatives and friends	52	51	52
Other*	22	25	23
Total	101	100	101
N	1,571	782	2,353

Source: Ministry of Labour employment survey 1973
* Other = mainly self-employed workers setting up on their own

Family and kinship influenced the recruitment process in both informal and formal sectors. In artisanal workshops, the family was the basis for recruitment into apprenticeships and for the mobilization of capital and client networks. Within the construction industry, the widespread practice of subcontracting relied heavily on personal recommendations. In the transport sector, access to microbus routes was limited by professional associations and the availability of places was passed by word of mouth to friends and relatives. In commerce there was a preference for trading relationships to be kept within the family, and access to the more prosperous jobs depended on possession of stalls and franchises that were sold amongst kinsmen. Kinship was the most common basis for pooling resources and many crucial items were acquired through inheritance.

In the formal sector, the vast majority of jobs in large enterprises were never advertised. Employers would rely on the existing workforce to pass the word around about forthcoming vacancies and used the recommendations of trusted workers as the means of selection. In addition, some would use an initial selection test (*prueba*) and a three-month trial period before finally committing themselves. The case studies suggest that it was mainly unskilled jobs that were filled in this way; higher skilled jobs were usually filled by internal promotion in which personal relationships were even more important. Many employers would head-hunt workers when they needed them, and there is evidence of poaching of labour between firms, especially at the highly skilled level (cf. Chaplin 1967). They would take good workers with them if they changed their line of business and send word to relatives when they needed extra hands.

It appears that the larger firms were increasingly relying on educational credentialism as an additional device for screening workers. Some required completed primary schooling as a minimum requirement for entry, and others were beginning to ask for secondary schooling. There is evidence of increased levels of education amongst the younger skilled workers in large firms. This may reflect rising levels of education generally, or an increasing supply of skilled workers which enabled employers to introduce an additional screening device. In any event, the rise of educational credentialism occurred *within* a system of personalistic and clientalistic recruitment and did not appear to have led to any decline in the importance of kinship connections.

In a few areas of the labour market the recruitment process was more casual. This applied particularly to jobs with high turnover, where conditions of work were particularly undesirable or badly paid and there was no skill or training involved. Examples include unskilled labouring, especially on construction sites, cleaning or assembly work in factories, sweatshop jobs and domestic service. In most of these cases employers were known to have vacancies and workers could obtain jobs by approaching employers directly. Some employers would advertise with employment agencies or put a card in the window of their premises. The most open labour market, in the sense of relying on impersonal mechanisms, was domestic service. Jobs were advertised through agencies, newspapers and with little cards in the front window – 'se necesita muchacha' (maid required). According to the maids I interviewed, these were generally the worst jobs – even in domestic service the best jobs could only be had by word of mouth. It appears then that personalization of recruitment was associated with the better, scarcer jobs. Can it be coincidence that most of these networks were 'male' and the casual labour markets 'female'?

Kinship networks interacted with market forces in the Lima labour market, operating as a vehicle for leverage and closure: knowing the right person might open up an opportunity for one person but closed it off for another. However, while these networks had the capacity to mobilize resources for kinsmen in general, they were highly gender segregated, they distributed resources to men and women differently and they transferred a gender-segregated ideology into the labour market.

Gender and processes of labour allocation

In chapter 4, I suggested that it was useful to analyse gender inequality in the family in terms of a division of labour, a distribution of resources, a distribution of power and a legitimating gender ideology. These elements all played their part in differentiating men's and women's position in the labour market. This occurred not only through indirect influences on demand and supply, but through the direct intervention of kinship networks in the labour market. The division of labour, and the gender ideology that underpinned it, affected the availability of men and women for work outside the home and the types of jobs that were considered appropriate for one or other sex. Socialization within the home fed into the recruitment process within the labour market. The distribution of resources in the family limited women's access to productive resources, especially in the informal sector. The distribution of power determined the degree of autonomy available to women, their ability to defend their own interests and their capacity to negotiate strategies for coping with wider economic change. Gender ideology both differentiated men's and women's labour in terms of value and status and legitimated this difference in terms of the ultimate solidarity of the family unit.

Just as there were contradictions within the structure and ideology of the family, as discussed in chapter 4, there were also contradictory effects for women in the labour market. There were different expectations as to whether or not married women should work and different ideas as to which jobs were acceptable; but all these elements were subject to the level of demand for women's labour. Thus gender segregation was as much due to the narrow range of options open to them as to the influence of the family over their supply characteristics.

Chapter 4 showed that manual women's participation in the labour market was low after marriage and childbearing, and data presented below provide further evidence of this. However, that chapter also pointed out that this could not necessarily be explained in terms of the dominant *machista* ideology which required married women to be confined to the home, for there were conflicting ideologies amongst the labouring class about this. Equally, if not more, influential was the view emanating from rural families that all members of the family should contribute to the household income. Moreover, women's kinship and neighbourhood networks could be mobilized to handle the childcare problem, if a good job could be found. We have also seen in chapter 6 that some married women managed to keep their jobs throughout the childrearing phase. Therefore, women's low labour force participation rates cannot be explained solely in terms of women's confinement to the domestic sphere.

Nevertheless, many women did have practical difficulties in combining work with raising a family, particularly those living in shanty towns miles from the commercial centres. These women were effectively limited to working at home, in the neighbourhood or in jobs where they could take children with them, such as street sales. According to Chueca (1982: 25) 68 per cent of working mothers in Villa El Salvador were working in the same neighbourhood. This restricted them to jobs with very low earnings and the vast majority were only doing it because their husband's earnings could not cover subsistence needs, because he did not have a stable job, or because they had been abandoned (Chueca 1982: 16).

Chapters 3 and 5 provided evidence of lower educational achievement amongst girls than boys, despite the fact that women's qualifications had been rising over successive generations. The family was responsible for continuing discrepancies between women's and men's educational levels because girls' education was still valued less than boys', and because girls were more likely to have to drop out of school to look after younger siblings. The family also affected girls' access to training because of the pattern of first entry into the labour market. Boys were sent into apprenticeships and would acquire a skill that would set them up for a range of later options, whereas girls were sent into domestic service, which interrupted their education, failed to provide them with a trade and oriented them towards long-term dependence on unskilled work. However, the role of educational differentials can be over-emphasized. We should remember that in some jobs, women were relatively overqualified compared with men (chapter 3), and open unemployment amongst women was higher at the higher educational levels.[1]

The evidence of overqualification, unemployment at higher educational levels and a desire to work amongst women currently not in paid work suggests that demand factors played an important role in limiting women's access to appropriate employment. There is some evidence that employers discriminated against women in various ways, for example, preferring single to married women, not considering them for training or promotion (e.g. Barrig 1982, Guzman and Portocarrero 1985). Chaplin (1967) argues that the introduction of protectionist labour legislation led to a drop in the demand for female labour. In other, more subtle ways too, gender segregation in the workplace influenced the demand for labour via the sex-typing of jobs. Personalistic recruitment networks confirmed and reproduced the allocation of men and women to 'men's' and 'women's' jobs.

Factors such as the physical separation between the home and the work-place, educational differentials and employer discrimination might go some way towards explaining the persistence of gender segregation in the formal sector, but it is not so easy to explain sex segregation within the informal sector, which was the major source of employment for women. Family and gender ideologies clearly influenced women's recruitment into domestic service, laundry or boardinghouse work because these activities replicated their own domestic roles and were largely carried out in their own or other people's homes. But why did women not enter some of the skilled informal sector occupations, such as shoemaking, tailoring, jewellery, metal-working or carpentry, which were also carried out in the home? In many cases apprenticeships were served in artisanal workshops appended to the house-hold and the family was the major source of tools, credit and clients. Could not girls have had access to these resources as well as boys? In fact, girls and women often *were* involved in such workshops; I have seen women help their husbands to stitch the soles to the uppers of shoes and machine up garments prepared for tailoring. Why then was this work not recognized publicly, why could women not set up in these trades on their own?

Gender divisions within the family affected women's access to jobs in the informal sector in a variety of ways. In chapter 4 we saw that there was a highly segregated domestic division of labour within the labouring-class family. Thus men did not cook even though they sold cooked food, women did not do construction work even though they were well accustomed to hard physical labour, and they did not make men's clothes even though they were dressmakers. Many artisanal workshops were appended to the home and were organized on the basis of family labour, but yet were strictly segregated.[2] This was especially true of apprenticeship. Boys worked with male *maestros* and girls with female ones. Tools and equipment associated with particular trades tended to be passed between kinsmen of the appropriate sex. Lobo provides evidence that inheritance of productive resources also followed gender lines. In one case cited, the house and contents of a deceased *maestro* went to his wife, but his tools and equipment went to the brother-in-law (Lobo 1982: 89). There is also evidence that client networks were gendered, making it difficult for women to establish themselves in a trade where the customers would expect to deal with men.

Although women had a certain authority within the family, it was confined to the domestic sphere – to control over other women and children, but not over adult men. This restricted women's ability to run workshops staffed by men and prevented them from taking over their husband's business as widows. One of Grompone's informants, who was the recently widowed wife of a garage owner, tells of the difficulties she had in carrying on the business after his death. Even though she had effectively run it for years after he became an alcoholic, she was unable to exercise independent authority in her own right. It was difficult for her to maintain control over the mechanics and to establish credibility with clients (Grompone 1985: 258–61). Gender segregation within the family therefore excluded women from certain family-based activities, particularly in the artisanal trades.

The one exception to this was commerce, where the whole household would be involved in the enterprise, men, women and children. Typically, the husband would rise at 3 or 4 a.m. and go to the wholesale market to buy vegetables; the wife would join him at the stall at around 6 a.m., having got the children up and ready for school. When the elder son or daughter got back from school at midday, they would take over from the father and work until the early evening. The prevalence of family labour in petty commerce is significant because it was the one line of business without a clear skill structure and apprenticeship system. But even here, women's access to productive resources and income was defined by their status within the family, i.e. as wives and daughters.

Even within their own sphere, such as dressmaking, women lacked the resources to establish a lucrative business. Women's claims on the domestic budget took second place after men's, and it was difficult for them to demand funds for large investments. Most women had to raise their capital by scrimping and saving from the housekeeping money ('me lo ahorre del diario'), although some were financed by their husbands. Few had held skilled factory jobs and commanded the high factory wages that men did, or were able to claim redundancy or severance pay. Women had little credibility to raise loans from banks. This lack of funds had the effect of limiting them to a very small scale of operation and less lucrative lines of business.

Gender inequality within the family therefore excluded women from resources and activities that would have been compatible with their domestic responsibilities. It limited their access to crucial resources – apprenticeships, equipment and tools, capital and the establishment of good client networks. It was also influential in defining the low status of women's activities. Thus cooking was not thought of as skilled unless it took place outside the home, and dressmaking, even though skilled, was not accorded as much status as tailoring. Women's limited access to 'good' informal jobs had far reaching implications because so many large enterprises drew their labour from this sector. Thus, if women could not obtain the appropriate jobs in the informal sector, their chances in the formal sector were slight.

In summary, gender segregation within the manual labour market was strongly affected by the family, not just because of its influence on women's supply characteristics (endowments and domestic constraints) and on the sex-typing of occupations and employers' demand for labour, but because of discrimination against women in the kinship networks that controlled access to productive resources within the informal sector.

WOMEN'S WORK AND THE HOUSEHOLD

Much of the literature on urban women in Latin America has focused on their contribution to household survival strategies, within a situation of economic crisis. It has been said that women's work acts as a 'subsidy' to the male wage or as a 'supplement' or 'reserve' in times of economic need (see chapter 2: pp. 30–1). These ideas are often situated within the broader discussion of women's contribution to the process of social reproduction (Bennholdt-Thomsen 1981, 1982, Redclift 1985). These debates are important not just because of how gender may contribute to the accumulation process but because men and women may share a common economic interest despite their very different positions in the labour market. There are various arguments here: first, women's contribution to household income enables capitalist employers to lower the male wage rate below subsistence level, and it therefore constitutes a 'subsidy' to capitalist profit (Roldán 1985). Another idea is that women's work 'dovetails' with men's, providing a supplementary source of income to offset periods of male unemployment – as in the case of construction workers who are prone to periods out of work (Moser and Young 1981). More recently, the literature on structural adjustment suggests that women have acted as a reserve labour force, driven out to work by poverty as household incomes sink (e.g. Joekes 1987). Although the analysis here is located in a period of economic growth rather than crisis, we might expect to find these effects amongst the poorer families.

Below I argue that although there was some evidence to support these hypotheses, it was slight in comparison with the larger pattern of economic inactivity amongst women. Women's labour force participation in households headed by men in manual jobs was generally low, lower than that of women in middle-class or wealthy families. Even when women did work, their contribution to total household labour income was small. On average, women contributed only 19 per cent of total household labour income and only 22 per cent of the total time spent in paid work by the household.[3] Thus their income-earning status was low within the family as well as in the labour market, and these two factors continually reinforced each other. This does not negate the fact that in many individual cases, women's contribution to household income was important, but statistically they were the minority. The predominant pattern was massive dependence on male earnings.

For the purposes of this analysis, the individuals in the Ministry of Labour 1974 survey were reaggregated into their original households. This created a file of 2,298 households containing all individuals of 14 years and over,[4] employed, unemployed and inactive. Fifty-four per cent of household members were heads of household and spouses, 29 per cent were sons and daughters and a further 17 per cent were parents, in-laws or other relatives. This file contains the entire Lima survey population, not merely the labouring class. Two main variables were created for identifying labouring-class families, although neither is entirely satifactory.[5] The first was aggregate household labour income, divided into four categories – poor (total household income was less than the minimum individual wage level), low (a range of one to two minimum wages), medium (two to four minimum wages) and high (more than four minimum wages). The second was a classification of households by occupation of the household head; this was a less inclusive variable since it omitted some 500 households whose heads were economically inactive or unemployed.

Table 8.2 gives the distribution of households between the different household income bands, the proportion of adults of 14 years and over who were economically active and the activity rates of different groups. It shows that economic activity rates were *negatively* associated with household income, rather than the reverse. There were marginally more adults in richer households and the activity rates were higher there as well. Female activity rates were low amongst all household income groups, amongst married and unmarried women and in all age groups, but they were especially low amongst the poorest households. The activity rates of sons and daughters were low mainly because of full-time education, but daughters' rates were lower than sons' (see table 8.5), further depressing the general female activity rate.

Female activity rates were low even where the male rates were low. In fact, the striking feature here is the very low *male* activity rates amongst the poorest households and the small number of economically active persons there. A fifth of this group were female-headed households, a larger proportion than in any other household income group, and the female activity rates in these households were much higher.[6] However, even where women's earnings were the most important source of household income, they were not able to rescue the family from poverty. These data indicate that poverty was fundamentally related to the lack of a male breadwinner. No amount of female labour force participation could compensate for this.

Table 8.3 shows that the occupation of the head of household was only a rough guide to aggregate household income and family social class. There was a considerable spread of income in all the occupationally defined households. Nearly two-thirds of those headed by persons in the two lowest occupational groups (sales, services and unskilled work) were in the poor and low-income groups, but 38 per cent were in the medium- and high-income groups. Fewer households headed by skilled and semi-skilled workers were

Table 8.2 Labour force participation measures by level of total household labour income (monthly)*, Lima 1974

	Level of monthly household income			
	Poor (<3,000 soles)	Low (3,000– 5,999)	Medium (6,000– 11,999)	High (12,000+)
% distribution of households (N=2,298)	22%	28%	31%	19%
x̄ no. of adults 14 yrs and over	2.2	2.7	3.3	4.0
x̄ nos economically active	0.6	1.3	1.7	2.2
Total household activity rate	33.6	56.6	58.6	59.7
Male activity rate	47.7	82.3	81.7	81.1
Female activity rate	18.7	22.9	30.0	36.0
Unmarried women's activity rate	21.4	30.7	34.0	37.3
Married women's activity rate	14.3	19.5	26.6	33.1
wives <25 yrs	11.5	10.5	23.7	39.3
wives 25–39 yrs	15.5	18.8	28.1	38.3
wives 40+ yrs	14.3	27.6	25.7	26.8

Source: Ministry of Labour employment survey 1974
* All measures are significant at the level of .0000

in the poorest group and more were in the low-income group, but *half* were in the medium- and high-income groups. This suggests that household income was being raised by extra income earners, just as it was lowered by the lack of a male breadwinner. However, as we shall see below, the additional incomes were more likely to come from sons and daughters than wives.

The data show that women's activity rates were more strongly associated with their husband's occupation than with the level of household income. For example, where the household head was employed in sales, services or unskilled labouring, the activity rates of both married and unmarried women were substantially higher (table 8.4). Moreover the rates increased with age, suggesting that women's ability to supplement their husband's earnings was restricted by domestic constraints earlier in the life cycle. Note, however, that this pattern applied only to the lowest occupational group, where the main

Table 8.3   Household income and occupation of head of household, Lima 1974

Level of household income	Occupation of household head			
	Sales Services Unskilled	Skilled Semi-sk. Drivers	Technicians Office workers	Prof. Managers Admin.
	%	%	%	%
poor (<3,000 soles)	28	9	5	2
low (3,000–5,999)	35	41	28	8
medium (6,000–11,999)	28	37	43	26
high (12,000+)	9	13	23	63
Total	100	100	99	99
No. of households	450	725	353	278

Source: Ministry of Labour employment survey 1974
* Excludes heads of household who were unemployed or inactive

breadwinner was *not* typically in formal sector employment; therefore the wife's contribution could not be said to be a 'subsidy' to a formal sector wage in this case. Moreover, this group was a minority of manual households; the participation rates of married women in the next, more 'capitalist' and more numerous group were extremely low. The data appear to provide more support for the 'reserve' thesis, i.e. that women's work is used to supplement low incomes. However, we should remember that many of the families in the sales and service category were not in the poorest group of families. A better explanation is that the enterprises in this sector provided more opportunities for family labour, as we shall see in the section below.

Without detailed data on household income and consumption, it is not possible to say precisely what contribution women's earnings made. However, these data suggest that on the whole it was small. In both the home and the labour market, therefore, women's economic role was weak, and these two confirmed each other. I believe that this dependence had the effect of subsuming women's own identity into the wider collectivity of the family and class.

OCCUPATIONAL DIVERSITY WITHIN THE HOUSEHOLD

This section looks at the extent to which labour market heterogeneity and mobility was reflected within the household. Was there a pattern of systematic coupling between male and female jobs? Were there 'sector-straddling' families where informal sector wives were supplementing the wages of

Table 8.4 Labour force participation measures by occupation of household head, Lima 1974*

	Occupation of household head			
	Sales Services Unskilled	*Skilled Semi-sk. Drivers*	*Technicians Office workers*	*Prof. Managers Admin.*
% distribution of households (*N*=1,806)	25%	40%	20%	15%
x̄ no. of adults 14 yrs and over**	2.9	3.1	2.8	2.9
x̄ nos economically active	1.7	1.6	1.5	1.5
Total household activity rate	65.2	58.2	59.3	57.6
Male activity rate**	84.4	85.3	85.7	84.5
Female activity rate	39.8	23.2	27.0	27.1
Unmarried women's activity rate	49.5	26.5	31.2	29.2
Married women's activity rate	31.9	20.7	25.2	26.1
wives <25 yrs	18.7	13.3	23.2	22.9
wives 25–39 yrs	30.0	23.8	23.4	29.7
wives 40+ yrs	40.9	19.9	30.6	22.3

Source: Ministry of Labour employment survey 1974
* Figures include female heads of household but exclude inactive or unemployed heads, both male and female
** Mean differences not significant, all other figures significant at the level of .0000

formal sector spouses, as in the 'subsidy' thesis? Were there 'lumpenproletarian families' where they all lived off various unskilled and dead-end jobs as in the 'dovetailing' thesis? Were there 'labour aristocrat' families whose wives spurned degrading female jobs such as vegetable sales or laundry work and confined themselves to 'respectable' work such as dressmaking? Were there 'proletarian families' where everyone had factory jobs or 'informal families' where they all contributed to the family enterprise? Was labour market mobility reflected in the household, with the younger generation already in office jobs still living with parents who were street pedlars?

The analysis here is restricted to male and female heads in *manual* employment. It compares the occupations of spouses, sons and daughters with that of the head of household. Table 8.5 shows once again the very high inactivity rates of spouses, daughters and, to a lesser extent, sons, even where the head was working in the lowest occupational groups. However, women

Table 8.5 Occupations of spouses, sons and daughters by occupation of household head (manual only), Lima 1974

| | Occupation of household head | | | |
	Service and unskilled work %	Petty traders %	Skilled Semi-skilled & drivers %	N
SPOUSES				
(inactive)	(78)	(72)	(80)	(659)
white collar	—	7	8	13
skilled, semi-skilled	11	7	28	39
petty trade	31	72	37	83
service, unskilled	58	14	26	52
N	116	155	575	846
SONS				
(inactive)	(61)	(50)	(64)	(324)
white collar	20	11	22	40
skilled, semi-skilled	51	35	50	99
petty trade	2	46	11	35
service, unskilled	27	8	17	38
N	105	103	328	536
DAUGHTERS				
(inactive)	(77)	(67)	(80)	(340)
white collar	20	31	40	36
skilled, semi-skilled	33	22	19	23
petty trade	13	34	23	26
service, unskilled	33	13	17	19
N	66	97	281	444

Source: Ministry of Labour employment survey 1974

were more likely to be active when the head of the household was in petty trade. In these households, there was also a tendency for other members of the family to be in the same line of work. Excluding inactives, almost three-quarters of the working wives and nearly half the sons were in petty trade as well as the household head. This confirms the fact discussed in chapter 5 that this occupation provided the only opportunity for household production in Lima.

In families with heads in unskilled labouring or service work there was also a tendency for the wives to work in the same occupational group, although they would have been in different activities because of gender segregation there (e.g. wives in laundry work, husbands in waiting, portering etc.). Those who were not in service work were in petty trade. Thus amongst those wives who were in paid work in these households, there was some dovetailing of unskilled and service occupations.[7]

Amongst families headed by persons in skilled and semi-skilled work, the rates of inactivity of spouses and adult children were higher. Interestingly, the spouses who were in paid work in this group had very diverse types of employment, with no particular tendency to concentrate in either factory work or skilled informal work, such as dressmaking. The majority of them were in sales and service work.[8]

Turning to the formal/informal division, about two-thirds of the wives who were in paid work were in the informal sector and there was little difference between households headed by skilled and unskilled workers in this respect. Wives who did work in the formal sector (shops and factories) were significantly more likely to be married to skilled workers. Thus there is some evidence for the existence of 'labour aristocrat' or 'proletarian couples'. However, there was an equal number of 'segment straddling' couples, where the wives of formal sector workers were in petty retailing and service work. Amongst sons and daughters there was a clear trend away from informal work, the major exceptions being daughters of unskilled workers and sons of petty traders.

There is much evidence of upward occupational mobility within these households, particularly between the generations. Excluding inactives, 20–2 per cent of the sons of skilled and semi-skilled and unskilled workers and 11 per cent of sons of petty traders were white collar employees. The figures were even higher for daughters: 40 per cent of the daughters of skilled & semi-skilled fathers were in white collar work, as were 31 per cent of the daughters of petty traders and 20 per cent of the daughters of unskilled and service workers. Clearly then, the investment in education by these young people, reflected in their inactivity rates, was paying off in terms of eventual employment. There was also evidence of mobility within manual work, but more amongst sons than daughters. Half the sons of unskilled and service workers were already employed in skilled and semi-skilled jobs and a third of the sons of traders were. More of the daughters were still in trade and service work. The best mobility opportunities for daughters were in offices rather than skilled manual work, which is further evidence of the bottleneck for women at the top of the manual labour market, identified in chapter 3. Thus the cross-class mobility described in that chapter was occurring in the heart of the labouring-class household, not to mention the wider kinship group.

The cumulative effect of individual occupational mobility together with changes in the domestic cycle was producing a process of *household* mobility as well. The increased income and occupational status of a middle-aged household head, together with the extra income contributed by teenage children, reduced the level of economic dependency and produced an improved standard of living for the whole household. This was visible in the shanty towns, as makeshift shacks were gradually replaced by single-storey and then double-storey brick buildings.

The above analysis demonstrates the diversity of labour market experience that was being brought into the household on a day-to-day basis. There was some evidence of a clustering of particular types of occupational experience within households, but these clusters were as likely to straddle labour market segments as to combine within them.[9] The main patterns were: (a) a tendency for household collaboration in petty trade and higher activity rates there; (b) a dovetailing between heads of household and their spouses in unskilled informal occupations (sales and services); (c) a slight clustering of heads, spouses and possibly sons in formal sector work; and (d) some straddling across the formal/informal divide by husbands and spouses. However, the extent of this clustering was offset by two other factors: first, the high inactivity rates of spouses and children, and second, the upward mobility between generations within the household, both within manual work and across the manual/non-manual divide.

It thus appears that women's role in supplementing men's economic activities has been overstated in the literature mentioned above. For most labouring-class wives, the common experience was that of being totally dependent on the earnings of a spouse and/or older children. Of those women who did work, the majority (78 per cent) were in informal activities in commerce and services yielding little income and often long hours. Such women were often supplementing the low earnings of men who were also employed in these sectors. But just as likely their husbands were in the better manual jobs – bus driving, skilled factory work etc. – and some were even married to non-manual workers. Only 37 per cent of wives working in sales and services were living with heads of household in the same occupational group; 46 per cent were in households headed by skilled and semi-skilled workers and 17 per cent were married to middle-class men. Thus, although these women were confined to a very restricted part of the manual labour market themselves, they had some indirect knowledge of better jobs through their husbands and children. As we shall see in the next chapter, women's perceptions of class divisions and attitudes towards other classes showed a similarity to men's that could only be explained by some mechanism of identification with male work experiences.

FAMILY, GENDER AND CLASS

We have seen that the family played a major role in differentiating men's and women's labour market position and thereby weakened women's contribution to the domestic economy. However, while women might have had a marginal position within the household as economic providers, they had a crucial role in the organization of consumption. It is worth considering this briefly in order that gender divisions in employment can be placed within the wider context of family life. At the ideological level, the division of labour between production and consumption roles was legitimated in terms of gender complementarity and reciprocity. Moreover there was a strong emphasis on family solidarity within both spheres. The struggle for livelihood was a family affair: getting a job was not just about pursuing individual self-interest, it was about sustaining immediate and extended kinship obligations. 'Honest work' and 'looking after the family' were central aspects of labouring-class morality: those who neglected their families provoked the strongest condemnation from both men and women. Many men mentioned the 'carga familiar' (the responsibility of maintaining a family) in the discussion of their position in the labour market:

'The *obreros* earn a miserable wage; what does it leave me for the children?'

'What can I say when I get home and the children are asking for bread?'

Equally, women's consumption activities were construed in terms of a collective struggle for physical and economic survival. Moreover, consumption activities were not the unique preserve of women; they involved extensive cooperation within the household and the local community. The sphere of consumption was one where individual, family and community interests converged. Housebuilding, for example, involved the cooperation of men and women in the nuclear and even extended family. It provoked community-wide collective action to invade land, and to pressurize the state for public utilities and other amenities. Housing was a communal good, a symbol of the family itself:

The self-builder attaches unusual importance to his property: declared ownership of land in these chaotically growing cities has almost a mystical significance, not only for the family itself, but for the community as a whole.... And the house on this land, built with so much effort, is an object on which the family lavishes its pride and stakes its new identity.

(Turner 1963: 391)

The reproduction of the family over time had great significance for the labouring class. Their energies were not just directed to the problems of day-to-day survival, but to securing a better future for their children. Mangin reports that 71 per cent of barriada residents agreed with the statement that 'one should sacrifice all for one's children' (Mangin 1967).

'I love my children and worry about them and their future and know that it is my responsibility to fight for them every day.'

(Lobo 1982: 129–30)

After housing, education was the main item of investment by the family, in terms of earnings foregone as well as the costs of uniforms, books etc. On occasion, it too required collective action at the community level to build the schools and pressurize the state for teaching resources.

The family was thus the basis for the struggle for livelihood, the pursuit of income-earning activities, better living standards and increased mobility chances in the future. This was achieved through the labour market and through the community. Kinship provided the organizational basis for co-operation and the normative standards of communal solidarity within and between households. Its goals, structure and values extended into the work-place and community through networks of reciprocity and collective action.

Many writers have pointed out that slums and shanty towns were socially heterogeneous and thus cannot be considered class-based communities (Lewis 1973, Dietz 1985, CIED n. d.). They contained some non-manual as well as manual workers, and formal as well as informal sector workers. This was partly an effect of the upward mobility process occurring within labour-ing-class families. Nevertheless, it is important to note that (a) wage labourers were the majority in most of these settlements, (b) many of those who were self-employed had been wage labourers earlier in their working lives, and (c) many of those in middle-class employment were sons and daughters of manual workers. Quite apart from the kinship connections linking individuals in different occupations and their shared conception of 'labouring work' as a basis for class identity, there was a common history of mobility within the labour market and shared struggles at community level to obtain rights to land and public services. Therefore there were plenty of bases for common class identity in these neighbourhoods.

Like the family, labouring-class communities combined internal diversity and inequality with shared norms and values embodied in notions of reciprocity. Community mobilizations were fundamentally based on the participation of families, in defence of the family, although they were also perceived as *class* struggles because they had to do with survival. The family was therefore central to the notion of class and community. Women's subordinate position within the family was constituted ideologically in terms of complementarity within the broader framework of family, community and class. Their mobilization on the basis of domestic roles and responsibilities was construed in terms of class and family interests even though it may also have reflected gender interests. Thus despite their economic dependence on men and their frequent experience of men's violence, women were more likely to defend the common class interests of the family than sectional interests based on gender. In the next chapter, we shall see how these interests were manifested in consciousness and political action.

9   Consciousness and political action

This chapter examines the nature of class consciousness and political action amongst the labouring class, with particular reference to the influence of labour market divisions, mobility and gender. I shall argue that there were common class identities and solidarities despite the internal segmentation created by heterogeneity and mobility. These attitudes were exhibited by informal sector workers as much as formal ones and women as much as men. Moreover, class was more important than gender as the basis for women's consciousness and action. This situation was underpinned by two factors: the unity of production and consumption within an overall situation of poverty and hardship, and the importance of the family in the struggle for livelihood and social progress. Despite this common consciousness, however, the labouring class was highly alienated from politics.

As mentioned in chapter 2, during the early 1970s there was a common stereotype in Latin America that the labouring class was organizationally weak, with a low level of solidarity class consciousness. It was said to exhibit a tendency for elitism, individualism, opportunism, deference and political apathy. There was a low level of participation in formal political organizations and within those that did exist, there was a susceptibility to manipulation by reformist or even reactionary political parties.

Labour market heterogeneity and the separation between the workplace and the community as independent spheres of action have played an important part in explanations of this situation. It has been argued that the workplace was the location for class action, but the community was the site for social movements which had a multi-class character (Portes 1985, Castells 1983). It has also been suggested men's actions mainly take place within the sphere of production (the workplace) and hence have to do with class while women's actions take place within that of consumption (the community) and are expressed in social movements (Moser 1987). In both sites, however, action is said to be fragmented by internal socio-economic divisions which produce a weak class consciousness and a clientelistic dependence on middle-class political agents. For example, the privileged position of formal sector workers produced an elitist and reformist consciousness, more concerned with the protection of sectional privileges than with political changes that might improve the situation of workers generally (e.g. Landsberger 1967). On the other hand, informal sector workers had different class interests from factory workers and their dispersion in scattered workplaces prevented the development of political consciousness (e.g. Sulmont 1977, Portes 1985). At the community level, preoccupation with consumption levels and social mobility was considered to have a divisive effect on consciousness and action, creating internal status divisions and emphasizing an ethic of individualism at the cost of collectivism (Safa 1974, Lloyd 1980).

Gender played a negligible role in these early discussions about the nature of class consciousness. Productionist theories assumed that women's low participation in the labour force and their concentration in informal activities while at work made for a low degree of class consciousness. Community studies indicated that since women were primarily involved in household consumption and more rooted in the community, they were prone to status striving and clientelistic dependence on charity organizations. Women were portrayed as politically apathetic, conservative and deferential.

The overall impression from these writings is of an internally divided, individualistic, acquiescent class; at best reformist, at worst conservative. Yet this image is contradicted by periodic conflagrations of mass strikes and street riots, the violence with which workers pressed their claims, and the high degree of lateral solidarity exhibited by workers' organizations in moments of crisis (Payne 1965, Bourricaud 1970). Community organizations were militant as well as reformist, and women were active participants in many of them. Such actions are not easily explained by the above literature.

Below I argue that the significance of labour market divisions was overemphasized in these theories and its separation from consumption was artificial. Production and consumption were indivisible as far as workers were concerned. Employment divisions were subsumed within the wider context of shared poverty, a reliance on hard physical labour and common antipathy towards the rich and powerful. Institutions such as the family and community played an important role in merging internal economic divisions and providing common sentiments of solidarity and opposition. However, there was a profound alienation from the political system, produced by years of government repression and political party sectarianism. This explains the low degree of political participation amongst manual workers better than a supposed lack of class consciousness.

Class identities amongst the labouring class in Lima had a populist character in that they stressed notions of common hardship rather than specific relations of production. They were implicitly radical in that they denied the moral legitimacy of the system of class privilege and political power, but the radicalism was latent because it was not yet expressed in class-based organizations. This is a very different picture from the apathetic, clientelistic picture painted by the literature of the 1970s.

METHODOLOGICAL NOTE

The findings reported here are based on an analysis of case study interviews in which standard 'class image'[1] material was gathered, i.e. how many social groups were perceived, how they were differentiated, the character of relations between them, the respondent's position in the class structure, whether social mobility was possible or desirable, etc. Respondents were also asked about the degree of help workers could expect from a range of different economic and political actors. All questions, with the exception of the last, were open-ended and coded after the interview had taken place.

I was particularly concerned that attitudes towards social class should not be influenced by current academic or political discourse. Therefore class identities were investigated via a social psychological projective technique which made no mention of the term 'social class'. Respondents were invited to identify an unspecified number of coloured cards with 'groups with the same problems and interests', and then to describe their associated characteristics.[2] Only when they had completed these images were they asked to locate the groups in social classes. In this way class identities were described using the referents that were most meaningful to the respondents.

Although it was possible to quantify much of the class image material, I found the language used in discussing class identities much more revealing. It conveyed the texture and sentiments of class relations more vividly than the quantitative analysis. In the following section, I shall provide some quotations from the questionnaires, in order to give a flavour of these sentiments. The translations are mine.

SUMMARY OF DATA ON CLASS IMAGES

The findings may be summarized as follows:

(a) The majority of respondents had an identifiable model of the social hierarchy and located themselves at the bottom of it. The term 'social class' was not frequently used in discussions about the identity and characteristics of social groups, nor were 'proletariat' or 'bourgeoisie' mentioned. However, it is clear from the way groups were described that respondents *meant* social class, i.e. they generally talked in terms of economic inequalities, power and privilege, suffering and exploitation.

The predominant model of the social hierarchy can be described as a 'work–wealth' model.

(b) There was remarkable uniformity in the self-identification of most manual workers, both in terms of how they described themselves and where they placed themselves; and the major basis for these identities was *work*. However, it is clear that they were referring to the physical and social nature of manual labour and its general relationship with poverty, rather than specific market situations or employment statuses. Excluding some 10 per cent who had no definable class image, the vast majority (84 per cent) identified themselves as *obreros* or *trabajadores* and only a small minority (16 per cent) as petit bourgeois or middle class. There was very little relationship between class images and labour market divisions, and scant support for the notion of a labour elite or an informal sector stratum set apart from the broad mass of manual workers. To the extent that any division within the working class was perceived, it was based on the *lack of work*, i.e. unemployment and criminal activities, rather than differences at work.

(c) Images of the overall class structure were very polarized between workers and the rich, with less notice taken of the middle class. Seventy-nine per cent of respondents mentioned the presence of a 'millionaire' class, while 43 per cent mentioned a middle class of office workers and bureaucrats. The major criterion for identifying the rich was *wealth* and this was related to property ownership. The middle class on the other hand was seen as a work-based class.

(d) Although there was some variation in the precise shape of the class models reported, there were remarkably uniform *sentiments* about the social and moral character of the different classes.[3] There was widespread antagonism towards the rich; feelings of respect or indifference towards the middle class; and a general belief in the moral superiority of the working class. There was little evidence of elitism, deference, social climbing or clientelism.

(e) There was considerable support for an ethic of self-improvement and this was described as a common goal amongst the poor. There was some ambivalence about cross-class mobility and a strong rejection of the values and culture of the wealthy. Most informants stressed movement within their class rather than moving into another, at least for their own generation.

(f) There was very little difference between the class perceptions of men and women; the basic shape of class images, class sentiments and the self-identification of class was the same. Therefore it is difficult to make the case for a gender-specific consciousness here.

THE SHAPE OF THE CLASS STRUCTURE

In all, fourteen different 'models' of class structure could be identified, but for simplification these have been collapsed into the seven models outlined below. Figure 9.1 shows that the majority had either a bipolar model which distinguished between rich and poor (A), or a tripartite model that included the middle class as well (B). Model C represents a small group with a bipolar image, defined in terms of the labouring class and the middle class only. Model D represents those who distinguished a small elite between the labouring class and the rich, distinct from the middle class, with which they identified. This group was based on informal sector employment and could be characterized as a petit bourgeoisie. As can be seen, this model was not common in the sample as a whole. Model E represents those who considered themselves members of the middle class, defined in terms of office workers or salaried employees. Again this was a very small group, half of whom were employed as shop assistants – a group whose inclusion in the study was always dubious (see Appendix). Finally, models F and G consisted of persons who could only talk about groups within their own class or who had difficulty identifying groups on any class criteria (e.g. drunks, vagabonds and gypsies). A few respondents mentioned groups below themselves, such as peasants, the unemployed etc. Since their class perceptions were the same as those in A, B, and F in all other respects, the extra groups are represented by the dotted boxes in these models.

Figure 9.1 shows that almost two-thirds of workers placed themselves in a class of *trabajadores* (labourers) which formed part of a wider hierarchy of social classes, and only 20 per cent located themselves above it. There was only a slight association between the perceived shape of the class structure and labour market divisions. On the whole, manufacturing workers were just as likely to perceive a tripartite structure as a bipolar one, and the same went for workers in commerce and services; only construction workers had a pronounced tendency for the latter model. The two-class model was equally prevalent amongst formal and informal sector workers: it was held by 54 per cent of men working in enterprises with more than twenty workers, 47 per cent of self-employed men and 50 per cent of self-employed women. Skill was a better predictor of the type of class image than enterprise size or employment status, a tripartite model being more frequent amongst skilled workers than unskilled ones. However, having a tripartite model did not mean that respondents located themselves in the middle class; two-thirds of skilled men, over half of self-employed men and 64 per cent of self-employed women who subscribed to a tripartite model identified with the lower class. Nor did it signify a more deferential attitude towards the class system, as we shall see below.[4]

Women's images did not differ much from men's, they were just as able as men to differentiate their position vis-à-vis other classes and just as likely to have a bipolar or a tripartite model of these classes. Slightly more women defined themselves as middle class, but these were not typically labouring-class women.[5] In any case, they were in the minority: two-thirds of all women identified with the labouring class.

model type	A	B	C	D	E	F	G
upper class	☐	☐		☐	☐		
middle class		☐	☐	[*]	[*]		
labouring class	[*]	[*]	[*]	☐	☐	[*]	[?]
underclass/ peasants	[ ][ ]	[ ][ ]				[ ]	

% distribution

	A	B	C	D	E	F	G
men	37	28	4	7	8	8	8
women	33	17	7	5	22	3	13
total	35	24	5	6	14	6	10

Figure 9.1 Class models of labouring-class men and women

Source: Author's case studies (unweighted)
* Respondent's location   ? no classes, unclassifiable

CRITERIA FOR THE IDENTIFICATION OF SOCIAL CLASSES

In considering how social groups were identified, we can look first at the terms used to name groups and then the criteria that were used to describe them more fully. The terms used for naming groups mainly rested on a combination of work and wealth. Over half the sample used specific or general occupational terms for the identification of their own group, 22 per cent mentioning very specific occupations, e.g. bricklayers, traders, and 34 per cent using general occupational terms such as *obreros*. Seventeen per cent used economic terms such as 'the poor'; 11 per cent used residential criteria such as 'we in the shanty towns'; a further 11 per cent referred to ethnic or locality factors such as *serranos* or *provincianos* (those from the mountains or provinces). Only one per cent mentioned political variables such as

unionists or political party members. There was little difference in the types
of criteria for class identification used by skilled and unskilled, or formal and
informal workers. All stressed the occupational and economic basis of their
own class identity and social differentiation generally. Women's criteria for
self-identification were similar to men's, with the majority stressing specific
or general occupational terms.

Respondents used similar criteria for identifying social groups other than
their own, and often they combined criteria. Table 9.1 lists all the criteria used
in describing different social groups and shows the predominant emphasis on
work and wealth. Although women tended to prioritize work and wealth as
much as men, they ranked other factors differently, placing more emphasis
on education, life style, residence and race, and less on political organization.

Table 9.1   Bases for differentiating social groups (percentage of men and women
mentioning each factor, multi-response), Lima 1974

	Men %	Women %
Wealth	75	81
Occupation	62	68
Capital/property	33	23
Life style	28	35
Organization	27	14
Education	20	32
Morality	17	21
Region/culture	12	12
Residential area	10	19
Nationality	9	6
Race	3	16
Other	12	7

Source: Author's case studies (weighted)

The class images of some respondents could be described as an ego-cen-
tred set of circles, having finer (mainly occupational) distinctions in the centre
and more general ones as they moved out. Thus within their own class they
would mention specific occupational groups (e.g. carpenters), in the proxi-
mate class general occupational groups (e.g. office workers), and on the
periphery, a general economic category such as 'the rich'. Other respondents,

particularly those with a two-class model, tended to contrast classes at a uniformly general level (e.g. 'rich and poor').

The notion of a 'work–wealth' model can be misleading in that it gives the impression that wealth comes from work. Yet according to these respondents, nothing could be further from the truth: the major division in Peruvian society was between those who had to work for a living and those who did not. This model did not prioritize production relations over consumption or vice versa, but saw them as indissolubly linked. The wealth of the rich was considered to be unearned and arose from property ownership, the exploitation of workers, and to a lesser extent from corruption and political manipulation. Eighty-three per cent of both men and women said that the basis of wealth was capital and property; and the way these were used produced poverty and suffering for workers.

> 'they are the powerful ones in society; they have everything because of their money; they inherit it; they make investments, they exploit workers' (textile worker)
> 'the rich set up enterprises according to their own criteria to make themselves richer. There are few who have made their money through work' (factory worker)
> 'they are the ones who do least and earn most; they are the great capitalists' (jeweller)
> 'they have power because of their capital' (tailor)
> 'the rich make and unmake people; they say whether I stay or go' (bricklayer)
> 'they have the destiny of the country in their hands. They live comfortably. They may have problems but they have a solution. They don't suffer at all. Their wealth gives them power. They have facilities to buy positions. They control poor leaders. They make political campaigns with their money' (tailor-outworker)

The vast majority of respondents identified themselves as 'labourers' using the terms 'obrero' or 'trabajador'. They did not talk of a labouring *class* as such, though the words did connote a social collectivity. Nor did these terms refer to a specific relation of employment, such as wage labourer. They literally meant labouring and toil, and this was also associated with struggle, suffering and poverty. *Trabajadores* included all manual workers, formal and informal, high wage and low wage, men and women. Even the self-employed counted themselves amongst them; the emphasis was on the fact that they worked (laboured), rather than that they worked for themselves. In the following quotations, all respondents are describing the labouring class and placed themselves in this group; the first six are from people who were self-employed or 'disguised' wage labourers.

'the *trabajadores* are poor, they sell to their customers, they depend on the owners (dueños), on foreigners' (market seller)

'the *obreros* are street traders like me' (newspaper vendor)

'the *obreros* are struggling to survive, they have a minimum wage but it isn't enough. They have poor living conditions' (barman)

'well, since I'm a bus driver, I'm an obrero as well' (owner of a microbus)

'I'm one of the *obreros*, *trabajadores* in all lines of work. We don't live well, we work hard all the time; we are poor because we are enslaved by work' (taxi driver)

'they have less economic resources, poor earnings, the burden of the family, there is nothing to turn to but their own labour. They are exploited. They have to submit themselves to the whim of the rich because of their work. They have to obey and grin and bear it' (*palanca* busdriver)

'we *obreros* only just get enough to live on' (skilled textile worker)

'the *obreros* work hard; there are no facilities, they live badly. They are exploited because of the great efforts they put in and the poor pay they receive' (factory worker)

'the *obreros* work hard, they are not recompensed for their work, they cannot improve things' (mechanic)

'we sweat a lot, and they pay us as little as possible, and that's how we live' (bricklayer)

'the *obrero* depends on others. He is exploited ... they don't appreciate the work he does ... he is only considered a brute force, a mere tool' (textile worker)

In all these discourses, 'work' was fundamentally related to poverty. Eighty per cent of men and women thought poverty was due to low incomes, exploitation or unemployment, rather than lack of education or powerlessness. Thus production and consumption were intimately connected. Some respondents emphasized the production side of this relationship, while others focused more on consumption, defining themselves as 'the poor', 'the humble ones' ('los humildes'), 'the people from the *barriadas*' etc. This type of language was more prevalent amongst less educated and more isolated workers, such as domestic servants and outworkers, and often, women.

'the poor live the worst life you can imagine, bad housing, bad food, some don't have work, they suffer, they live in precarious houses' (bricklayer)

'we are the poor – we struggle to survive, we have no means to defend ourselves' (tailor)

Surprisingly little reference was made to ethnicity or provincial origins in the identification of social classes. However, this was much more frequent amongst women, particularly domestic servants.

'the ones with money are white, conceited, spoilt, they abuse the *cholos*. We are the *cholos*, people without luck, obliged to work in order to survive, we are swindled' (domestic servant)

'the *trabajadores* are us *mestizos*. We work in order to live and even so they pay us little. We are on the breadline for everything' (shop assistant in an ironmonger's shop)

'we are the *provincianos*, the *trabajadores* with least status' (factory worker)

'the *trabajadores* are *serranos* like me; it is some time since I've been to my homeland but I don't forget (plumber)

Within the work–wealth model, the salaried middle class was perceived as an intermediate group, reliant on their labour power, like workers, but occupying a higher level because of their different type of work and better educational levels ('más cultura'). Workers perceived much less of a divide between themselves and the middle class and were more favourably disposed towards them, although some thought they had an easier life. This reflects the blurring of the boundaries between the two, which was mentioned in chapter 3.

'they work as office workers, they live according to their salaries, they are good people, well educated' (electrician)

In terms of criteria for social differentiation then, the major division was between those who lived off property and capital and those who worked for a living. Amongst the latter, a distinction was made between manual and non-manual workers and their associated status and life styles. However, divisions *amongst* manual workers in terms of wage labour and self-employment, informal and formal sector work, and male and female occupations played a negligible role in the definition of labouring-class identity.

CLASS SENTIMENT

Class identities were underpinned by a strong sense of moral community. Work was a source of positive morality – humility, honesty, trustworthiness etc. The propertied classes were immoral because they did not work; they were politically corrupt, arrogant, deceitful, not to be trusted. There is no doubt about the suspicion and hostility that was felt towards the 'clase alta'.

'they think they are lords, the all-powerful, the only ones that matter' (upholsterer)

'they see a person and they treat him badly, they think he is beneath them, they think that money can buy everything, they don't look at who you are, they are arrogant' (mechanic)

'you can't trust them, you have to watch them' (bricklayer)
'they exploit and enslave people, they deceive the obrero' (solderer)
'the rich look at you as if you were a piece of rubbish. We are despised by them' (airport porter)

In contrast, the moral superiority of the labouring class was stressed. Workers were more honest, straightforward, dependable, helpful to one another etc. Their solidarity was the product of common experiences of hard physical labour, the struggle to house and feed a family, and helping each other out.

'the *trabajadores* are more humble, more honest, but the trabajador thinks he is worth less than others, he undervalues himself' (mechanic)
'the *obrero* is more faithful, more sincere. There is more union, more harmony amongst the poor' (postman)
'I am of the *obrero* people, I can say the truth with my people, you are always yourself when you're with your own people' (bricklayer)
'arriving at work is like being with the family, we love each other, we help each other' (bricklayer)
'I trust them because they are the ones who support each other' (taxi driver)
'I trust the *trabajadores* because we suffer like they do, we earn our daily bread with the sweat of our brow' (driver)

The role of 'honest work' as the source of working-class morality was demonstrated by the attention occasionally drawn to 'thieves and layabouts' who attracted moral condemnation:

'there are people who are lazy, delinquents, they like to do nothing, they don't work, they rob people'
'they don't have morals or shame'
'there are robbers, people who don't want to work, lazy people' (various)

There was a latent radicalism in this dual class morality since it implied an oppositional element in class attitudes and questioned the basic legitimacy of the social order. This was a far cry from the image of deference and clientelism portrayed by the literature mentioned above, and it would explain the violence of class confrontations when they did occur.

DIFFERENTIATION AND MOBILITY

There was some recognition of differences amongst workers in terms of occupations and levels of income, but these were not the basis for separate class positions. When respondents were asked to place these different groups into classes, they were all located in the labouring class:

'I am one of the *trabajadores* in general, according to what jobs they do some earn more, others earn less' (delivery boy)

There was widespread recognition of the fact that working-class families were trying to 'progress', 'improve themselves' etc. However, this too was viewed as movement within the class, it was a case of a common struggle to rise out of poverty and to improve living standards, rather than to abandon their own class.

'the *obreros* live off their work, they hope to progress economically' (lorry driver)
'the people from the villages are good people who are just trying to live better' (bus driver)
'you always try to better yourself; you've always got to aspire to something' (carpenter)

Most respondents thought that they had achieved more than their own parents and were better off in Lima than where they were born. Moreover, as we saw in chapter 3, most desired further mobility for their children (see also Briones and Mejía (1964) and Collier (1976b)). However, many thought that further mobility was not possible or even desirable for themselves, particularly if it implied a rejection of their own moral and cultural community.

'I would have to change my style of life and work' (mechanic)
'it is impossible to change your trade, let alone your group. I'm OK as I am' (jeweller)
'I wouldn't like to change groups, although get nearer, yes, with luck and some money. But not spiritually' (taxi driver)
'change groups? No – they have other feelings' (solderer)
'I would have to force myself to join the entrepreneurs, I wouldn't like to exploit people' (bootblack)

The search for better jobs and higher living standards was perceived as a legitimate common goal for workers, as long as it did not involve a departure from labouring-class morality and culture. Indeed, aspirations to 'progress' and a 'better life' could be said to be a class goal as much as an individual one. The fact that the middle class was seen as a work-based class, distinct from the rich, meant that upward mobility did not have to imply betraying the culture of 'working people'.

GENDER AND CLASS CONSCIOUSNESS

Women's class images were very similar to men's; there was little evidence that they were any less class conscious than men, or more conservative. There were differences amongst women, just as there were amongst men, but the general tendencies were the same. They had both bipolar and tripartite models of the class structure, they mainly identified with a labouring class composed of a variety of manual jobs, they opposed this class against a wealthy propertied class and they perceived the main criteria of social differentiation to be work and wealth. They expressed the same sentiments of moral community with their own class and moral condemnation of the rich. Here are some examples:

'the *trabajadores* have to work in factories or in private houses, they don't live well, they have poor wages' (washerwoman)

'we are the *obreros*. We earn less than others but we work harder. We don't get the value of what we produce' (textile worker)

'the poor are all the *trabajadores*, they earn little, they are deceived, they don't have good jobs. I am one of the self-employed, people who look after their own business without depending on anyone, but it also involves a lot of suffering and bad pay' (female restaurant owner)

'the poor live badly, but they are more peaceful, more noble, there is understanding amongst them' (shirtmaker)

'the *obreros* suffer the most, they only just manage to survive on what they earn and they are badly treated. I am one of them' (domestic servant)

'the *obreros* are good industrious people, who only do the right thing. They make us work like animals. The *patrón* squeezes the last drop out of us' (shirtmaker)

'the rich are the ones who have everything, they don't worry about the rest of us, they are hypocrites. The lower class are the ones who don't have anything, they are *empleados*, *obreros*. They go straight from their work to their homes, they are more sincere' (street pedlar)

'the rich are comfortably off, surrounded by everything, exploiting the poor. They are selfish, despotic, they abuse us. They trample on the poor' (dressmaker)

'businessmen give work but pay little. They live off our labour, and they, yes, they earn a lot' (servant)

At the margin, women were slightly more prone than men to identify themselves as middle class, to emphasize status factors such as living standards, education and ethnicity, and to be more judgemental in terms of class sentiment. However, this should not necessarily be interpreted as a 'bourgeois' consciousness. Most of those who located themselves in a middle group did so because of an awareness of greater poverty than their own rather than because of elitism.

'I am one of those with an average level of earnings, we work in order to survive, we educate our children. We are exploited, they make us work overtime and pay a miserable wage. Then there are the poor, who live in misery, they eat only once a day, they live amongst straw matting, they have to beg, they don't progress' (dressmaker)

'there are the rich, the middling ones and the poor. The rich have money, good clothing, cars, large mansions. The middling ones are struggling. There are days when we don't have a whole housekeeping allowance, there are things we want to buy but we can't. The poor can't even buy bread. I have seen people go days without eating. If I were to go to a rich person for help, he wouldn't give me anything, but a poor person would even if it meant a sacrifice' (knits jumpers for neighbours)

'businessmen do what they want with the *obreros*, they exploit them, they own the capital. Salaried employees have more advantages at work. The *obreros* are ordered about by the foreman, who might be a tyrant or a good person. The Federation of Obreros protects *empleados* and *obreros* from the *patrón*' (commissioned saleswoman)

Like men, women saw production and consumption as two sides of the same coin, although they were often more aware of the consumption side because of their role as managers of consumption in the family and their awareness of neighbours with economic difficulties. Their perception of the gulf between the rich and the poor was also experienced through the sphere of consumption, in domestic service. In this occupation, many women had suffered bad treatment, status derogation and racism and these experiences were very influential in their perception of class relations. It led to a particular emphasis on the moral elements of class, especially the immorality of the rich. There was little evidence of deference and status striving amongst these women. If anything, their class sentiments were more fiercely oppositional than the men's, more hostile towards the rich and having more solidarity with their own kind:

'the rich are white, conceited, spoilt, they abuse the *cholos* all the time, and the bad thing is that nobody punishes them. They live in great mansions with great luxury and they spend money just for the sake of it. They take everything for themselves and don't leave anything for the poor. The professionals think they know everything and despise those of us who haven't studied. The *cholos*, that's us, people without luck, obliged to work in order to survive, we are swindled, we cannot educate ourselves because we don't have the money' (domestic servant)

'those with money are white, they live in luxury and spend money for the sake of it. They swindle their servants. Their children are spoilt and treat us badly. They are hardly ever at home and want us to do everything for them. All the rich treat us badly, saying that we are only servants and that's what they pay us for. We are *trabajadores* because we work in order to survive. We can't study, buy anything or do anything. We can't change groups because we are poor and have a different skin colour. I wouldn't like to change because if I became rich all of a sudden, I would treat people badly, and I don't want to' (servant)

Women's attitudes were influenced by past experiences of domestic service as well as by their current type of employment. It is likely that these memories would also be present amongst women who were not economically active, and therefore it should not be assumed that such women lacked a work-based consciousness. Amongst the women who were in paid work, the activities of other members of the household, whose experiences were very different from their own, were often reflected in their attitudes and perceptions. Many of those who identified with factory workers, bus drivers, salesmen etc. had fathers, brothers, husbands, and sons in these occupations. This produced a much broader definition of class identities than might have been expected from their own narrow range of labour market positions.

There was little evidence of gender consciousness in these data. Women never mentioned gender as a specific aspect of inequality or deprivation, nor did men. When the family was mentioned, it was always in terms of common interests rather than different ones. To be fair, gender interests and gender consciousness were not specifically investigated in this research, and it is possible that a different set of questions might have produced different answers. However, in all the open-ended discussions about inequality, the discourse was not about men and women but about family and class.

SUMMARY

The above analysis has shown that most manual workers shared a common identity as members of a broad labouring class which included formal and informal sector workers and men and women. This identity rested on several factors: first, the fact that workers chose to stress the common aspects of work which had to do with physical effort, drudgery and status, rather than differences in employment conditions, skill or income; second, the fact that most of them had been exposed to a variety of different types of jobs in their own working lives; and third, occupational diversity within the household and extended family.

The family played an important role in facilitating the development of this common class identity. It provided a framework for the pooling of resources from the labour market, the organization of household consumption and the development of longer term mobility strategies. It was the main agency through which the struggle for livelihood and the escape from poverty – the two main sources of labouring-class identity – were achieved. It was the source of an ideology that legitimated solidarity between individuals with unequal access to resources. Finally, it provided a mechanism through which the struggles of individual families and households were extended to wider groups in the workplace and community.

> Family solidarity shades into community solidarity, reinforced by the frequent practice of endogamy.
>
> (Anderson *et al.* 1979: 15–16)

POLITICAL ACTION AMONGST THE LABOURING CLASS

Studies of political action amongst the labouring class in Lima have tended to confirm the picture of a weak, apathetic and clientelistic class. Trade unions were reported to have a low level of union membership, ideological divisions between and within unions, and union leaders tended to enter into patron–client relations with political parties or even the government in power (see e.g. Haworth 1983, Sulmont 1977). In the shanty towns, studies stressed the individualism of squatters and their preoccupation with internal status rankings within the community (Lloyd 1980). Goldrich *et al.* (1967) reported a low level of politicization amongst them, and Mangin (1967) claimed that while community organizations were capable of mobilizing extensive support during the early phases of shanty-town formation, they tended to atrophy over time. Collier (1976a) provided evidence of a long history of paternalistic relations between these organizations and the government in power.

In the following pages I shall argue that the forms of class consciousness outlined in the previous pages were more indicative of political alienation than passivity or cooptation, and this alienation was a product of the political system rather than internal labour market divisions. I shall also show that women were politically active within both the workplace and the community, although their actions were usually subordinated to male leadership and organization. However, in both spheres their actions were defined in class rather than gender terms, even when gender roles were an important basis for mobilization. I do not want to overstate the case for radicalism and militancy amongst this class, for there clearly were problems in this respect; I merely wish to challenge the view that economic divisions within the class were responsible for a weak consciousness and ineffective forms of action.

The class images and attitudes described above portray a populist radicalism in two senses. First, there was a perception of profound inequality between rich and poor, an awareness that this inequality was linked to opposed economic interests and a rejection of its normative legitimacy. Second, labouring-class identities were framed in general terms that overrode occupational and labour market differences, providing a wide basis for solidarity. Dependence on work and the struggle against poverty made for common bonds between formal and informal sector workers and between men and women.

These subjective perceptions might be expected to be a basis for radical collective action. Yet there was considerable cynicism about political institutions. This was demonstrated in the case study data by the responses to a question about who helped workers most. Just over a third of the sample thought unions helped workers a lot, a fifth thought they helped a little and the remaining two-fifths, that they did not help at all. A fifth of them thought the government helped a lot, a third thought they helped a little, and the rest not at all. Political parties fared very badly: less than 10 per cent thought they helped a lot or a little, and 90 per cent thought they did not help at all. There were very few differences between men and women in these responses or between formal and informal sector workers.

Other studies carried out during that period found similar attitudes. Goldrich *et al.* (1967) reported that respondents in two Lima shanty towns showed a high degree of alienation from political parties and scepticism about the degree of help that could be expected from the government. There was more opposition to the political system than in comparable Chilean shanty towns, more interclass hostility and more disposition to condone violence as a means of settling political questions. Yet only about a fifth were registered members of an opposition party. Collier (1976b) reported similar results from a city-wide survey in 1967.

On the other hand, there was evidence of lateral support within the labouring class, although much of it was informal. Most of my case studies said that their friends and relatives helped them more than formal political groups, and of the latter, there was more support for unions than for political parties or the government. There was a high degree of participation in unions and community associations in terms of attendance at meetings and support for protest action (Briones and Mejía 1964: 54, Roman de Silgado 1981: 319–20, Dietz 1980: 99). The cynicism regarding political institutions was thus directed to the middle-class agents and their clients, rather than to political protest as such.

Alienation from the political system was an effect of strong intervention by the state and national political parties in the workplace and the community. This, in turn, was the product of a general weakness of political institutions in Peru. Traditional oligarchic domination had been undermined but the new industrial/commercial bourgeoisie was not strong enough to set up an alternative power base on its own. Most political parties had to rely on interclass alliances or support from the military for access to power. The fragility of these alliances meant that for most of this century Peru had alternated between weak civilian government and military dictatorships.[6]

This political instability was a reflection not only of the absence of a bourgeois revolution but also the failure of populism.[7] In many Latin American countries the industrialization process saw the rise to power of populist parties which drew widespread support from the labouring class and to a great extent furthered its interests. Peru had an important populist party in the APRA,[8] but it failed to gain the presidency until 1985. As a result, the labouring class was subject to intermittent repression and courtship by competing political contenders, many of whom were too weak or too sectarian to represent their interests effectively.

Up to the 1930s, labouring-class action was mainly contained within anarchist and anarcho-sindicalist organizations, and there were some spectacular gains in the 1912–19 period (Stein 1980, Blanchard 1982, Sulmont 1977). In the late 1920s two political parties were formed which would vie for labouring-class support: the Peruvian Communist Party[9] and the APRA. The PCP followed an orthodox Marxist line, focusing its attention mainly on miners and industrial workers. APRA was a 'broad front' party which promoted a cross-class alliance involving rural and urban workers, students, intellectuals, and some middle-class groups such as teachers and bank workers. Both parties were active in the labour movement, competing for the allegiance of union leaderships and sponsoring their own union federations and confederations. However, both parties suffered severe repression, especially between 1933 and 1940 and 1949 and 1954, which had a moderating effect on their strategy during the periods of relative freedom which followed.

From the 1930s, the APRA was a major contender in national politics, commanding a significant vote in national and municipal elections. Although it did not win the presidency, it had control over Congress in 1945–8, 1956–62 and 1963–8. It is said that the military coups of 1949, 1962 and 1968 were effected to prevent APRA coming to power, and many pro-labouring class reforms were introduced in order to undermine its support. APRA had a highly organized and centralized party apparatus, with an explicit populist ideology.[10] Throughout the 1950s and 1960s, it dominated the labour movement and the student movement, and it controlled the leadership of many clubs and associations in the shanty towns.[11]

However, during the 1960s it became progressively more reformist in ideology and more instrumental in its political alliances,[12] so the Communist Party gained strength, especially in the unions. A number of breakaway groups formed new parties on the left, with Trotskyist, Maoist or Castroite allegiances.[13] These parties were small but extremely active in promoting political action amongst rural and urban workers. The parties of the urban middle class, formed in the 1950s, also looked to the labouring class for support.[14] By the early 1970s there were four main union confederations, each linked to a particular political party.[15] In the shanty towns too, community organizations faced continual intervention from competing political groups with different ideologies and agendas (see Bayer 1969). Thus there was little scope for independent action for the labouring class either in the workplace or the community.

Because of the weakness of political institutions, most governments in power adopted varying degrees of repressive and corporatist control of the labouring class. Repression involved arrests and deportation of leaders, non-recognition of unions and community associations, bribery and proscription of political parties and unions. Vertical control was achieved by strong government intervention in the housing and labour markets and the establishment of government-sponsored organizations. Via the Ministry of Labour there were strict controls on the formation, internal organization and activities of unions, and a tendency for government intervention in the collective bargaining process (see Payne 1965). Labour legislation, social security and wage policy were used as measures to contain workers' demands, especially in military regimes which had proscribed union activity, e.g. Benavides (1933–9) and Odría (1948–56).

In the shanty towns, governments again combined repressive and cooptive measures, ranging from eviction and relocation to formal or informal authorization of occupancy, the granting of land titles, *remodelación* (street planning), the installation of public utilities, schools and clinics, and the formation of dwellers' associations (see Collier 1975, 1976a, Henry 1978). In some governments, particularly those of Odría (1949–56) and Velasco (1968–75), these practices were used explicitly to build support for the government and undermine the unions.[16]

At both workplace and community level, political organizations within the labouring class were small, fragmented and dispersed, and this fostered dependence on political party support which in turn encouraged confrontation with the state. Payne (1965) noted that strikes and union-led demonstrations were used as a means of political protest, rather than just focusing on employment issues. Action in the communities often involved violent confrontations with the state, not just in the process of invasion, but in later demonstrations and representations (Collier 1975, 1976a, Henry 1978, Skinner 1981). Political vulnerability fostered a tendency for tactical negotiation with specific political agencies (see Bayer 1969 and Skinner 1981 for case studies), which has been interpreted as clientelism and cooptation (e.g. Castells 1982). However, this was an instrumental rather than deferential clientelism and attributed little legitimacy to the political agents involved. As Dietz (1980) has pointed out, from the squatters' point of view it worked as a strategy for obtaining services. When it did not, there was a shift towards more radical action (Skinner 1981).

There was little evidence of class-based voting in the slums or shanty towns;[17] but neither was there widespread support for the establishment, as was claimed by some early writers (e.g. Patch 1967, Bourricaud 1970). In general, intervention in labouring-class organizations by political parties did not translate into votes. In the presidential elections of 1963, the shanty town vote was split between the three main political contenders: approximately two-fifths supported the party of 'modernization and growth' (Belaunde), a third, the 'populist oligarch' (Odría) and a quarter, APRA. In the municipal elections of 1963 and 1966, in which APRA joined forces with Odría's party, this coalition received 41–4 per cent of the shanty town vote, but Belaunde's party received the same.

Voting patterns amongst urban workers did not support any specific political alternative decisively, either conservative or radical. Rather their votes have been split between the different options, reflecting the national pattern of voting. This suggests that a range of different factors were affecting their electoral behaviour, not least a strong tactical approach to voting, specific benefits received from different political agencies, and national political and economic policies.[18] A recent study of differences in political attitudes amongst squatters also maintains that they were not related to socio-economic differences; radicalism was fundamentally associated with education and participation in unions and local associations (Stokes 1991), i.e. by the wider matrix of social and political institutions.

Ironically, although political party intervention was a source of partisan divisions between workers, it did facilitate lateral solidarity between different groups of workers and between workplace and community organizations. Plant and enterprise unions were affiliated to industrial or regional federations and these in turn to large confederations, which provided a broad base of support. For example, in 1973, there was a strike of about 5,000 workers in the Federation of Leather and Shoeworkers in support of three separate union conflicts: a wage demand of the Diamante workers (one of the two biggest shoe factories in Lima), a lockout in the smaller Red Rose factory, and a demand for better working conditions by the Bata–Rimac shop workers. This industrial federation thus provided political linkages between non-manual shop assistants and manual workers in small and large factories. General strikes called by regional federations and confederations commanded an even broader base of solidarity, including many informal sector workers. This solidarity was expressed in press statements, public mYetings, demonstrations, strikes and picketing.[19] Whether or not such displays of solidarity were effective, they were defining a common political interest that cut across labour market divisions.

There have been few studies of the links between unions and community associations, but scattered evidence indicates that they did exist. As already indicated, APRA was active in both spheres. The Peruvian office of the AIFLD[20] encouraged aprista unionists to take up leadership roles in the community so that they would be more familiar with community-level problems and be more influential there (Douglas 1972). Many invasion leaders were in fact union leaders. Henry (1978: 167–8) provides several instances when squatter communities supported union struggles. For example, in 1975 they demonstrated in support of a factory occupation in Hilado-Vitarte and against police repression during another strike in Naña. In 1976, a conflict with a supplier to a textile factory led to a road being blocked for eight hours by workers and community residents. In Villa El Salvador, Comas and El Planeta, residents supported a teachers' strike by running soup kitchens, picketing schools and participating in demonstrations (Skinner 1981: 169, Andreas 1985: 101–2). The workplace and the community could thus produce mobilization around similar interests and issues.

GENDER, CLASS AND POLITICAL ACTION

In general, political action by the labouring class during the 1970s was dominated by men. However, women were not politically passive; they participated in strikes, demonstrations, land invasions and communal protests. Women's actions were restricted to very specific spaces within the political arena, defined by their location in the labour market and their role in the family and community, but within these spaces there was scope for political protest. However, their action was generally in a supporting rather than a leadership role.

Ideologically, labouring-class women were caught between conflicting traditions originating from the bourgeois and peasant families. As we saw in chapter 4, women were passive participants in the formal decision-making structure of the peasant communities, but they were active in broadly based patterns of inter-household and communal participation. This translated into strong female support in crisis situations such as land invasions, 'marchas de sacrificio' and regional strikes (Andreas 1985). In the same way, women of the urban labouring class engaged in a range of formal and informal political activities, albeit in a subsidiary role to men.

However, government institutions and political parties which intervened in labouring-class organizations worked with bourgeois assumptions of female passivity and domesticity (cf. Chaney 1979). Women's participation within most political parties was ghettoized into women's sections or committees concerned with women's issues and access to central leadership positions was denied or discouraged (see the testimony of Magda Portal, one of the early aprista leaders, in Andradi and Portugal 1979). APRA itself placed great emphasis on the family as a political unit and established an enduring tradition of family activism which incorporated women. However, this was within a highly patriarchal conception of the family, in which women had second-class status.[21] Male unionists and community leaders who had served their political apprenticeship within APRA could hardly fail to be influenced by these notions.

As we saw in chapter 5, union membership in the formal sector was as high amongst women as amongst men. However, most union leaders were men; around 1978, only 7 per cent of them were women. Women who did become active in unions were usually directed towards 'female' activities such as taking minutes or organizing social functions (Andradi and Portugal 1979: 103–4, Guzman and Portocarrero 1985: 110). The scope for women's participation in unions was limited by the highly gender-segregated nature of the workplace; hence women were mainly active in those industries that were large employers of women, e.g. clothing and pharmaceuticals. In these industries, women had more chances of occupying leadership positions and were active in calling strikes, staging demonstrations and promoting factory occupations (see testimony of Vilma Mazuelos in Andradi and Portugal 1979: 105–17, also Andreas 1985: 127–33). However, they relied on support from wider federations that were dominated by men.

Women had an important role in the community because of their active participation in inter-household reciprocity networks, especially in the immediate aftermath of invasion e.g. getting water, guarding each other's houses, shopping, looking after neighbours' children etc. They were even involved in communal construction activities, such as building roadways, laying pipes, and installing cables (Blondet 1990: 29–32). Women were active supporters of community organizations and participated in marches and demonstrations to request services from the government (Blondet 1990: 31, Andreas 1985, my own case studies). During the 1980s, as a result of the acute economic crisis in the shanty towns, food aid programmes were channelled through women and many soup kitchens were set up and organized by them; there were over 7,000 in Lima in 1993.

As mentioned, political action in the shanty towns was heavily controlled by external agencies and these were generally oblivious to women's political role in the community. Women were targeted by external agencies, not as a source of political support, but as a vehicle for the distribution of charity aid and socialization into middle-class values. Religious, charity and welfare institutions, as well as political parties and government agencies, mobilized women through the formation of mothers' clubs. These were mainly concerned with homemaking activities, such as craft work, child welfare, cooking and nutrition, religious activities, charity gifts etc. Women could occupy leadership positions in these clubs, but usually in a clientelistic relationship with middle-class women (Blondet 1990: 34–8). Women's participation in these clubs was thus based on their domestic roles and was not intended to have political impact.

The main decision-making body in the communities was composed of 'padres de familia' who were assumed to be *male* household heads. These associations were important politically since they often controlled access to plots, lobbied the government for public services, collected money for community investments etc. Many of them were connected to political parties such as APRA which assumed that the leaders would be men and that women would merely provide logistical support. During the 1970s, the new structure of community representation set up by the Velasco government (SINAMOS) explicitly prohibited political activists from leadership positions, but it also restricted these positions to household heads and therefore excluded married women. External influences on political participation in the shanty towns therefore tended to confine women to very female-specific issues and to marginalize them from major decision-making processes. This tendency would change dramatically in the 1980s with an increased politicization of women's activities in the community and more autonomy from outside agencies (see Andreas 1985).

In both the workplace and the community then, women's political actions were generally subordinated to men's, and were confined to female-specific political spaces i.e. 'female' factories and 'mothers' clubs'. However, although women's action was either segregated from men's or was subsidiary to it, women did not view their actions as separate from men's; but rather, as complementary to them, forming part of a joint defence of the family, a common struggle for livelihood. Radcliffe (1988) has argued that even within their female-specific spheres, women saw themselves as part of a class struggle in alliance *with* men rather than part of a feminist struggle *against* men. In the early 1970s, feminism was barely present as a political movement,[22] but even after the burgeoning of feminist organizations in the 1980s, she maintains that they were sceptical about any alliance with middle-class feminists.

CONCLUSION

This chapter has examined the relationship between labour market divisions, class perceptions and political action. The analysis has shown that work was the core element in labouring-class identity; it was the basis for differentiation from other classes and the source of labouring-class morality. However, the definition of 'labourer' was extremely broad and paid relatively little attention to differences of employment status, type of enterprise or level of skill and income. The terms 'obrero' and 'trabajador' which were crucial to the identification of 'labouring class' were synonymous with economic insecurity, physical effort, bad treatment by employers and poverty. Although differences within these categories were recognized, they were not considered a basis for *class* divisions.

The stress on 'labouring work' as a common element amongst a group with varying labour market positions may have been a product of the diversity of work experience in individual work histories and in the household. Chapters 6 and 7 showed that many of those who were currently in wage labour had been self-employed and vice versa, and that most of those who had reached better positions in the manual labour market had done so by working their way up through much less desirable jobs. Chapter 8 revealed great occupational diversity in the labouring-class family.

While work was the core of labouring-class identity, it was strongly linked to consumption. Work was inseparable from physical and economic survival, from the struggle for housing, decent living standards, and long-run mobility. This link between consumption and production was mediated by the family, providing a common basis for class identity. Family and kinship also facilitated access to jobs and consumption goods, and was a basis for formal and informal collective action within the workplace and the community. Therefore the family was, in a sense, a class institution.

The linking of work with consumption may have radicalized class consciousness, for while few workers would have experienced direct exploitation by capitalist entrepreneurs because of the small size of the formal sector, many had observed the vast gap in wealth and standards of living between the rich and the poor. Many of those working in the services sector would have been able to experience these differences at close quarters. Moreover, the kinds of confrontation witnessed between squatters and bureaucrats in struggles over housing and urban services confirmed perceptions about the contradictory interests of the rich and the poor.

However, while class images, attitudes and sentiments involved a radical rejection of the class hierarchy, these attitudes were not translated into autonomous class action designed to change the situation. I have argued that this was the product of alienation from the political system, produced by years of repression and political party sectarianism, rather than because of a lack of class consciousness or cooptation into vertical patronage arrangements. Such arrangements did occur, but they were the product of a cynical instrumental approach to political demand-making.

The second question addressed in this chapter has been whether women's very different position in the labour market, compared with men's, produced a distinguishable class consciousness and whether their role in the family produced forms of action around gender rather than class interests. We saw that women's class perceptions differed very little from men's, they too stressed work as the major source of class identity, and they described it in the same terms as men. There is some evidence in their actual discourses that they identified with men's work situations as well as their own, which may have reflected the occupational diversity within the household and their dependence on male breadwinners. The fact that 'labouring work' was defined so generally meant that women's employment situation would not have been distinguished from men's, in any case.

Women were extremely active within the sphere of consumption, and these actions were primarily linked to their domestic roles. Undoubtedly, women's activities in this sphere were serving their 'practical gender interests' and were generally supportive of the gender division of labour rather than challenging it. However, some consumption activities involved cooperation between spouses and between members of the extended family, and it is difficult to say whether they represented the interests of women rather than the family. Moreover, since (a) consumption played such a central role in the definition of *class* identities, (b) it was structured in terms of complementarity and cooperation within the *family*, and (c) the family itself was perceived as a class institution, women's actions within the sphere of consumption can also be seen as a manifestation of *class* action. The fact that these mobilizations were mainly led by men further emphasizes the point that they were carried out in the name of family, and by extension, of community and class.

It would not be right to give an impression that the labouring class of Lima was simmering with frustrated revolutionary consciousness. Clearly few workers had a well-thought-out analysis of the roots of their poverty and oppression, and even if they had, there were still formidable obstacles to the formation of a class-based political party. However, the alternative picture of an apathetic, deferential, individualistic mass was just as wrong. The reality was somewhere between the two.

10 Conclusions

This book has examined the relationship between class and gender in the context of rapid industrialization in Peru. It has particularly focused on the nature of differentiation and mobility within the labouring class and its effects on class consciousness and political action. It has come up with a picture very different from that depicted by the literature of the time which stressed marginality, a weak and deferential class consciousness and ineffectual political action. It has shown that the growth process was not as exclusionary as was assumed, there was much less marginalization, a greater spread of income growth and more fluidity in class structure. To be sure, the benefits of growth were distributed unequally, but the poor were definitely a part of the process. Only a very small proportion of the urban labour force had stagnant real earnings during the period – probably less than 10 per cent of the squatter population according to Lewis (1973).

There was much less polarization between formal and informal sectors than conventionally assumed. The formal sector had generated a greater range of employment opportunities, especially for white collar employment; in fact the fastest growing occupations were in the middle class. There was little evidence of an 'uncontrolled' expansion of the informal sector; it was buoyant rather than depressed, with some earnings that were comparable with those in the formal sector. There was a great range of variation within the two sectors and some overlap between the two.

There was also high occupational mobility during this period. In fact, it was the fluidity of class structure, rather than its rigidity, that was remarkable. Between 1940 and 1972 the labour force had quadrupled in size, with extremely rapid growth in the absolute size of both the middle and labouring classes. This growth was fed by migration and occupational mobility. In 1974, 61 per cent of those currently in white collar jobs were of labouring-class or peasant extraction and 46 per cent of those in manual jobs were from peasant families. Nearly two-thirds of the total workforce were upwardly mobile between generations, and much of this mobility involved movement between two or more occupational classes. Within generations there was also some mobility, although it was more confined to movement within classes.

All social classes were affected by the process of economic growth, diversification and mobility. The economic interests of the propertied class – the oligarchy – became more diverse as its members moved away from land to industrial, commercial and financial concerns, and new recruits were absorbed. However, it retained a stable class core through kinship and inheritance, and thus maintained its dominance over the status order in Peru. The middle class had become more of a 'salariat' than a bourgeoisie in the classical Marxist sense, lacking the latter's economic power and independence, and reliant on the state and capital investments by the oligarchy or foreign capitalists. A large group were dependent on public sector employment, which had expanded greatly as a result of the Velasco government reforms: 41 per cent of all non-manual employees and 52 per cent of professionals and technicians worked for the state. Another important group were managers or administrators of private, often foreign-owned, firms. Only a small proportion were independent entrepreneurs. As a result of high mobility into the middle class, it had only a small class core and its class identity was fractured and unstable.

The boundary between the middle class and the labouring class was becoming increasingly blurred by overlapping earnings and upward mobility. Some of the middle class stressed the traditional status boundary between the two, aping the attitudes and customs of the oligarchy, especially their disdain for manual, non-'white' labour. Others were more loyal to their roots and advocated social justice and structural reforms. The economic dependency of this class and the high proportion of upwardly mobile recruits account for its inability to develop a stable bourgeois political party and the radicalism of many groups such as teachers and bank clerks. In the early 1970s left-wing movements were mainly supported by middle-class unions and students.

The labouring class was more affected by heterogeneity and mobility than any other class. It was scattered between a variety of different forms of production: 60 per cent were in small informal enterprises, 19 per cent worked in large formal ones, and the rest were in between. The majority were experiencing some form of wage dependence, but not all in capitalist enterprises. Wage work or quasi-wage work were to be found in informal as well as formal enterprises, and encompassed almost two-thirds of the total manual workforce. The remaining third were self-employed and a tiny fraction were unpaid family workers. If we exclude domestic servants and wage workers in the informal sector, we are left with 39 per cent who were formal sector wage workers. Nearly half of these were in large firms with wage levels and working conditions that might merit the description of a 'labour elite'. Only a fifth of the total manual workforce were in this latter group.

The work history data provide evidence of considerable movement between these categories. These data show that (a) the experience of wage work was more widespread than in the cross-sectional data, and (b) the stable proletarian and informal cores were smaller. The vast majority of the labouring class had had some experience of wage work, but this was a transitional state they moved in and out of. Only a very small proportion had had continuous employment in wage labour or in the formal sector, and the proletarian core of wage workers with exclusive experience of this type of employment was probably less than 10 per cent of the total manual workforce. By the same token, only a small proportion of this class had been confined to informal sector work (19 per cent), and the self-employed core was even smaller (7 per cent).

Chapter 5 showed that there were skill hierarchies with both formal and informal sectors, closely associated with earnings differences, which provided the basis for mobility within and between sectors. Nearly half of over 30-year-olds had reached the status of *maestro*, and less than a third were immobile or downwardly mobile in skill terms. Since mobility was correlated with earnings and was oriented towards self-employment, a majority of manual workers could look forward to higher incomes, higher skill and more autonomy towards the end of their working lives.

The overall picture in Lima was not one of mass marginalization within squalid shanty towns, nor one of a rigid division between privileged factory workers and an impoverished lumpenproletariat. Rather it was a fluid kaleidoscope of workers who moved between a variety of work situations in the course of their lives. Wage work was a common experience for many of them, especially as young apprentices and trainees, as factory workers and building labourers; but it was not an enduring experience, for it would probably be followed by self-employment. Nor was it the totalizing, monolithic experience that it was in communities dominated by mines and plantations. Some migrants had worked in such places prior to arrival in Lima, but for a great many, wage work was experienced in small or medium enterprises, often in the employment of kinsmen and countrymen.

However, this was a labouring class that understood very well the power of capital over workers and the vulnerability of propertylessness, and was well aware of the dominant ethos of disdain for all forms of manual employment, whether wage labour or self-employed. It was a class that aspired to a modern urban life style and used modern institutions, such as education and self-help organization in order to achieve it; but it was also a class with a strong petty entrepreneurial ethos, that struggled to liberate itself from dependence on employers by moving into self-employment. This was a heterogeneous class, but one that shared common experiences of migration and mobility and common struggles for housing and education. Thus while cross-sectional differentiation may have been a source of division, common mobility experiences and life styles were a source of solidarity.

GENDER DIVISIONS WITHIN THE MANUAL LABOUR MARKET

This book has shown that gender was a major source of segmentation within the working class, one that crosscut other axes such as skill and enterprise size. Indeed, much of the variation within the formal and informal sectors and within wage employment and self-employment was attributable to gender. Men and women were located in quite different parts of the manual labour market: men were in the more productive and high wage sectors, the more skilled jobs, the larger enterprises and the more lucrative forms of self-employment. Only a few women could expect to get well-paid factory jobs or to establish themselves as successful self-employed dressmakers. Most started off in the lowest paid job of all – domestic service – and on marriage became trapped into home-based self-employment or outwork which both yielded little income. Women's trajectories show a much smaller proletarian core and a larger informal one. Moreover, most women's experience of wage work was in 'quasi-wage' employment such as domestic service and outwork rather than in capitalist enterprises. Women were much less successful than men in charting an upwardly mobile career through wage labour into self-employment, few of them reached *maestra* status either in the factories or in self-employment and many more were confined to unskilled and poorly paid jobs over their entire lives.

The pattern of female employment had a depressive effect on the overall structure of employment. Excluding women (a third of manual workers) reveals a picture that corresponds more closely to a 'classical' form of proletarianization: greater concentration in the secondary sector, in medium and large enterprises, in capitalist wage work and in highly skilled, highly paid and unionized jobs. Mobility patterns show a larger proletarian core and less continuous dependence on informal sector work.

GENDER SEGREGATION AND THE FAMILY

Gender inequality in employment was related to the highly polarized pattern of occupational sex segregation: jobs were dominated by one sex or the other and this was true within both formal and informal sectors. Whereas 'male' occupations showed great diversity in terms of economic sector, enterprise size, skill level and employment status, 'female' ones were restricted in number and more confined to low-wage, low-skilled and undercapitalized jobs. This affected opportunities for career progression over the lifetime.

Conventionally, theories of gender segregation in employment have distinguished between demand and supply factors, largely stressing supply. There is a particular emphasis on women's role in the family, particularly their domestic constraints. However, we must remember that just over half of manual women were single – working as domestic servants or in 'female' factory jobs. Moreover, many women were excluded from types of informal sector work that would have been compatible with their domestic roles. The family was indeed important in explaining gender inequalities in employment, but its influence was not restricted to domestic constraints.

In my view, women's supply characteristics have been overemphasized in explaining their position in the labour market. In Lima, education had become a legitimate aspiration for labouring-class girls and the educational gap between manual men and women had been closing over the generations. Many women were relatively overqualified for some of the jobs they did, compared with men.

The labouring-class family did have a segregated division of labour between men and women, which made men responsible for breadwinning and women for childrearing and food provisioning; however, there was also an expectation that married women should contribute to household income if possible and extended kin networks could be mobilized to redistribute domestic tasks if necessary. The work histories showed that some women returned to work after a break for childrearing and remained in the workforce for a considerable period. There was also a minority who continued working throughout their lives, despite marrying and having children. These data suggest that the lack of opportunities for employment was at least as important as their educational qualifications or domestic constraints in explaining women's low labour force participation.

In reality, demand and supply are very intertwined and the family affects them both. It limits women's availability for work, their acquisition of skill, and their level of aspirations; but through its influence on gender ideology it also affects employers' expectations as to the kind of work that is appropriate for women, the way they are slotted into the division of labour at work, whether their jobs are defined as skilled etc. This may not amount to explicit discrimination; it is a more subtle mechanism that feeds into the process of occupational sex-typing and subsequently reinforces established patterns of supply and demand (cf. Scott 1986b).

In the formal sector, women were concentrated in labour-intensive, assembly functions or in work that was connected to the clothing industry. There was a preference for young unmarried girls, although many married women also worked there. Men did not work in these jobs, despite doing other types of assembly work and many of them working as tailors. Women's jobs were labelled unskilled or semi-skilled, despite the fact that they were deemed to have special aptitudes for it and many of them had higher than average qualifications. The sex-labelling of these jobs thus owed more to gender ideology than to domestic constraints.

The informal sector could offer a reasonable alternative to formal sector employment. However, despite the fact that such work was often carried out at home or in places where children could also be looked after, women were largely absent from this part of the informal sector. A major reason for this was that the crucial conditions for successful self-employment – access to apprenticeships, capital, clients and information – were obtained through a kinship system which discriminated against women.

While the family was not necessarily opposed to women working, it had very firm ideas about appropriate work for boys and girls, and men and women. Boys were sent at an early age to work as *ayudantes* or *aprendices* alongside a male adult, but girls were sent into domestic service or clothing sweatshops. The exclusion of girls from informal sector apprenticeships had far-reaching implications since it impeded their movement into the formal sector via a craft trade, their access to further training within the formal sector and the possibility of saving wages to finance movement into self-employment. Even when women did have the requisite training, however, the informal networks that provided access to loans, tools, markets and clients were all male and difficult for women to break into.

In summary, women's confinement to the disadvantaged parts of the manual labour market was associated with patterns of sex segregation within both informal and formal sectors. These patterns were influenced by gender divisions within the family not only because of women's supply characteristics, but through the incorporation of gender roles into the structure of work, and in the case of the informal sector, by gender segregation within the kinship system itself. Women's exclusion from the lucrative parts of the formal and informal sector had negative implications for pay and conditions in the few areas that were left to them. Faced with such a narrow range of alternatives, it is hardly surprising that the participation rates of married women were low.

What were the political implications of this segregation for women? Should men and women be treated as separate classes? If so, how do we deal with the fact that they were married to each other and that the family itself lay at the root of the gender division? How did women's gender interests, arising from their own position in the family and the labour market, relate to the class interests they shared with other male workers and the male members of their own households?

Women's weak position in the labour market meant that in most cases their contribution to household income was limited; they were massively dependent on male earnings. Children were more likely to supplement the male breadwinner than wives – but these were older teenagers, often up-wardly mobile ones. The popular image of women and young children eking out a living to keep the family from poverty only applied to a minority of families during the early 1970s. Labouring-class families were much keener to keep their children in school, hoping they would some day realize the dream of becoming doctors and lawyers.

The implications for women were clear. They were better off sustaining the common class interest of the family than pursuing sectional interests of gender. The structure of labour market opportunities was biased towards men, and there was enough growth in the economy to permit relatively good earnings and mobility opportunities for them. Women's efforts were there-fore geared to fighting for improved consumption levels, encouraging their children into upward mobility and maintaining the ideology of solidarity and reciprocity which would mean that they would be provided for. The labour market and the family thus interacted to produce a convergence of class and gender interests.

This conclusion is supported by the fact that men and women shared similar class identities. The common element to both was their dependence on low incomes and hard work, whatever the job. Women with little experi-ence of factory work, such as domestic servants, identified themselves as part of the *clase trabajadora* (labouring class), as did taxi drivers and street pedlars. This identity was common to workers in many different types of employment, women or men. Moreover, they all had a common (hostile) perception of the propertied class, whom they blamed for their own poverty and suffering. This raises a set of more general questions about the relation-ship between employment and class consciousness, and the need to modify the concept of class itself.

ECONOMIC AND SOCIAL CLASS

In chapter 1, I argued that the theoretical integration of class and gender required the concept of class to be broadened to include aspects of consump-tion and status. This broader concept should be distinguished from the narrower one based on production relations, using the term *social class* for the former and *economic class* for the latter. A useful elaboration of the distinction between economic and social class was made by Giddens (1973) in an attempt to theorize the linkages between class structure and political action. He argued that while classes were not actual social groups, they could not be treated as mere aggregates of individual positions, since this could not explain how consciousness and action were formed. Some process of group formation must emerge out of the common interactions and experiences that were generated by economic class and this provided the crucial mediating mechanism that fostered common consciousness and action.

An early version of the concept of 'structuration' was advanced to describe the process whereby economic positions generated 'clusters of social groupings'. Giddens mentions mobility and the labour process as two such mechanisms. However, he also suggests that distributional processes such as neighbourhood segregation may play a role.

> But without dropping the conception that classes are founded ultimately in the economic structure of the capitalist market, it is still possible to regard consumption patterns as a major influence upon class structuration.
>
> (Giddens 1973: 109)

For Giddens, social class refers to processes of social interaction and segregation created by both production and consumption, which convert economic positions into 'structured social forms'. This theory provides us with the possibility of linking individual positions in the sphere of production with more broadly based distributive and status groupings such as the family and community. This is crucial for women who are not in paid work, who have no class position within a productionist framework.

Giddens's definition of social class is vague and hinges more on a discussion of the different processes of structuration than on social class as an entity. He is not explicit about the basis for membership or the appropriate unit of analysis. However, a good summary definition would be that social classes are broad-based social collectivities defined by common location in the structures of production and distribution, power and status.

Giddens suggests that structuration is a variable process; therefore social classes will differ in their coherence, visibility and boundedness. This depends on the degree of segregation and closure created by production and distribution and whether class has merged with other social divisions such as ethnicity. Social classes may also be identified by the institutions, cultures and symbol systems that are typically associated with such groupings. This is particularly relevant in Peru where the distributive system (e.g. housing) had created more rigid boundaries than the labour market, where aspects of rural culture had been reproduced within labouring-class communities and where the majority were mestizos.

In the minds of manual workers in Lima, production and consumption were indissolubly linked. Work was a strategy for survival for all of them, not just for women. The struggle to feed and house a family was part and parcel of the struggle for livelihood. The concept of 'suffering' was central to their definition of class identity and this meant suffering at home (i.e. living in poverty) as much as at work. The family was the mediating institution between individual production roles and collective consumption. The search for a better job was as much for the benefit of the family as for the individual; providing for the family was an important part of labouring-class morality. In this respect the family was a class institution.

This argument does not imply that the family was a homogeneous unit, or that the organization of consumption within it was egalitarian. The division of labour within the family resulted in some inequality of consumption according to gender and seniority. However, we must remember that although the burden of domestic labour fell on women, men also had a role to play, not only in supplying the main source of income, but in contributing to consumption itself (e.g. building work, repairs etc.). Moreover, many consumption goods were communal (e.g. housing). In the squatter settlements, the pursuit of these communal consumption goods involved the mobilization of the whole family, and often involved extended kin as well.

It may be useful to think of the family as an alliance group, whose members have some common interests and some different ones, and amongst whom there are divisions as well as solidarities. This makes it possible to see how the family can be a source of common *class* identity for its members, women as well as men. Women's domestic roles are the basis of both a gender interest and a class interest. Women identified with their men not just because they were dependent on the male breadwinning wage, but because they had a vested interest in defending the consumption level of the family as a whole. This was reinforced by the strong ideology of family solidarity which coexisted with internal gender inequalities.

Labouring-class communities were largely networks of extended families, sharing a common struggle for livelihood. Even social mobility was defined as a collective goal. The search for better jobs and prospects was not seen as an individualistic attempt to cross into another class, but simply a desire to raise their standard of living ('procurar vivir mejor'). This was a family goal and a class goal. Thus family and community were both spheres where production and consumption were brought together, and where common experiences and aspirations were collectivized and reaffirmed. Thus despite considerable occupational diversity within the family and community, workers chose to stress their common dependence on manual labour and precarious living conditions rather than specific jobs or aspects of work.

There is a strong status element in this conception of labouring-class identity. According to Weber, status refers to the structure of prestige and honour in society and is an expression of social values rather than economic interests. It is principally manifested in style of life (including education and occupational prestige), social networks ('restrictions on social intercourse') and various symbols and rituals which act as status 'markers'. Status is also associated with social privileges and politico-legal entitlements such as citizenship, which are underpinned by power structures (Turner 1988). Status positions are ranked hierarchically, and relations between those in different positions in the hierarchy are characterized by deference and respect (towards superiors) and derogation (towards inferiors).

There is an ambiguity in Weber's theory about the precise relationship between status and class. He suggests that the two are analytically, if not empirically, distinct, but that they may merge under certain conditions. Many contemporary scholars suggest that the two should be seen in combination (e.g. Giddens 1973, Turner 1988: 12). Status is deeply embedded in work and power relationships, it is a prime motivation in occupational mobility, and contributes to class consciousness and action.

One factor that these manual workers had in common, even those working in the most isolated conditions, was low social status. This was a product not only of economic relations between classes, but of the way that these relations had been intertwined historically with cultural and ethnic differences, and reinforced by relatively brutal forms of political domination. The wounding experience of social derogation comes through in much of the consciousness data. It was the arrogant, patronizing, racist attitudes of the rich that provoked most hostility and resentment – and workers knew that their work, their life style, their culture and colour were all elements of their social class identity.

CONSCIOUSNESS AND POLITICAL ACTION

In the 1970s, the labouring class was involved in political action on two fronts: unions and neighbourhood movements. The Marxist class framework saw these as separate political arenas, with only unions constituting the proper place for class action. The development of a concept of *social class* makes it possible to interpret neighbourhood mobilizations as a form of class action, and women's participation in these actions can be seen as a reflection of class interests as well as gender interests. Scattered evidence of solidarity between unions and community organizations is a manifestation of the structural link between production and consumption and between social and economic class.

However, the fact remains that during the 1970s at least, political action within the labouring class was fragmented. At the time, commentators suggested that this was because of a poorly developed class consciousness due to economic heterogeneity and a tendency towards deference and clientelism. In chapter 9, I argued that the class attitudes and sentiments of the manual workers I interviewed exhibited a latent radicalism, because of the strong hostility towards the rich and the lack of legitimacy attributed to the existing social order. However, this radicalism was not expressed in enduring class-based political organizations and action. I argued that this lack of political participation was not because of differences of interest arising from economic divisions amongst manual workers, although fragmentation and dispersal would have made organization difficult. Rather it was because of a long history of repression and intervention by external agents in labouring-class action.

CONJUNCTURAL SPECIFICITIES

The situation described in this book was a product of several specific conjunctural factors: first, the extent of growth in the economy generally. This was an uneven pattern of growth and it was concentrated in the city and the formal sector, but it spread to the urban informal sector and to the countryside. Second, there was a highly interventionist state at the time, which created substantial public sector employment and thus fuelled the process of upward mobility into the middle class and the demand for many informal sector services. Third, many urban workers were first-generation migrants who had maintained their links with the countryside and continued to support kinship networks and principles of reciprocity which enabled them to integrate rapidly into the urban economy. The fact that such networks were able to deliver material resources may also have been a reason for their strength and vitality.

Finally, the size of the 'urban labour surplus' may have been limited by growth in the peasant economy and a highly selective migration process. Kinship played a major role here: as we saw in chapter 4, kinship networks heavily influenced the process of migration to Lima, recruitment into the labour market and access to housing. They spread information out from Lima about the scope for opportunities there, and often recruited labour directly. Many migrants did not move to Lima until they had a job fixed up. Thus the migration process was finely tuned to levels of employment in the city. On the other hand, the kinship system was also the vehicle for a return flow of remittances from the city to the countryside, which further stimulated the process of growth there.

As a result of the complex interrelationships between the family and economy in Peru, class and gender were highly intertwined. This was the case in all social classes, not just the labouring class. In the latter case, kinship was a crucial mechanism for economic survival in the face of poverty. Yet it was also the source of profound gender inequalities. On the other hand, gender implied solidarity as well as inequality. Therefore women's subordination within the labouring class was subsumed under the broader class interests of the family both materially and ideologically.

Appendix
Data sources

This book uses three main data sources: national population censuses, employment surveys, and my own case studies. Reliable censuses had taken place in 1940, 1961 and 1972. The Ministry of Labour had been doing regular employment surveys since 1967, based on a sample frame of about 3,000 households drawn from all social classes. The analysis in this book is based on two surveys that had taken place in 1973 and 1974. These data sets consisted of individual cases aged 14 years and over, economically active and inactive. From the 1974 survey I was able to create a household data set by reaggregating the individual cases into their original households. From the total sample interviewed in the 1973 survey, the manual population was extracted for detailed analysis. This then served as a proxy universe for the selection of 192 case studies for re-interview in 1974. The following figure shows the relationship between these different sources of data.

NATIONAL CENSUSES (1940, 1961, 1972)

EMPLOYMENT SURVEYS

1973 survey
7,425 active/inactive individuals
3,588 employed individuals
2,377 employed manuals ————————▶ CASE STUDIES
192 manual workers

1974 survey
7,342 active/inactive individuals
3,642 employed individuals ————————▶ HOUSEHOLD DATA SET
2,298 households

Figure A1 Levels of analysis and data sources

NATIONAL POPULATION CENSUSES

National population censuses provide the sole basis for longitudinal analysis of employment in Peru since labour force surveys were only introduced in the mid-1960s. However, considerable problems were involved in making inter-censal comparisons because of changes in definitions and levels of aggregation of the data. Fortunately, the censuses had become progressively more disaggregated over the years which made it possible to reconstruct the data for better comparability (the worksheets are published in Scott 1988). The most important changes concerned the definition of economic activity (which changed in 1961) and the classification of the labour force by economic sector (which changed in 1972). Minor alterations also occurred with respect to employment status (1961) and occupational groups (1981). In all cases, the data could be adjusted to overcome these problems and the figures presented in the book are thus unaffected by definitional changes.

MINISTRY OF LABOUR EMPLOYMENT SURVEYS

The Ministry of Labour employment surveys were established under the guidance of Michigan State University in 1965. The first surveys took place in 1967, 1969 and 1970, and were repeated annually or even six-monthly during the early 1970s. Most of them were carried out in urban areas only, particularly in Lima and seven other major cities. During my fieldwork period in Peru there were four surveys: August/September 1972; March/April 1973 (NE); August/September 1973 (NF) and March/April 1974 (NG). I used data from the NE and NG surveys.

The Ministry surveys were based on a multi-stage stratified area sample, originally constructed in 1965 and updated and improved in 1971–2 on the basis of the pre-census register of households. The sample frame consisted of Primary Sample Units (based on regional administrative units, of which Lima was one), and Secondary Sample Units containing around 100 households. In Lima, at the time of the March 1973 survey, there were approximately 6,000 SSUs, stratified according to the type of housing and socio-economic level of the inhabitants. From these a random sample of 376 SSUs was drawn to serve as the frame for the selection of a sample of households. In each SSU approximately nine households were selected giving a total of around 2,500 households and a probability of selection of one per 225 houses. Within each selected household, every individual of 14 years and over was interviewed.

The March 1973 survey covered 2,376 households with a sample population of 7,425 persons of 14 years and over and an employed labour force of 3,588. The response rate was 94.8 per cent for households and 94.0 per cent for individuals (Ministry of Labour 1974: x–xvii). The March 1974 survey had a total of 7,342 cases aged 14 or over, 3,642 of whom were in employment and 3,700 were inactive or unemployed.

The 1973 survey was used to select the manual population for detailed quantitative analysis. This was done on the basis of the job descriptions in the Directory of Occupations (SERH 1966), at the three-digit level of classification. The criterion was that the work should involve a major amount of manual physical labour. In most cases this was unambiguous; however, there was a problem with sales workers. I wished to include street vendors, market traders and family workers in small front-room shops in the shanty towns, but not those working in department stores, on the grounds that only the former had comparable working conditions and labour market situation to manual workers. Where the occupational code could not distinguish these two situations, the minimum wage was used as an additional filter to screen out the latter group. This filter was not altogether successful and a small number of salaried women in small stores remain an ambiguous category in these data.

THE CASE STUDIES

The possibility of re-interviewing a subset of informants from the March 1973 employment survey provided an excellent opportunity to combine qualitative and quantitative research methods. It offered the means to select the case studies on a representative basis and to cross-check data between the two sources. However, this method required that the case studies should be heads of household and/or spouses in order to permit easy identification of the original informants.

For theoretical reasons, the case studies were stratified by economic sector, employment status and sex. However, the manual sample population was unevenly distributed between these categories which, given the upper limit of 200 cases for selection, would have given too few cases in some of the more interesting cells. Therefore I decided to select an equal number of cases for interview in each of the cells, and use the original sample cell size expressed as a fraction of 192 as a weight for more general quantitative analysis.

The subfile of manual workers selected from the original 1973 sample consisted of 2,377 individuals and 1,241 heads of household or spouses. The latter group were distributed according to the three stratification criteria as shown in table A1.

Allowing a generous margin within each cell for wastage, 344 addresses were selected by systematic random procedures. There were difficulties in tracing 21 per cent of the cases and there was a further rejection by 8 per cent.

Table A1   Distribution of the proxy universe for case study selection, Ministry of Labour employment survey, March 1973

	Men		Women		Total
	Wage labour	Self-employed	Wage labour	Self-employed	
Manufacturing	119	79	51	31	280
Construction	27	32	1	—	60
Transport	35	56	—	—	91
Commerce	31	146	30	161	368
Services	57	48	263	74	442
Total	269	361	345	266	1,241

Within each cell, the target quota was twelve, producing the distribution shown in table A2.

There were some differences between the Ministry of Labour sample and the case study data set because the case studies were heads of household or spouses. The case studies overrepresented older age groups and underrepresented formal sector workers. Whereas 44 per cent of men in the Ministry sample were under 30 years, only 26 per cent of the case study men were; and 30 per cent of the men in the first group were over 40, whereas 47 per cent of the latter group were. The differences were less marked for women because domestic servants were classified as head of their own household: 56 per cent of women in the Ministry sample were under 30 compared with

Table A2   Distribution of case studies interviewed by criteria for selection, February–July 1974

	Men		Women		Total
	Wage labour	Self-employed	Wage labour	Self-employed	
Manufacturing	12	12	12	12	48
Construction	12	12	—	—	24
Transport	12	12	—	—	24
Commerce	12	12	12	12	48
Services	12	12	12	12	48
Total	60	60	36	36	192

48 per cent of the case studies, but the case studies had more in the 30–39 group – 33 per cent compared with 22 per cent. In the Ministry sample, formal sector jobs were 17 per cent of the total, whereas in the case studies they were only 11 per cent.

PROBLEMS IN THE DEFINITION OF EMPLOYMENT DATA

An analysis of differentiation and mobility in the labour market requires careful definitions of 'work', 'employment', 'job' and 'earnings'. In a country where a considerable amount of economic activity is conducted within the household, where labour services are often unpaid and hired labour may involve some payment in kind (e.g. food and lodgings), there is considerable ambiguity in the definition of these terms. This is particularly the case for women, whose activities in the home may contribute significantly to the output and earnings of others (e.g. husbands), even though they are unremunerated and not considered by official survey organizations – or even by the women themselves – to be 'working'.

Defining 'jobs'

In Lima there were three categories of work: *ayuda*, *cachuelo* and *trabajo*. *Ayuda* referred to the general notion of 'helping out', but it was also one of the categories of unpaid reciprocal labour used in the countryside and found frequently in the city. It included domestic activities within the nuclear household, child labour inside and outside the household and some services exchanged between extended kinsmen. These activities were defined by custom rather than contract and monetary remuneration was not normally involved.

Cachuelos are best translated as 'odd jobs' or 'sidelines'. Unlike 'ayuda' they were remunerated activities and did not usually involve reciprocal favours. They were occasional in nature and seen as supplementary to the main job, implying that they took up little time or yielded little income, or both. Typical *cachuelos* included weekend work, occasional services performed for friends or clients, extra work derived from the main job etc. Such activities were considered *cachuelos* whether or not the individual had a main job.

Trabajo was the word used to refer to a 'proper job' or a 'main job'. It almost always involved payment in cash and a formal or informal contract. Workers would talk of having a job in a contractual sense ('tengo un trabajo'), but they also used the term to refer to paid work in general, as in 'looking for work' ('buscando trabajo'). The distinctions between these categories of work can be illustrated thus: 'Esto no es trabajo, señorita, es un cachuelo nomás' (This isn't a job, miss, it's just a sideline), 'No tenía trabajo todavía, sino ayudaba a mi padre en su taller' (I didn't have a job yet, I was just helping my father in his workshop).

In both the censuses and the surveys, 'employment' included the category of 'unpaid family workers', provided that they worked a minimum of fifteen hours a week or a third of a normal working day. This had the merit of recognizing some of women's unpaid work within family enterprises, although the hours cut-off may have excluded the more casual activities. However, in the employment surveys this cut-off was only applied at the coding stage, and not always then, so a higher level of casual work was included. The Ministry of Labour enquired about 'other work' additional to the main job, but did not use the local argot term, *cachuelo*. According to their data, only 5 per cent of the workforce had second jobs. In my case studies, odd jobs were asked about using the local term. This produced a higher proportion – 27 per cent – although it was lower than expected.

Most Peruvian agencies involved in the collection of labour force data were aware of the difficulties in defining economic activity. The Ministry of Labour data was generally of higher quality than the censuses because they had a specialized field staff and more sophisticated survey instruments. The employment surveys reported a slightly higher level of economic activity than the census (about 5 per cent higher), particularly amongst the self-employed, women and the middle aged. This suggests that they were picking up more married women working at home than the census, although it is still possible that there was some underestimation of casual activities.

Earnings data

There are great difficulties in obtaining precise data on earnings in a country like Peru, because of the large amount of informal sector employment. Webb (1976) evaluated a number of different Peruvian sources of income data and concluded that the Ministry of Labour surveys underestimated income levels compared with family budget surveys, inflating the number of poor households. He suggests that the main reason for the discrepancy was that the Ministry of Labour survey used the previous week as the period of reference and had no control questions on expenditure. Other surveys were based on the whole range of the family budget and over a whole year. Another reason may be that the Ministry of Labour considered domestic servants separately from the households where they worked and lived, as head of their own household. Their large number and very low wages would have significantly depressed household incomes at the lower end of the distribution.

Assessing the incomes of the self-employed is notoriously difficult because of the instability of their earnings, the lack of formal budgeting and the fact that accounts are not separated from family housekeeping. There is no way of knowing whether self-declared earnings were higher or lower than the declared levels amongst this group. The Ministry of Labour had no data on overtime, although it did ask about 'normal' hours. According to the case studies only 3 per cent did overtime, but this is probably an underestimate. About a fifth of the sample was paid in kind as well as cash (e.g. food and lodgings, as in the case of maids), although very few (2.5 per cent) were paid in kind only.

There is probably some margin of error in the estimation of manual earnings reported in this book. However, a comparison of the earnings data in different surveys suggests that this margin was small and non-random, for there were remarkable consistencies between different data sets.

WORK HISTORY DATA

The most obvious problem with retrospective data is that of memory recall – how accurately do people remember their life and work histories, do they forget short-term or undesirable events, can they date them precisely? The life history technique used in these case studies was pioneered in Texas (see Balan *et al.* 1969, 1973) and developed in the Peruvian context by Long and Roberts (1984) and Laite (1981). This technique maximizes memory recall in two ways: first, it takes the informant through his/her occupational history chronologically from the beginning, covering every job up to the present, and second, it asks about a range of other biographical data occurring throughout the individual's lifetime, which act as prompts for the completion of the work history. The one drawback is that the technique relies on collecting information year by year, so changes within one year are not easily recorded.

I had two means of cross-checking these data: first, with the work history data in the Ministry of Labour sample – there were only two cases of inconsistency between the two data sets. Second, a month by month record of job changes that had occurred during the previous year indicated that while there was some variation in *volume* of activity over the year, i.e. number of hours worked and *cachuelos* undertaken, there were very few short run changes in main jobs during the year.

Jobs and job changes in the work history data

A data set was created comprising all jobs in the case study work histories (999). A similar data set was constructed from the Ministry of Labour survey, which included up to four jobs in the last decade, and the first job. However, these two data sets are not comparable. First, the case studies contained complete work histories starting at different times in the past, while the

Ministry histories were confined to the last ten years. Second, completed jobs were a much larger proportion of the total in the case studies (81 per cent) whereas in the Ministry data they were only half. This produced a significant age bias, with a larger proportion of jobs being done by young people amongst the case studies: teenage jobs were 29 per cent of the total here whereas in the other data set they were only 15 per cent. On the other hand, jobs held by the over-40s were only 17 per cent compared with 28 per cent in the Ministry sample. These differences affected the figures on job duration, since they were highly correlated with age.

Ideally, current jobs should be excluded from duration analysis because they are incomplete, but this produces other biases by underrepresenting certain groups of people and types of jobs. It excludes first-time job-holders who tend to be young and casual workers and it leaves out many workers in the older age groups who have been a long time in their jobs. Thus it underrepresents the young and the old and jobs of very short and very long duration. After an analysis of the costs and benefits of omitting non-termi-nated jobs from both data sets, I considered it preferable to include them in the analysis prepared for chapter 6. This was less of a problem in the case study data because fewer informants were in their first jobs (19 per cent).

Notes

2 Class, gender and the informal sector

1 In most Latin American countries there was a literacy requirement for suffrage, which ruled out a large proportion of the rural population. In the cities the exclusion was less – about 10 per cent in Lima in 1972.

2 In neo-classical economics, a labour surplus can be said to exist when it is possible to draw labour away from one sector of the economy with no loss of output. The marginal product of labour in this sector is assumed to be zero. In Marxist theory, a labour surplus is the excess of labour over that required by existing technology and capital stock to produce currently demanded levels of goods and services.

3 The famous ILO report on employment and incomes in Kenya (ILO 1972) was the first to put forward a policy of labour-intensive growth based on support for the informal sector.

4 Hart was one of the few who included illegal activities in the definition of informal employment (Hart 1973). Most other studies refer to registered activities, which happen to be small in scale. This usage differs again from that used in countries like Britain which include non-marketed goods and services (e.g. DIY) and tax evasion.

5 For critiques of the informal sector see Breman 1976, Bromley 1978, Moser 1978, Bromley and Gerry 1979, Nelson 1979, Mazumdar 1981, Kannappan 1985, Connolly 1985.

6 Custom markets exist where the producer has a regular clientele who patronize him or her, regardless of lower prices elsewhere. They may do this because of high quality goods or services, easier credit, or personal loyalty.

7 This position has been particularly associated with the work of PREALC. For a review see Tueros 1985.

8 Portes and Walton (1981) went so far as to say that the system of accumulation in the Third World *depended* on the role of petty commodity producers which, as Schmitz (1982) pointed out, is a bit like the tail wagging the dog.

9 For a comprehensive review of the marginality debate, see Kay (1989: 100–24).

10 Populism was a cross-class movement that relied heavily on support from the urban labouring classes. See chapter 9.

11 Recently, such issues have been taken up by Eckstein (1989).

3 Growth, inequality and mobility

1 'Non-manual' includes professionals, managers, technicians and office workers and is used synonymously with 'white collar' or 'middle-class' employment. All other urban occupations are 'manual' and are referred to as 'working-class' occupations. See Appendix for further details.

Official Peruvian statistics did not have a good classification of occupations in the 1970s and it did not permit an easy identification of manual/non-manual work. Half the occupational groups were based on skill distinctions and half on economic sectors. Thus sales and service occupations had a mix of manual and non-manual workers in them. A new classification was produced by myself and a research group at the Ministry of Labour which has a consistent ranking of skill, income and education. For details of the classification see Suárez 1975. This classification is used for all analysis of Ministry of Labour data in this book.

2 In Peru, the census definition of 'urban' includes district capitals regardless of size, some of which are under 2,000. In 1972, a World Bank mission calculated an urbanization statistic based on the 2,000 limit alone which gave a figure of 53 per cent urban. Of these 44 per cent were living in Lima (World Bank 1979b: 83).

3 Peru's exports included a variety of mineral ores, guano (fertilizer), rubber, sugar, cotton, coffee, wool, fishmeal and oil.

4 When industrial promotion laws were passed in 1940 and 1959, they were vague and diffuse; the degree of protection was very low and did nothing to harm the interests of the exporters. On the contrary it encouraged them to diversify into manufacturing (GIECO 1972).

5 Export-processing included pulp, paper and chemicals from cane, metal products from mineral ores and oil derivatives. Export-processing contributed about a quarter of industrial output during the 1960s (Thorp and Bertram 1978: 262)

6 By 1972 imported consumer durables had fallen to 3 per cent of imports. About half of industrial output was capital and intermediate goods (Thorp and Bertram 1978: 270). In 1968, around 77 per cent of output in intermediate goods and engineering and half of consumer goods output was controlled by foreign and mixed companies (Thorp and Bertram 1978, citing Espinozo and Osorio 1972).

7 The highest rates were between 1960 and 1966 when they reached 11.6 per annum.

8 By 1972, public expenditure represented 12 per cent of GDP.

9 In 1974, Lima accounted for 71 per cent of all industrial establishments, 73 per cent of the industrial labour force and 73 per cent of industrial output (Economic Census 1963 and Manufacturing Census 1974). The supply of local investment capital and commercial bank credit was concentrated there (World Bank 1979b: 101). Most government services, such as health, education and the armed forces, were located in Lima.

10 In 1972, the next largest cities after Lima were (rounded figures): Arequipa 305,000, Trujillo 254,000, Chiclayo 190,000, Chimbote 160,000, Huancayo and Piura 127,000, Cuzco 121,000 (World Bank 1979b: 83).

11 In Peruvian official statistics, the port of Callao, which is now surrounded by the city, has a separate constitutional status and is excluded from the figures for Lima. In this book, the statistics for Lima are based on an amalgamation of the figures for the Province of Lima and the Constitutional Province of Callao. For further details see Scott (1988).

12 Population of 6+ years in work or actively seeking work in Lima.

13 In 1963, 91 per cent of all personal service establishments had less than five persons per establishment.

14 Enterprises with five to nineteen workers accounted for only 7 per cent of total remunerations, 5 per cent of gross output and 5 per cent of value added, while those with over a hundred workers accounted for 71 per cent of sales, 72 per cent of output and 74 per cent of value added. (Manufacturing Census 1974).

15 These data are based on the national censuses, reclassified for comparability. The procedures that were used to permit intercensal comparisons are given in Scott (1988).

16 Census data do not permit the identification of wage earners in enterprises with less than five employees and are thus excluded. They were 28 per cent of the informal sector on my definition. See discussion pp. 46–7.

17 Formal employment is defined here as all wage and salaried employment. It would include a small production of wage earners working in small establishments who would normally form part of the informal sector. In 1974 they were 13 per cent of all wage earners.

18 Since the occupational data in the 1940 census could not be compatibilized with later classifications, the analysis of changes in occupational structure has to be restricted to the 1961–72 period.

19 See Appendix for a discussion of possible underestimation of family labour.

20 The 1974 manufacturing census shows that average labour productivity in the largest group (500+ workers) was 242 per cent above that of the smallest (five to nine workers) and the average wage was 166 per cent greater (Manufacturing Census 1974). The industrial statistics for the same year give similar differentials.

21 According to the 1973 industrial statistics (unpublished) average labour productivity for industry as a whole was 297 soles. Leaving aside the petroleum and iron and steel industries which had productivity rates of over 1,000, six industrial branches had levels of near or over 400 – industrial chemicals, beverages, rubber, electrical machinery, consumer chemicals and non-ferrous metals. On the other hand, glass, shoes, leather products, wood, wooden furniture and clothing were all under 200. In these industries even the largest firms had low rates and thus a low differential between them and the smallest establishments.

22 Including ineligibles, the proportion of the total labour force unionized in Lima in 1973 was only 21 per cent. The proportion in the manual labour force was similar (Ministry of Labour 1974: 52).

23 There was legislation covering minimum wages, employer–employee contributions to social security, paid holidays, separation payments, pensions etc. There was specific provision for women covering maternity leave, equal pay, limits on the length of the working day and week, and other controls over working conditions. Much of this legislation dated from 1918 and was specific to certain industries or occupations (Mesa-Lago 1978). In 1972 labour stability laws were introduced which made it difficult to fire workers who had been employed for more than three months. In 1974 this was repealed in the case of export manufacturers.

24 Many of the self-employed made voluntary contributions to the social security system. In 1970 new legislation extended social security to domestic servants. However, there was widespread evasion.

25 This was gleaned from case studies and newspaper cuttings; see also De Soto (1986).

26 From case study data; see chapter 5.

27 Only 19 per cent of total informal sector employment was in manufacturing.

28 Of total informal sector employment, 68 per cent was in commerce and services.

29 According to the CISEPA/SERH study, only 23 per cent of the small establishments surveyed said that their products were destined for the immediate neighbourhood and almost half of these were bakers. The rest sold their products all over Lima (Vega-Centeno 1973).

30 The CISEPA/SERH study reported that 41 per cent had a regular clientele on whom they could depend for custom. According to Reichmuth, 25 per cent of informal clothing enterprises were charging more than their formal sector competitors (Reichmuth 1978: 125, 168–9).

31 See Scott (1988) for a review of the debate over Peruvian census definitions of female labour force participation.

32 Ministry of Labour survey data for 1974 give women a higher proportion of employment – 32 per cent.

33 These occupations were: teachers (three categories), obstetricians, nurses, dieticians, social workers, secretaries, dressmakers, hairdressers, domestic servants, washerwomen, cooks, lodging-housekeepers, and chambermaids. They provided employment for almost two-thirds of women and all of them were over 50 per cent 'female'.

34 A 'female' occupation is defined here as one with a simple majority of women; this meant considerable overrepresentation of women since even at the lower limit (50 per cent), it was much above their overall share of employment (32 per cent).

35 Further disaggregation of this group would place secretaries in an inferior position with respect to male clerks thereby confirming the diagonal polarization for this class too.

36 Unfortunately, there are no longitudinal studies of income trends which differentiate between male and female earners. However, Webb's data is suggestive. Since all urban incomes were rising in real terms during the period of growth (even that of domestic servants, who are specifically mentioned), we can assume that the incomes of most women workers rose.

37 From 1900 school enrolments rose three times as fast as population, reflecting one of the world's highest rates of educational expansion this century. By 1963, Peru was devoting a larger share of GNP to education than any other country in Latin America bar Cuba and Puerto Rico (Hunt 1971: 394). It ranked sixth out of nineteen Latin American countries in the coverage of the school age population by the educational system – despite its low per capita income and high population growth rates (Gall 1974).

38 The proportion in different occupational groups who wished a professional job for their son was as follows: professionals 73 per cent, technicians 71 per cent, office workers 67 per cent, skilled and semi-skilled workers 64 per cent, sales workers 69 per cent, service workers 58 per cent, unskilled workers 53 per cent (Lima 1974 data).

39 The educational level of employed women differed from that of the female population as a whole because of the varying pattern of female labour force participation. The proportion with secondary levels of education was smaller, that with further education was larger. Illiteracy was lower because it predominated in older age groups who had ceased to work.

40 Of the whole sample, 64 per cent would like a professional job for their son, but only 37 per cent wanted one for their daughter; 15 per cent would like a technician's job for their son compared with 36 per cent who would like one for

their daughter; and 7 per cent wanted an office job for their son compared with 16 per cent who wanted one for their daughter (Ministry of Labour 1974 data).

41 In this section I shall use the term *class* mobility to refer to movement between the broad non-manual, manual and peasant classes, and *occupational* mobility to refer to the one-digit occupational groups. (In many studies the latter are referred to as classes.)

42 Most mobility in advanced industrial societies is short distance, i.e. between adjacent occupational groups (Heath 1981).

43 This was because of the demographic structure of the workforce which was weighted towards younger groups.

44 Sales work is located beneath skilled and semi-skilled work here because the average level of earnings and education for the group as a whole was below the other group. However, it is likely that male shopkeepers who had been able to purchase large amounts of stock and equipment with their indemnity payments would have been at the top of the distribution, significantly above the mean. In this sense, it may be misleading to portray it as downward mobility (see chapter 7, pp. 157–61).

45 However, these constraints may have varied over the generations amongst women and many of the older women may not have worked at all.

46 Women actually had a *higher* proportion of cross-class mobility than men (90 per cent compared with 80 per cent), but more of it consisted of movement out of the peasantry into unskilled and service work.

47 The term 'class core' refers to those offspring who are in the same occupational groups now as their fathers were.

48 See the large literature on regional associations in Lima (Doughty 1970, Long 1973, Jongkind 1974, Skeldon 1977b, Altamirano 1984).

49 The fact that each improvement in amenities in the shanty towns had to be won by self-help and collective action, often involving confrontation with the state, helped to promote a common sense of solidarity.

50 Hence the emphasis on these issues by radical and populist political parties, including Velasco, who mounted an entire bureaucracy devoted to the issue of participation (SINAMOS).

4 Family, gender and the labouring class

1 For a comprehensive survey of the literature on women and the family in Latin America see Lavrin (1987); for an example of anthropological kinship studies see Bolton and Mayer 1977; for a review of the literature on household strategies see Schmink 1984; systematic analyses of *machismo* are rarer but see Youssef (1974), Pescatello (1973), Nash and Safa (1980), and various Peruvian writings, for example Barrig (1979).

2 This issue has recently been taken up, for example, by Harvey and Gow (1994).

3 These assumptions and claims were made in the feminist writings of the 1970s and were subsequently heavily criticized (e.g. Barrett 1980).

4 Alternative terms include the 'sex-gender system' (Rubin 1975) or 'gender subordination'. The first of these does not indicate any inequality between men and women and the second is too vague about its source.

5 The Spanish Crown was concerned at the amount of profligacy and illegitimacy in the colonies. Marriage was thought to introduce social order, and it was made a condition of access to *encomiendas* (see Schurz 1964: 284, Burkett 1978: 115,

Lockhart 1968: 152–5). *Encomiendas* were grants of rights to the labour (but not the land) of groups of Indians, made by the Crown to conquistadores or settlers. They were the main source of wealth in early colonial times.

6 By 1563, 468 out of 500 *encomenderos* were married, and most of them had Spanish wives. These women played a crucial role in the consolidation of the Spanish culture amongst the dominant classes and in urban colonial society generally. For observations on the association between marriage, class and race see Lockhart (1968: 157, 210), Burkett (1978: 116, 1977: 20, 24).

7 Ever since *encomenderos* were given rights over Indian labour, women's labour was drafted in for domestic service, and this often involved sexual services (Burkett 1978: 109–12). Immediately after colonization, Catholic missions were established in many Indian communities and on the *haciendas*. Apparently priests were amongst the most licentious of the Spanish colonials (Schurz 1964: 262–4, Youssef 1974: 91).

8 Many middle-class youths would initiate their sexual lives with the domestic servants in the household (Arnold 1978, Sindicato de Trabajadores del Hogar 1982). Peasant women were often abused by *hacendados* as were schoolgirls in rural areas by school teachers (Babb 1985).

9 There was an increasing immigration of a new class of European entrepreneurs (see Wilson 1984, 1986), and European governesses were being imported for elite girls (Barrig 1979: 43–4).

10 This ideology was espoused with particular fervour by the small-town petit bourgeoisie who were striving to establish a boundary between themselves and the surrounding (Indian) peasants and urban workers (Wilson 1985).

11 Women's inheritances were more likely to consist of houses, jewellery or cash, rather than productive capital or land. If they did inherit land, they were likely to be bought out by their brothers (Wilson 1984).

12 In Peru, the Catholic Church retained a powerful influence on political, educational and welfare institutions, in contrast with other Latin American countries (e.g. Argentina, Mexico) where it lost influence after the Independence period (Schurz 1964).

13 Barrig cites writings by Catholic priests in the 1960s: 'A woman wants to be able to admire the financial ambitions of her husband ... it is part of the support and security she needs as a woman. A woman who has to help her husband economically feels her femininity to be cheated' (Barrig 1979: 27).

14 According to Chaney (1973: 134), only a third of women of voting age were registered as voters in the mid-1960s in Peru.

15 The husband was the legal representative and decision-maker of the *sociedad conjugal*, responsible for its domiciliary and economic well-being. Wives had 'the right and obligation to attend personally to the home'(article 162) and required their husbands' permission to work outside the home (article 173). They retained rights over their personal property (dowry and inheritance), but the joint property of the family, which included women's earnings from work, was controlled by the husband. The mother and father had joint responsibility for their children (*patria potestad*), but where there was disagreement between them, the father's will prevailed. The recognition of illegitimate children by their father resulted in a loss of maternal rights for the mother. Longstanding consensual unions were considered de facto *sociedad conjugal*, and the women were not entitled to any of its property (Roca and Rodriguez 1978).

16 There was great diversity in rural social structures in Peru, especially with regard

to kinship institutions (Bolton and Mayer 1977). It is something of a travesty to reduce this diversity to a single pattern. I shall concentrate on those features that were common in the southern *sierra*, which was an area of relatively dense peasant settlement and one that had best preserved its traditional institutions.

17 There is an extensive literature on forms of reciprocity amongst the Andean peasantry, see Mayer 1974,1977, Alberti and Mayer 1974, Brush 1977a, 1977b, Orlove 1977, Bolton and Mayer 1977, Isbell 1978, Guillet 1980).

18 On the role of kinship reciprocity in structuring links between agriculture and other sectors of the economy, and between the countryside and the town, see Mayer (1974), Smith (1975, 1979, 1984), Isbell (1974, 1977), Campaña (1982). On the role of kinship generally in affecting migration patterns see Bradfield (1973), Skeldon (1974,1977a), Radcliffe (1986a, 1986b).

19 One of the principal organizational units in the bilateral kinship system is the sibling group, which has strong bonds of loyalty and reciprocity. Siblings would have close relationships with their nephews and nieces and strong rights over their labour.

20 In the traditional division of labour men were associated with the heavy labour involved in cultivation and construction, while women were concerned with planting, the storage and marketing of produce, food provisioning and domestic budgeting (Nuñez del Prado 1975a, 1975b, 1982, Skar 1979, Bourque and Warren 1981, Deere 1982, Radcliffe 1986a, 1986b). Textile and herding activities were usually, but not always, considered to be women's work.

21 Children started agricultural work at 6 or 7 years; girls entered domestic service at 9 to 10 years (see chapter 6).

22 Despite the extensive research on *compadrazgo* there has been remarkably little detailed analysis of gender differences. This observation is based on anecdotal evidence.

23 Resources in the different networks were used for different purposes: women's off-farm wages were used for consumption whereas men's were used for productive investment (Campaña 1982: 17). Women controlled the resources derived from children's migration, especially from girls in domestic service (Radcliffe 1986b).

24 On the whole, male outmigration resulted in an increasing burden of work for women (Deere 1982, Villalobos 1978, Campaña 1982, Radcliffe 1986a). Deere (1982) suggests that traditional forms of gender segregation began to break down as a result of this, especially amongst the poorer peasant families. In the Mantaro valley, which was one of the regions most exposed to socio-economic change, women were becoming responsible for most of the agricultural and commercial activities on the farm (Campaña 1982). However, they were still excluded from the major decision-making processes of the community (Campaña 1982, Saràvia 1982).

25 In Inca times, women held political and religious offices, so the principle of complementarity applied to these spheres as well as the economy (Silverblatt 1978). However, under Spanish-colonial rule, these offices were abolished, leaving women bereft of independent representation. The new political offices in the communities and on the *haciendas* were all 'male' (Silverblatt 1980: 169–72). This institutional exclusion severely eroded women's political and moral authority.

26 It has been argued that family violence should be set in the context of wider historical patterns of aggression between families, community and classes in the

sierra. Bolton (1972) shows that aggression there was high, as manifested by homicide, assault, verbal abuse, theft and litigation.

27 According to Caravedo *et al.* (1963: 254), between a fifth and a quarter of the migrants in an inner-city slum were runaways.

28 However, although girls were permitted to make sexual unions prior to marriage such unions were patterned and promiscuity frowned upon (Boyden, personal communication). Controls over married women's sexuality took the form of opposition by men to birth control (Bronstein 1982).

29 Evidence on the stability of marriage is contradictory. In one view, marriages were stable and divorce rare (Carter 1977: 211, Skar 1979, Isbell 1978). Stycos, however, cites a number of references that mention marital instability in the *sierra* (1968: 229); see also Bolton (1972: 64).

30 Most of the data in this section are drawn from studies of particular labouring-class neighbourhoods or occupational groups; they are therefore illustrative but not necessarily representative. They also cover quite a long time span within the growth period, although the remarkable similarity in the findings suggests that the patterns were relatively stable throughout.

31 Many families married legally in response to pressure from the state and the Catholic Church. For example, marriage certificates were occasionally required by schools (Pimentel 1983: 64) and by agencies responsible for distributing housing sites in the shanty towns (Boggio 1970: 122–3, 135, Barrig 1982: 159, 218, Lobo 1982: 140). During the early 1970s, as part of a campaign to 'integrate' the poor into urban society, mass marriages were organized in the shanty towns (Collier 1976a: 114, Fernández 1983: 5–6). According to Fernández, 30 per cent of those legally married had participated in mass marriages.

32 In Ciudad de Dios in 1955 the proportions were 66:34 (Matos Mar 1966: 67); in El Agostino they were 67:33 (cited by Lobo 1982: 140); in Cuidadela Chalaca they were 63:37 (Lobo 1982: 140); in Virgen del Buen Paso they were 72: 28 (Boggio 1970: 123); in Pamplona Alta they were 71:29 (Fernández 1983: 4).

33 In Flora Tristan neighbourhood, only 5 per cent of families had six children or more (Anderson *et al.* 1979: 16). In Pamplona (Sara-Lafosse 1978: 16) 5 per cent had eight or more.

34 The seven working-class districts were: Comas, El Agostino, La Victoria, Rimac, San Juan de Miraflores, San Martin de Porres, and Villa Maria del Triunfo.

35 Buvinic and Youssef considered Peru to have a 'low' proportion of female-headed households (calculated at 10–14 per cent) (cited by Sara-Lafosse 1978: 15).

36 It is difficult to obtain data on unmarried mothers because they were usually absorbed into the households of their own kin (Boggio 1970: 120). In Mendocita unmarried mothers were only 2 per cent of all adult women (Caravedo *et al.* 1963: 21) and in Ciudad de Dios they were 8 per cent (Matos Mar 1966: 67). Boggio and others report that considerable pressures were brought to bear on men who impregnated single women to set up a consensual union or formally marry the girl (Boggio 1970: 118–19).

37 It is difficult to assess the amount of casual informal activity carried out by married working-class women in their homes. Lobo reports such activities as raising pigs and chickens, cooking for neighbours, looking after neighbours' children, renting out magazines, charging for viewing the television, etc. (Lobo 1982:53).

38 Studies of working children show that just under half came from an 'ordinary' nuclear family. Around 23–6 per cent came from single-parent families (mainly

headed by mothers); and the rest lived with other relatives or unspecified persons (Oort de Sanchez 1983: 73, Alarcón 1986: 22, Mansilla 1986: 103–5).

39 Children were subjected to physical violence from teachers in the schools (Pimentel 1983: 25, 36).

40 In Mendocita, 20 per cent of reported crime was associated with drunkenness, and approximately 10 per cent of the sample were said to be alcoholic (Caravedo *et al.* 1963: 72).

41 Some 50 per cent of fathers from rural areas and 50 per cent of those from the *sierra* used physical punishment, compared with 29 per cent of fathers from urban areas and 38 per cent from the coast (La Jara 1983: 12–13).

42 Note that Pimentel's sample had a very high proportion of persons from rural backgrounds: 90 per cent of the men and 86 per cent of the women were migrants; and of these, 79 per cent of the mothers and 71 per cent of the fathers were of peasant origin (Pimentel 1983: 29).

5 Divisions amongst the labouring class

1 The unemployed are omitted from this entire analysis because of a lack of data on the previous job.

2 Migrants made up 74 per cent of men and 71 per cent of women workers. Both groups were mainly from district, provincial or departmental capitals (80 per cent).

3 The minimum wage went up from 2,400 soles to 3,000 soles between the two Ministry of Labour surveys (1973 and 1974). For this reason a different figure may be cited according to which survey is being used.

4 These were mainly domestic servants, street sellers and storekeepers.

5 These data contradict a common notion that women predominate absolutely in the informal sector. They were, however, overrepresented there, i.e. their share of informal employment was greater than their share of total employment.

6 Salaried workers were included in the manual sample if they worked in informal enterprises and earned less than the minimum wage (see Appendix).

7 Informal earnings as a proportion of formal earnings was 85 per cent for men and 55 per cent for women; women's earnings as a proportion of men's was 42 per cent in the informal sector and 65 per cent in the formal sector.

8 The figure for the smallest size group is inflated by the inclusion of the self-employed, who had much higher earnings than wage workers in this group. When the former are excluded, the means fall to 2,327 and 1,144 soles respectively, which signifies a quantitative jump at this end of the range also.

9 Activities that are normally thought of as services e.g. repairs were classified according to the industry with which they were associated e.g. manufacturing, construction, rather than with services. This meant that the number of men in self-employed services was very small.

10 There were more pronounced differences in the coverage of men and women in enterprises with 5–99 workers.

11 Throughout this section, skill distinctions are taken at face value – i.e. on the basis of socially recognized definitions. I do not consider whether these categories are inherently skilled or not, nor how they acquired the definitions that they did.

12 One informant had worked with a *maestro* for many years, but he was never shown how to cut cloth without a pattern. In desperation he took to unpicking the clothes he had sewn up during the day, to get the original pattern. Once he had mastered (*sic*) this, he was able to set up on his own.

13 In domestic service there was an internal hierarchy based on status rather than skill: at the top was the *mayordomo* (butler), then came housekeeper, nanny, cook and finally, maid. A cook would earn 2,000 soles, a nanny 1,900 and a maid 1,200.

14 The Ministry of Labour survey asked whether the respondent had ever learnt a trade. The question did not ask how he or she learnt the skill for their *present* job or whether the trade learnt was for that job. According to the responses, only 29 per cent said they had 'ever learned a trade', 36 per cent of the men and 17 per cent of the women.

15 This figure is an adaptation of the one originally published in Scott (1979).

16 There were only nineteen semi-independent workers in the case study sample. Their average daily wage was 162 soles, whereas that of the independent self-employed was 154, and that of wage labourers, 131 soles.

17 A *colectivo* is a saloon car run as a bus on a specific route, taking up to five passengers.

18 A few men were in this situation also, but they were mainly old men or ones who had fallen on hard times.

19 They normally only had a tiny room and a bathroom, perhaps with only cold water. See Bunster and Chaney 1985: 55.

6 Mobility within the labouring class I: aggregate patterns

1 The Ministry of Labour survey had data on up to four jobs held during the previous ten years and the informant's first job. However, little information was elicited about these jobs, only occupation and economic sector. The dating of the beginning and end of each job was not extensively probed, therefore the duration data may be unreliable. In terms of the actual jobs reported, however, a crosscheck against the case studies re-interviewed from the Ministry of Labour sample revealed only two discrepancies.

There are several differences in the structure of the two work history data sets. The case studies had a higher proportion of completed jobs and included child labour. The Ministry of Labour sample had a higher proportion of non-completed (current) jobs. This gave a bias towards older age groups and longer job durations in the latter case.

2 Child labour was defined as work performed by children under the age of 14, without a wage, for relatives.

3 The reason for the discrepancy between fathers' and mothers' involvement in agriculture is that a high proportion of fathers (29 per cent) were dead or had deserted the home at the time when the respondent started work.

4 Of men, 53 per cent reported child labour but only 33 per cent of women. There may be a gender bias here because girls' labour in the household was not considered work.

5 Of the men, 48 per cent had started work in the *sierra* and 19 per cent on the coast (the rest in Lima).

6 In the case study data, economic sector was defined in terms of the type of activity associated with the job, rather than the enterprise; thus drivers are classified in transport whether they worked as distributors for factories and shops, private chauffeurs or bus drivers. This has only a minor effect on the distributions between sectors, but makes more sense in terms of identifying similar occupational skills and career linkages.

7 A two-sector categorization was necessary here because of the large number of possible combinations and the small number of cases.

8 This figure only rose to 34 per cent when women under 30 were excluded.

9 The high-income group were those with three times the minimum wage.

10 See Appendix for a discussion of some of the technical problems involved in the analysis of job changes and job duration.

11 In a study of factory workers, 68 per cent had spent 80–100 per cent of their working life in their current trade and 77 per cent had had less than five jobs during the last decade (Briones and Mejía 1964: 32–3).

12 Bendix and Lipset defined a low mobility rate as 0 to 1.9 job changes per decade, medium mobility as 2 to 4.9 changes and high mobility as over 5 changes (Bendix and Lipset 1964: 159).

13 There was a strong correlation between age and job duration in this data set (0.53), slightly higher than in the case histories.

14 The data on numbers of jobs held for men was as follows: skilled workers 6.6, unskilled 4.2; wage workers 6.1, self-employed 5.3; formal workers 6.5, informal workers 5.0. The tendencies for the women were the same, but the range of variation much lower: skilled workers 3.7, unskilled 3.5; wage workers 3.5, self-employed 3.4; formal workers 3.9, informal workers 3.3.

15 Job duration data in the case study data set are based on all jobs in the work histories (999), not just current jobs (see note 1).

16 This discrepancy may have been because of the underrepresentation of current (incomplete) jobs, compared with the Ministry of Labour data (see note 1).

17 An equation based on the case studies, regressing enterprise size, self-employment (dummy), skill, age and income on job duration produced an r^2 of 0.19. Age accounted for 15 per cent of total variation. Sex contributed an infinitesimal amount once these other factors were controlled for and was not statistically significant.

18 The duration of the working life is calculated by the simple addition of all years worked since first job (including child labour), minus total years not in employment.

19 The inclusion of men and women in this equation widened the gap between the mobile and the immobile, the former having a slightly longer working life and more job changes, but the statistical significance of this relationship remained weak (correlation coefficient = 0.17, p = 0.08).

7 Mobility within the labouring class II: career paths

1 In 29 per cent of the cases, the father was absent at the time when the informant started work.

2 Those currently in manufacturing had slightly higher levels of education than those in other sectors. Nearly three-quarters had completed primary schooling, several had some secondary schooling and there were no illiterates.

3 Only firms that had a specific quality component linked to brand names (e.g. Van Heusen shirts) insisted on a firm-specific training for their workers.

4 Thirteen out of the twenty-four construction workers had not finished their primary schooling, and a further seven (i.e. less than a third) had completed the cycle, but had no secondary schooling.

5 See Appendix (p. 224) for the definition of manual jobs.

6 A *bazar* is a small multi-purpose shop, selling toys, cigarettes, magazines etc.

8 Employment, family and class

1 Female unemployment rates were 50 per cent higher amongst women with secondary education than amongst those with primary education. These rates were also 50 per cent higher than the unemployment rates of men with secondary schooling (Scott 1986a: 331).

2 The historical origins of this segregation probably lie with the guilds and were linked to their political activities (see Wilson 1986, Blanchard 1982).

3 This information is based on the whole sample, thus it includes middle-class families as well. However, since female activity rates were *higher* amongst middle-class families, and the sex-differentials in earnings lower, we can suppose that women's contribution in labouring-class families would have been even lower.

4 These data exclude economic activities undertaken by children aged between 8 and 14 years.

5 Income is not a reliable indicator of class because of the high degree of variance; occupation is a better indicator, but the class position of the *family* can't be defined solely by the occupation of the household head.

6 The situation of female-headed households in this data set is ambiguous since a third stated they were married or cohabiting. It is difficult to say whether they did in fact have a male breadwinner to support them. The activity rate of these women was 44.1 per cent which is still low, so some may have been living off a male income, or they may have been middle-class widows living off pensions.

7 Three-quarters of female-headed households were in sales and service work, although they were actually only a minority of all heads of household in these two occupational groups (22 per cent).

8 There were some construction workers in this group – suggesting the possibility of 'dovetailing'. However, they were only a small minority and would certainly not account for the whole pattern.

9 More disaggregated categories would facilitate a finer measurement of patterns of coupling and intergenerational mobility. A longitudinal analysis would reveal how these processes changed as individuals moved around in the labour market and household composition changed.

9 Consciousness and political action

1 On class images see Lockwood (1966), Bulmer (1975), Davis (1979) and Graetz (1983).

2 The wording was as follows: 'Let's finish with a game. You know our country is made up of groups of people who have the same problems, the same interests, but they are different from other groups who have other problems and interests.... Let's suppose that each of these cards represents one of these groups. Could you tell me who they are?...' The use of strongly coloured cards helps to focus the respondent's images and encourages personal identification with the representations of society that emerge in the discussion. They are not told how many cards there are and only take as many as they want.

3 There has been some discussion about the stability of class images. However, Graetz's (1983) maintains that class sentiments are more stable than images.

4 Lockwood (1966) and others have suggested that a tripartite model is deferential rather than oppositional.

5 Most of these women were downwardly mobile, or were married to middle-class husbands or were themselves in jobs that were on the margin of manual employment, e.g. shop assistants.

6 Peru had military dictatorships in 1914–15, 1930–1, 1933–9, 1948–56, 1962–3 and 1968–80.

7 Definitions of populism vary, but it usually refers to a political movement which aims to represent 'the people' as the main agent of social transformation. 'The people' is a vague category but is usually assumed to be composed primarily of the urban labouring class. In practice, populism has relied on a cross-class alliance between organized labour, white collar workers, students, parts of the state bureaucracy and the industrial bourgeoisie. Its ideology is usually reformist rather than revolutionary and the goal is growth, modernization, and redistribution. For a further review see Roxborough (1984), Dix (1985).

8 APRA stands for Alianza Popular Revolucionaria Americana (Popular Revolutionary American Alliance). It was formed in 1924 by Raul Haya de la Torre, a young student activist, while in exile in Mexico. It appeared in Peru as the PAP (Partido Aprista Peruana) when he returned in 1930.

9 The Communist Party was founded by Mariátegui as the Peruvian Socialist Party in 1928, but after affiliation to the Third Communist International in 1930, it changed its name to the Peruvian Communist Party.

10 In the early years, APRA's ideology was anti-oligarchic, anti-military, anti-clerical and anti-imperialist. It had a broad range of activities, educational and cultural as well as political (Kantor 1953).

11 In the shanty towns, APRA would set up youth clubs, mothers' clubs, housing associations etc. Alan Garcia, who became president of the Aprista government in 1985, was once a legal adviser to squatter invaders (CIED n.d.).

12 For the 1963 and 1966 elections, APRA formed an alliance with Odría (who had been responsible for extensive repression of apristas during the early 1950s). From 1963, APRA was also receiving support from the AFL-CIO via ORIT (Organizacion Regional Interamericana de Trabajadores) and the AIFLD (American Institute for Free Labour Development). The American support was to help APRA promote an anti-communist and reformist trade unionism (Payne 1965: 200, McIntyre 1972: 455–461).

13 Apra Rebelde was formed in 1960, the MIR in 1962, Bandera Roja in 1964, Vanguardia Revolucionaria in 1965, and Patria Roja in 1968.

14 The Partido Democrata Cristiana was formed in 1955, Acción Popular in 1956 and the Movimiento Social Progresista in 1956. Acción Popular formed Cooperación Popular, which promoted community development in urban shanty towns and in rural villages. The Christian Democrats formed a union confederation in 1955 and were active in charity work in the shanty towns.

15 The main confederations were: the CGTP (communist), the CTP (aprista), the CNT (Christian Democrat) and the CTRP (pro-Junta). In the early 1970s, the most powerful confederation, in terms of number of affiliates, strikes and man-days lost in strikes, was the CGTP (Sulmont 1977: 321).

16 See Collier (1975, 1976a) on Odría's government, and Stepan (1978), Dietz (1980) and Skinner (1981) on the activities of SINAMOS (National System of Social Mobilization) during the Velasco period.

17 Voting was obligatory in Peru, although there was a literacy qualification. In the Lima shanty towns, 85 per cent of those eligible to vote were registered and did vote (Collier 1976b: 36).

18 Although some writers have attributed the vote for Odría to his cooptive practices in the shanty towns, his macro-economic policies did in fact generate employment for manual workers, especially in the construction industry. The vote for Belaunde cannot be explained in terms of cooptive practices since he showed little interest in the shanty towns. He did, however, promise industrial growth and modernization.

19 These observations are based on a review of newspapers during the period (mainly *El Comercio* and *Expreso*).

20 AIFLD = American Institute for Free Labor Development. See note 12.

21 A motion at the second congress of the APRA party in 1948 stated: 'women are not active members of the Party, they are only companions, because they do not have the status of citizens' (Magda Portal in Andradi and Portugal 1979: 217). This may have referred to the fact that women still did not have the vote at the time. Nevertheless, as Magda Portal said, they were militating alongside the men and being imprisoned and deported, so they should have been considered full political partners.

22 The first feminist organization was ALIMUPER, founded in 1973.

References

Acker, J.R. (1973) 'Women and social stratification: a case of intellectual sexism', *American Journal of Sociology* 78 (4): 936–45.

Alarcón Glasinovich, W. (1986) *Pobreza urbana y trabajo infantil.* Mimeo. Lima: Radda Barnen.

Alberti, G. and Mayer, E. (eds) (1974) *Reciprocidad e intercambio en los Andes peruanos.* Lima: Instituto de Estudios Peruanos.

Altamirano, T. (1984) *Presencia andina en Lima metropolitana.* Lima: Fondo Editorial, Pontifícia Universidad Católica del Peru.

Anderson, J.M., Figueroa Galup, B. and Mariñez, A. (1979) *Child Care in Urban and Rural Peru.* A report presented to the Overseas Education Fund of the League of Women Voters. Lima.

Anderson Velasco, J. (1982) 'La red informal en las estratégias de supervivencia en barrios pobres de Lima'. Paper presented to the Congreso de Investigación acerca de la Mujer en la Region Andina. Lima, 7–10 June 1982.

Andradi, E. and Portugal, A-M. (eds) (1979) *Ser mujer en el Peru.* Lima: TOKAPU Editores.

Andreas, C. (1985) *When Women Rebel: the Rise of Popular Feminism in Peru.* Westport, CT: Lawrence Hill & Co.

Arnold, K. (1978) 'The whore in Peru', in S. Lipshitz (ed.) *Tearing the Veil.* London: Routledge and Kegan Paul.

Babb, F.E. (1985) 'Men and women in Vicos, Peru: a case of unequal development', in W. Stein (ed.) *Peruvian Contexts of Change.* New Brunswick: Transaction Books.

Balan, J., Browning, H.L., Jelin, E. and Litzler, L. (1969) 'A computerized approach to the processing and analysis of life histories obtained in sample surveys', *Behavioural Science* 14: 105–20.

Balan, J., Browning, H.L. and Jelin, E. (1973) *Men in a Developing Society.* Austin, TX: University of Texas Press.

Barrett, M. (1980) *Women's Oppression Today.* London: Verso.

Barrig, M. (1979) *Cinturon de castidad.* Lima: Mosca Azul.

Barrig, M. (1982) *Convivir: la pareja en la pobreza.* Lima: Mosca Azul.

Bayer, D.L. (1969) 'Urban Peru – political action as sellout', *Transaction* 7(1): 36, 47–54.

Beaulne, M. (1974) *La industrialización por sustitución de las importaciones en el Peru 1958–1969.* Mimeo. Lima: ESAN.

Bendix, R. and Lipset, S.M. (1964) *Social Mobility in Industrial Society*. Berkeley, CA: University of California Press.

Benería, L. (1979) 'Reproduction, production and the sexual division of labour', *Cambridge Journal of Economics* 3: 203–25.

Benería, L. and Roldán, M. (1987) *The Crossroads of Class and Gender*. Chicago: University of Chicago Press.

Bennholdt-Thomsen, V. (1981) 'Subsistence production and extended reproduction', in K. Young, C. Wolkowitz and R. McCullagh (eds) *Of Marriage and the Market*. London: CSE Books.

Bennholdt-Thomsen, V. (1982) 'Subsistence production and extended reproduction. A contribution to the discussion about modes of production', *Journal of Peasant Studies* 9 (4): 241–54.

Bernstein, H. (1979) 'African peasantries: a theoretical framework', *Journal of Peasant Studies* 6: 421–43.

Blanchard, P. (1982) *The Origins of the Peruvian Labour Movement 1883–1919*. Pittsburg: Pittsburg University Press.

Blondet, C. (1990) 'Establishing an identity: women settlers in a poor Lima neighbourhood', in E. Jelin (ed.) *Women and Social Change in Latin America*. London: Zed Books.

Boggio, K. (1970) *Estudio del ciclo vital en Pamplona Alta*. Mimeo. Lima: Cuadernos Desco.

Bolton, R. (1972) *Aggression in Qolla Society*. Unpublished PhD dissertation, Cornell University.

Bolton, R. (1974) 'El abusivo y el humilde', *Allpanchis* VI: 42–78.

Bolton, R. and Mayer, E. (eds) (1977) *Andean Kinship and Marriage*. Washington, DC: American Anthropological Association.

Booth, D. (1985) 'Marxism and development sociology: interpreting the impasse', *World Development* 13 (7): 761–87.

Bourque, S.C. and Warren, K.B. (1981) *Women of the Andes*. Ann Arbor, MI: University of Michigan Press.

Bourricaud, F. (1970) *Power and Society in Contemporary Peru*. London: Faber and Faber.

Boyden, J. (1983) *The Transformation of Production in and the Economic Development of a District in the Central Peruvian Andes; 1700–1979*. Unpublished PhD dissertation, London School of Economics.

Boyden, J. (1985) *Children in Development: Policy Programming for Especially Disadvantaged Children in Lima, Peru*. Oxford: Report for UNICEF and OXFAM.

Bradfield, S. (1965) 'Some occupational aspects of migration', *Economic Development and Cultural Change* 14 (1): 61–70.

Bradfield, S. (1973) 'Selectivity in rural–urban migration: the case of Huaylas, Peru', in A. Southall (ed.) *Urban Anthropology*. New York: Oxford University Press.

Brass, T. (1986) 'The elementary strictures of kinship: unfree relations and the production of commodities', in A.M. Scott (ed.) *Rethinking Petty Commodity Production*, special issue of *Social Analysis*, no. 20: 56–68.

Breman, J. (1976) 'A dualistic labour system? A critique of the "informal sector" concept', *Economic and Political Weekly* 2 (48): 1870–6, and (49): 1905–8. Reprinted (1985) in R. Bromley (ed.) *Planning for Small Enterprises in Third World Cities*. Oxford: Pergamon.

Briones, G. and Mejía Valera, J. (1964) *El obrero industrial*. Lima: Universidad Nacional Mayor de San Marcos.

Bromley, R. (ed.) (1978) *The Urban Informal Sector*, special issue of *World Development* 6 (9/10).

Bromley, R. (1982) 'Working in the streets: survival strategy, necessity or unavoidable evil' in A. Gilbert *et al. Urbanization in Contemporary Latin America*. Chichester: John Wiley.

Bromley, R. and Gerry, C. (1979) *Casual Work and Poverty in Third World Cities*. Chichester: John Wiley.

Bronstein, A. (1982) *The Triple Struggle: Latin American Peasant Women*. London: War on Want Campaigns Ltd.

Brush, S.B. (1977a) 'Kinship and land use in a northern sierra community', in R. Bolton and E. Mayer (eds) *Andean Kinship and Marriage*. Washington, DC: American Anthropological Association.

Brush, S.B. (1977b) *Mountain, Field and Family: the Economy and Human Ecology of an Andean Valley*. Philadelphia, PA: University of Pennsylvania Press.

Brydon, L. and Chant, S. (1989) *Women in the Third World*. Aldershot: Edward Elgar.

Bulmer, M. (ed.) (1975) *Working Class Images of Society*. London: Routledge and Kegan Paul.

Bunster, X. and Chaney, E.M. (1985) *Sellers and Servants: Working Women in Lima, Peru*. New York: Praeger.

Burkett, E. (1977) 'In dubious sisterhood: race and class in Spanish Colonial South America', *Latin American Perspectives* IV (1 and 2): 18–26.

Burkett, E. (1978) 'Indian women and white society: the case of sixteenth century Peru', in A. Lavrin (ed.) *Latin American Women: Historical Perspectives*. Westport, CT: Greenwood Press.

Campaña, P. (1982) *Estudio preliminar de la condición y participación económica de la mujer en el Peru rural*. Mimeo. Paper presented to the Congreso de Investigación de la Mujer en la Región Andina, Lima, 7–10 June 1982.

Campaña, P. and Rivera, R. (1984) 'Highland Puna communities and the impact of the mining economy', in N. Long and B. Roberts (eds) *Miners, Peasants and Entrepreneurs*. Cambridge: Cambridge University Press.

Caravedo, B., Rotondo, H. and Mariategui, J. (1963) *Estudios de psiquiatria social en el Peru*. Lima: Ediciones del Sol.

Carbonetto, D., Hoyle, J. and Tueros, M. (1985) *Sector informal urbano en Lima metropolitana*. Lima: Centro de Estudios para el Desarrollo y la Participación (CEDEP).

Carbonetto, D., Hoyle, J. and Tueros, M. (1988) *Lima: sector informal*. Lima: Centro de Estudios para el Desarrollo y la Participación (CEDEP).

Cardoso, F.H. (1972) 'Dependency and development in Latin America', *New Left Review* no. 74.

Carter, W.E. (1977) 'Trial marriage in the Andes?', in R. Bolton and E. Mayer (eds) *Andean Kinship and Marriage*. Washington, DC: American Anthropological Association.

Castells, M. (1982) 'Squatters and politics in Latin America: a comparative analysis of urban social movements in Chile, Peru and Mexico', in H. Safa (ed.) *Towards a Political Economy of Urbanization in Third World Countries*. Delhi: Oxford University Press.

Castells, M. (1983) *The City and the Grass-Roots: A Cross-cultural Theory of Urban Social Movements*. Berkeley, CA: University of California Press.

Castillo Rios, C. (1985) *Los niños del Peru*, 4th edn. Lima: Librería Importadora, Editora y Distribuidora.

Central Bank (1966) *Cuentas Nacionales del Peru 1950–65*. Lima: Banco Central de Reserva.

Central Bank (1976) *Cuentas Nacionales del Peru 1960–69*. Lima: Banco Central de Reserva.

Chaney, E.M. (1973) 'Women in Latin American politics: the case of Peru and Chile', in A. Pescatello (ed.) *Female and Male in Latin America*. Pittsburgh: University of Pittsburgh Press.

Chaney, E.M. (1979) *Supermadre: Women in Politics in Latin America*. Austin, TX: University of Texas Press.

Chaney, E.M. and Schmink, M. (1980) 'Women and modernization: access to tools', in J. Nash and H. Safa (eds) *Sex and Class in Latin America*. New York: Bergin Publishers.

Chant, S. (1991) *Women and Survival in Mexican Cities*. Manchester: Manchester University Press.

Chaplin, D. (1967) *The Peruvian Industrial Labour Force*. Princeton, NJ: Princeton University Press.

Chueca, M. (1982) *Mujer, familia y trabajo en Villa El Salvador*. Paper presented to the seminar Analisis y Promoción de la Participación de la Mujer en la Actividad Economica. Lima, 2–5 March.

CIED (Centro de Información, Estudios y Documentación) (n.d.) *Partidos y conciencia en las barriadas*. Lima: Pontifícia Universidad Católica del Peru.

CISM (Centro de Investigaciones Sociales por Muestreo) (1967) *Barriadas de Lima*. Lima: Ministry of Labour.

Collier, D. (1975) 'Squatter settlements and policy innovation in Peru', in A.F. Lowenthal (ed.) *The Peruvian Experiment*. Princeton, NJ: Princeton University Press.

Collier, D. (1976a) *Squatters and Oligarchs*. Baltimore: Johns Hopkins University Press.

Collier, D. (1976b) *Squatter Settlements and the Incorporation of Migrants into Urban Life: the Case of Lima*. Mimeo. Center for International Studies, Massachussetts Institute of Technology.

Connolly, P. (1985) 'The politics of the informal sector: a critique', in N. Redclift and E. Mingione (eds) *Beyond Employment*. Oxford: Basil Blackwell.

Cook, S. (1984) *Peasant Capitalist Industry. Piecework and Enterprise in Southern Mexico Brickyards*. Lanham, New York: University Press of America.

Cutler, A.J., Hindess, B., Hirst, P.Q. and Hussain, A. (1977, 1978) *Marx's Capital and Capitalism Today* (two vols). London: Routledge and Kegan Paul.

Davis, H.H. (1979) *Beyond Class Images*. London: Croom Helm.

Deere, C.D. (1982) 'The division of labor by sex in agriculture: a Peruvian case study', *Economic Development and Cultural Change* 30 (4): 795–811.

De Janvry, A. and Garramon, C. (1977) 'The dynamics of rural poverty in Latin America', *Journal of Peasant Studies* 4 (3): 206–15.

De Soto, H. (1986) *El otro sendero*. Lima: Editorial El Barranco. Translated (1989) as *The Other Path*. London: I.B. Taurus.

Dietz, H.A. (1980) *Poverty and Problem-Solving under Military Rule*. Austin, TX: University of Texas Press.

Dietz, H.A. (1985) 'Political participation in the barriadas: an extension and reexamination', *Comparative Political Studies* 18 (3): 323–55.

Dix, R.H. (1985) 'Populism: authoritarian and democratic', *Latin American Research Review* XX (2): 29–52.

Dos Santos, T. (1970) 'The concept of social classes' *Science and Society* 38: 166–93.

Doughty, P. (1969) 'La cultura del regionalismo en la vida urbana de Lima', *America Indigena* XXIX (4): 949–81.

Doughty (1970) 'Behind the trade of the city: provincial life in Lima, Peru' in W. Mangin (ed) *Peasants in Cities*. Boston, MA: Houghton Miffin.

Douglas, W.A. (1972) 'El gremialismo auspiciado por Estados Unidos', in D. Sharp (ed.) *Estados Unidos y la Revolución Peruana*, pp. 475–502. Buenos Aires: Editorial Sudamericana. (First published as *US Foreign Policy in Peru*.)

Eckstein, S. (ed.) (1989) *Power and Popular Protest: Latin American Social Movements*. Berkeley, CA: University of California Press.

ECLA (1959) 'The industrial development of Peru', *Analysis and Projections of Economic Development*, vol. IV. ECLA.

ECLA (1971) *Income Distribution in Latin America*. ECLA.

Edwards, E.O. (1974) *Employment in Developing Nations*. New York: Columbia University Press.

Edwards, R. (1979) *Contested Terrain*. London: Heinemann.

Elson, D. and Pearson, R. (1981) 'Nimble fingers make cheap workers: an analysis of women's employment in Third World export manufacturing', *Feminist Review* 7: 87–107.

Ennew, J. (1986) 'Mujercita y Mamacita: girls growing up in Lima', *Bulletin of Latin American Research* 5 (2): 49–66.

Escobar, G. (1973) *Sicaya*. Lima: Instituto de Estudios Peruanos.

Espinozo Uriarte, H. and Osorio Torres, J. (1972) *El poder económico en la industria*. Lima: CIES, Universidad Nacional de Federico Villareal.

Favre, H. (1977) 'The dynamics of Indian peasant society and the migration to coastal plantations in central Peru', in K. Duncan and I. Rutledge (eds) *Land and Labour in Latin America*. Cambridge: Cambridge University Press.

Fernández, B. (1983) *Unión y estabilidad conyugales* Mimeo. Lima: Pontifícia Universidad Católica del Peru, Departamento de Ciencias Sociales.

Figueroa, A. (1984) *Capitalist Development and the Peasant Economy in Peru*. Cambridge: Cambridge University Press.

Fitzgerald, E.V.K. (1976) *The State and Economic Development: Peru since 1968*. Cambridge: Cambridge University Press.

Fitzgerald, E.V.K. (1979) *The Political Economy of Peru 1956–78*. Cambridge: Cambridge University Press.

Fritsch, W.R. (1962) *Progress and Profits: the Sears Roebuck Story in Peru*. Washington, DC: Action Committee for International Development Inc.

Gall, N. (1974) 'Peru's education reform. Part I', *American Universities Field Staff Report*. West Coast South America Series, vol. XX1, no. 3.

Garnsey, E. (1978) 'Women's work and theories of class stratification', *Sociology* 12 (2): 224–43.

Germani, G. (1964) *Política y sociedad en una época de Transición*. Buenos Aires: Paidós.

Gerry, C. and Birkbeck, C. (1981) 'The petty commodity producer in Third World cities: petit bourgeois or "disguised" proletarian?', in F. Bechhofer and B. Elliott (eds) *The Petite Bourgeoisie: Comparative Studies of the Uneasy Stratum*. London, Macmillan.

Gianella, J. (1967) *Marginalidad en Lima metropolitana*. Lima: DESCO.

Giddens, A. (1973) *The Class Structure of the Advanced Societies*. London: Hutchinson.

GIECO (Grupo de Investigaciones Económicas) (1972) *Industrialización y políticas de industrialización en el Peru*. Lima: Universidad de Ingeniería.

Goldrich, D., Pratt, R.B. and Schuller, C.R. (1967) 'The political integration of lower class urban settlements in Chile and Peru', *Studies in Comparative International Development* III (1): 3–22.

Goldthorpe, J. (1983a) Women and class analysis: in defence of the conventional view', *Sociology* 17 (4): 465–88.

Goldthorpe, J. (1983b) 'Social mobility and class formation: on the renewal of a tradition in sociological enquiry', paper presented to the ISA Research Committee on Social Stratification and Mobility, Amsterdam.

Goldthorpe, J. (1984) 'Women and class analysis: a reply to the replies', *Sociology* 18: 491–9.

Graetz, B.R. (1983) 'Images of class in modern society; structure, sentiment and social location', *Sociology* 17 (1): 79–96.

Gregory, P. (1986) *The Myth of Market Failure: Employment and the Labor Market in Mexico*. Baltimore: Johns Hopkins University Press.

Grompone, R. (1985) *Talleristas y vendedores ambulantes in Lima*. Lima: DESCO.

Gugler, J. (1982) 'Overurbanization reconsidered', *Economic Development and Cultural Change* 31 (1): 173–89.

Guillet, D. (1980) 'Reciprocal labor and peripheral capitalism in the Central Andes', *Ethnology*, 19 (2): 151–67.

Gurrieri, A. (1971) 'La mujer joven y el trabajo en el Peru', in A. Gurrieri, E. Torres-Rivas, J. Gonzales and E. de la Vega (eds) *Estudios sobre la juventud marginal latinoamericana*. Mexico City: Siglo XXI.

Gutiérrez, R. (1984) 'From honor to love: transformations in the meaning of sexuality in colonial New Mexico', in R.T. Smith (ed.) *Kinship, Ideology and Practice in Colonial New Mexico, Latin America*. Chapel Hill, NC: University of North Carolina Press.

Guzman, V. and Portocarrero, P. (1985) *Dos veces mujer*. Lima: Mosca Azul for Flora Tristan.

Harris, O. and Young, K. (1981) 'Engendered structures; some problems in the analysis of reproduction', in J. Llobera and J. Kahn (eds) *The Anthropology of Pre-Capitalist Societies*. London: Macmillan.

Hart, K. (1973) 'Informal income opportunities and urban employment in Ghana', *Journal of Modern African Studies* 11: 61–89.

Harvey, P. and Gow, P. (1994) *Sex and Violence: Issues in Representation and Experience*. London: Routledge.

Haworth, N. (1983) 'Conflict or incorporation: the Peruvian working class, 1968–76', in D. Booth and B. Sorj (eds) *Military Reformism and Social Classes*. London: Macmillan.

Haworth, N. (1984) 'Proletarianisation in the world order: the Peruvian experience', in B. Munslow and H. Finch (eds) *Proletarianisation in the Third World*. London: Croom Helm.

Heath, A. (1981) *Social Mobility*. London: Fontana.

Heath, A. and Britten, N. (1984) 'Women's jobs do make a difference' *Sociology* 18 (4): 475–90.

Henry, E. (1978) *La escena urbana: estado y movimientos de pobladores 1968–1976*. Lima: Fondo Editorial/Pontificia Universidad Católica del Peru.

Hindess, B. (1987) *Politics and Class Analysis*. Oxford: Basil Blackwell.

Holton, R.J. (1989) 'Has class analysis a future? Max Weber and the challenge of liberalism to gemeinschaftlich accounts of class', in R.J. Holton and B.S. Turner (eds) *Max Weber on Economy and Society*. London: Routledge.

Humphrey, J. (1982) *Capitalist Control and Workers' Struggle in the Brazilian Auto Industry*. Princeton, NJ: Princeton University Press.

Humphrey, J. (1987) *Gender and Work in the Third World*. London: Routledge.

Humphries, J. and Rubery, J. (1984) 'The reconstitution of the supply side of the labour market: the relative autonomy of social reproduction', *Cambridge Journal of Economics* 3: 203–25.

Hunt, S. (1971) 'Distribution, growth and government economic behaviour in Peru', in G. Ranis (ed.) *Government and Economic Development*. New Haven, CT: Yale University Press.

Hunt, S. (n.d.) Real wages and economic growth. Chapter 4 of unpublished manuscript.

ILO (1972) *Employment, Incomes and Inequality: A Strategy for Increasing Productive Employment in Kenya*. Geneva: International Labour Office.

Isbell, B.J. (1974) 'The influence of migrants upon traditional social and political concepts: a Peruvian case study', in W.A. Cornelius and F.M. Trueblood (eds) *Latin American Urban Research*, vol. 4. Beverly Hills, CA: Sage.

Isbell, B.J. (1977) '"Those who love me"': an analysis of Andean kinship and reciprocity within a ritual context', in R. Bolton and E. Mayer (eds) *Andean Kinship and Marriage*. Washington, DC: American Anthropological Association.

Isbell, B.J. (1978) *To Defend Ourselves: Ecology and Ritual in Andean Village*. Austin, TX: University of Texas Press.

Jelin, E. (1967) 'Trabajadores por cuenta propria y asalariados: distinción vertical y horizontal?', *Revista latinoamericana de sociología* no. 3: 388–410.

Jelin, E. (1976) 'Orientaciones e ideologías obreras en América Latina', *Estudios Sociales*, no. 3. Buenos Aires: CEDES.

Jelin, E. (ed.) (1990) *Women and Social Change in Latin America*. London: Zed Books.

Joekes, S. (1987) *Women in the World Economy: an INSTRAW Study*. New York: Oxford University Press.

Jolly, R., de Kadt, E., Singer, H. and Wilson, F. (eds) (1973) *Third World Employment*. Harmondsworth: Penguin.

Jongkind, F. (1974) 'A reappraisal of the role of regional associations in Lima, Peru', *Comparative Studies in Society and History* XIV: 471–82.

Kannappan, S. (1985) 'Urban employment and the labor market in developing nations', *Economic Development and Cultural Change* 33 (4): 699–729.

Kantor, H. (1953) *The Ideology and Program of the Peruvian Aprista Movement*. Los Angeles, CA: University of California Press.

Kay, C. (1989) *Latin American Theories of Development and Underdevelopment*. London: Routledge.

Laclau, E. and Mouffe, C. (1985) *Hegemony and Socialist Strategy: Towards a Radical Democratic Politics*. London: Verso.

Laite, J. (1981) *Industrial Development and Migrant Labour*. Manchester: Manchester University Press.

La Jara, E. (1983) *Socialización de los hijos del migrante de la sierra*. Mimeo. Lima: Pontifícia Universidad Católica del Peru, Departamento de Ciencias Sociales.

Landsberger, H.A. (1967) 'The labor elite: is it revolutionary?', in S.M. Lipset and A. Solari (eds) *Elites in Latin America*. Oxford: Oxford University Press.

Latin American and Caribbean Women's Collective (1980) *Slave of Slaves*. London: Zed Books.

Lavrin, A. (1987) 'Women, the family and social change in Latin America' *World Affairs*, 150 (2): 109–28.

Leeds, A. (1969) 'The significant variables determining the character of squatter settlements', *America Latina* 12 (3): 44–86.

Leeds, A. (1973a) 'Political, economic and social effects of producer and consumer orientations toward housing in Brazil and Peru: a systems analysis', in F.F. Rabinowitz and F.M. Trueblood (eds) *Latin American Urban Research*, vol. 34. Beverly Hills, CA: Sage.

Leeds, A. (1973b) 'Locality power in relation to supralocal power institutions', in A. Southall (ed.) *Urban Anthropology*. New York: Oxford University Press.

Leeds, A. (1974) 'Housing settlement types, arrangements for living, proletarianization and the social structure of the city', in W. Cornelius and F. Trueblood (eds) *Latin American Urban Research* no. 4. Beverly Hills, CA: Sage.

Lehmann, D. (ed.) (1982) *Ecology and Economy in the Andes*. Cambridge: Cambridge University Press.

Lewis, R.A. (1973) *Employment, Income and the Growth of the Barriadas in Lima, Peru*. PhD dissertation, Latin American Studies Program, Cornell University.

Little, A.D. Inc. (1960) *A Program for Industrial and Regional Development of Peru*. A report to the government of Peru.

Lloyd, P. (1979) *Slums of Hope*. Harmondsworth: Penguin.

Lloyd, P. (1980) *The 'Young Towns' of Lima: Aspects of Urbanization in Peru*. Cambridge: Cambridge University Press.

Lloyd, P. (1982) *Third World Proletariat?* London: Allen and Unwin.

Lobo, S. (1976) 'Urban adaptation among Peruvian migrants', *Rice University Studies*, vol. 62 (3): 113–30, Summer.

Lobo, S. (1982) *A House of My Own: Social Organization in the Squatter Settlements of Lima, Peru*. Tucson, AZ: University of Arizona Press.

Lockhart, J. (1968) *Spanish Peru 1532–1560*. Madison, WI: University of Wisconsin Press.

Lockwood, D. (1966) 'Sources of variation in working class images of society', *Sociological Review* 14 (3): 249–67.

Lomnitz, L. (1977) *Networks and Marginality*. New York: Academic Press.

Long, N. (1973) 'The role of regional associations in Peru', in M. Drake *et al.* (eds) *The Process of Urbanization*. Milton Keynes: Open University.

Long, N. and Roberts, B. (eds) (1978) *Peasant Cooperation and Capitalist Expansion in Peru*. Austin, TX: University of Texas Press.

Long, N. and Roberts, B. (eds) (1984) *Miners, Peasants and Entrepreneurs*. Cambridge: Cambridge University Press.

Lopes, J.R.B. (1964) *Sociedade industrial no Brasil*. São Paulo: Difusão Européia do Livro.

MacEwen, A. (1974) 'Differentiation among the urban poor: an Argentine study', in E. De Kadt and G. Williams (eds) *Sociology and Development*. London: Tavistock.

McIntyre, W.J. (1972) 'La política obrera de Estados Unidos y Peru', in D. Sharp (ed.) *Estados Unidos y la Revolución Peruana*. Buenos Aires: Editorial Sudamericana (first published as *US Foreign Policy in Peru*).

Mallon, F.M. (1986) 'Gender and class in the transition to capitalism: household and mode of production in central Peru', *Latin American Perspectives* 13 (1): 147–74.

Mangin, W.P. (1959) 'The role of regional associations in the adaptation of rural population in Peru', *Sociologus*, new series, 9 (1): 23–35.

Mangin, W. (1967) 'Latin American squatter settlements: a problem and a solution', *Latin American Research Review* II (3): 65–98.

Mangin, W. (ed.) (1970) *Peasants in Cities: Readings in the Anthropology of Urbanization*. Boston, MA: Houghton Mifflin Co.

Mansilla, M.E. (1986) *Los Petisos*. Lima: Radda Barnen.

Marshall, G., Rose, D., Vogler, C. and Newby, H. (1988) *Social Class in Modern Britain*. London: Allen and Unwin.

Martinez, H., Prado, W. and Quintanilla, J. (1973) *El éxodo rural en el Peru*. Lima: Centro de Estudios de Población y Desarrollo.

Matos Mar, J. (1966) *Estudio de las barriadas limeñas (1955)*. Lima: Department of Anthropology, Universidad Nacional Mayor de San Marcos.

Mayer, E. (1974) *Reciprocity, Self-Sufficiency and Market Relations in a Contemporary Community in the Central Andes of Peru*, PhD dissertation, Cornell University.

Mayer, E. (1977) 'Beyond the nuclear family', in R. Bolton and E. Mayer (eds) *Andean Kinship and Marriage*. Washington, DC: American Anthropological Association.

Mayer, E. and Alberti, G. (eds) (1974) *Reciprocidad e intercambio en los Andes peruanos*. Lima: Instituto de Estudios Peruanos.

Mazumdar, D. (1976) 'The urban informal sector', *World Development* 4: 655–79.

Mazumdar, D. (1981) *The Urban Labour Market and Income Distribution: A Study of Malaysia*. Oxford: Oxford University Press for the World Bank.

Meillassoux, C. (1972) 'From reproduction to production', *Economy and Society* 1 (1): 93–105.

Mercado, H. (1978) *La madre trabajadora*. Estudios de Población y Desarrollo. Serie C no. 2.

Mesa-Lago, C. (1978) *Social Security in Latin America*. Pittsburgh: University of Pittsburgh Press.

Miller, R.U. (1971) 'The relevance of surplus labour theory to the urban labour markets of Latin America', *Bulletin of the International Institute of Labour Studies*, vol. 8: 221–45.

Mingione, E. (1985) 'Social reproduction of the surplus labour force: the case of Southern Italy', in N. Redclift and E. Mingione (eds) *Beyond Employment*. Oxford: Basil Blackwell.

Ministry of Industry and Tourism (1973) *Estadística Industrial*. Lima: Ministerio de Industrias y Turismo.

Ministry of Labour (1973) *Tabulaciones sobre ingresos de la población en el Peru*. Lima: Dirección General de Empleo, Ministerio del Trabajo.

Ministry of Labour (1974) *Estudio de la mano de obra en las areas urbanas del Peru (1973)*. Lima: Dirección General de Empleo, Ministerio del Trabajo.

Molyneux, M. (1985) 'Mobilization without emancipation? Women's interests, the state and revolution in Nicaragua', *Feminist Studies*. 11 (20): 227–54.

Morley, S.A. (1982) *Labor Markets and Inequitable Growth*. Cambridge and New York: Cambridge University Press.

Moser, C.O.N. (1977) 'The dual economy and marginality debate and the contribution of micro-analysis: market sellers in Bogota', *Development and Change* 8 (4): 465–89.

Moser, C.O.N. (1978) 'Informal sector or petty commodity production: dualism or dependence in urban development?', *World Development* 6 (9/10): 1041–64.

Moser, C.O.N. (1981) 'Surviving in the suburbios', *Bulletin of the Institute of Development Studies* 12 (3): 19–29.

Moser, C.O.N. (1987) 'Mobilization is women's work: struggles for infrastructure in Guayaquil, Ecuador' in C.O.N. Moser and L. Peake (eds) *Women, Human Settlements and Housing*. London: Tavistock.

Moser, C.O.N. (1989) 'Gender planning in the Third World: meeting practical and strategic gender needs', *World Development* 17 (11): 1799–825.

Moser, C.O.N. (1993) *Gender Planning and Development*. London: Routledge.

Moser, C.O.N. and Young, K. (1981) 'Women of the working poor', *Bulletin of the Institute of Development Studies* 12 (3): 54–62.

Nash, J. and Fernandez-Kelly, M-P. (eds) (1983) *Women, Men and the International Division of Labour*. Albany, NY: State University of New York Press.

Nash, J. and Safa, H. (1980) *Sex and Class in Latin America*. NY: Bergin.

Nelson, J. (1979) *Access to Power*. Princeton, NJ: Princeton University Press.

Nun, J. (1969) 'Superpoblación relativa, ejercito industrial de reserva y masa marginal', *Revista Latinoamericana de Sociología* 5 (2): 178–235.

Nuñez del Prado, D. (1975a) 'El rol de la mujer campesina quechua', *América Indígena* (Mexico) 35 (2): 391–401.

Nuñez del Prado, D. (1975b) 'El poder de decisión de la mujer quechua andina', *América Indígena* (Mexico) 35 (3): 623–30.

Nuñez del Prado, D. (1982) *El papel de la mujer campesina en los Andes y su contribución a la economia familiar*. Paper presented to the Congreso de Investigación de la Mujer en la Región Andina, Lima, 7–10 June 1982.

O'Laughlin, B. (1977) 'Production and reproduction: Meillassoux's Femmes, Greniers et Capitaux', *Critique of Anthropology* 8(2): 3–32.

ONE (Oficina Nacional de Estadística) (1979) *Encuesta nacional de fecundidad del Peru 1977–78*. Lima: ONE.

Oort de Sanchez, A.C.M. (1983) *Niños que trabajan*. Undergraduate thesis, Department of Social Work, Pontifícia Universidad Católica del Peru, Lima.

Orlove, B. (1974) 'Urban and rural artisans in Southern Peru', *International Journal of Comparative Sociology* XV (3): 193–211.

Orlove, B. (1977) 'Inequality among peasants: the forms and uses of reciprocal exchange in Andean Peru', in R. Halperin and J. Dow (eds) *Peasant Livelihood*. New York: St Martins Press.

Ortiz, A. (1983) *El trabajo de la mujer casada*. Mimeo. Lima: Department of Social Sciences, Pontifícia Universidad Católica del Peru.

Pahl, R.E. (1989) 'Is the emperor naked? Some questions on the adequacy of sociological theory in urban and regional research', *International Journal of Urban and Regional Research* 13 (4): 709–20.

Pan American Union (1950) *The Peruvian Economy*. Washington, DC: Pan American Union.

Pastore, J. (1982) *Inequality and Social Mobility in Brazil*. Madison, WI: University of Wisconsin Press.

Patch, R. (1967) 'La Parada, Lima's market. A study of class and assimilation', *American Universities Field Staff Reports*. West Coast South America Series, vol. 14, parts 1–3.

Payne, J.L. (1965) *Labor and Politics in Peru*. New Haven, CT: Yale University Press.

Peace, A. (1979) *Choice, Class and Conflict*. Brighton: Harvester Press.

Perlman, J. (1976) *The Myth of Marginality*. Berkeley, CA: University of California Press.

Pescatello, A. (ed) (1973) *Female and Male in Latin America*. Pittsburgh: University of Pittsburgh Press.

Pimentel, C. (1983) 'Problemas psicológicos de los niños y represión familiar y escolar en la barriada', in C. Pimentel, M. del Pilar Remy, L. Millones, C. Checa and C. Aramburú, *Peru: la población diversa*, Serie Investigación I. Peru: Ediciones Amidep.

Portes, A. (1985) 'Latin American class structures: their composition and change during the last decades', *Latin American Research Review* XX (3): 7–39.

Portes, A. and Walton, J. (1981) *Labor, Class and the International System*. New York: Academic Press.

Powell, S. (1970) 'Political participation in the barriadas: a case study', *Comparative Political Studies* 2 (2): 195–215.

PREALC (1978) *Sector informal: funcionamiento y políticas*. Santiago: Organización Internacional del Trabajo.

Prieto de Zegarra, J. (1980) *Mujer, poder y desarrollo en el Peru*, vol. I. Lima: Dorhca.

Quijano, A. (1974) 'The marginal pole of the economy and the marginalized labour force', *Economy and Society*, 3: 393–428.

Radcliffe, S.A. (1986a) 'Gender relations, peasant livelihood strategies and migration. A case study from Cuzco, Peru', *Bulletin of Latin American Research* 5 (2): 29–47.

Radcliffe, S.A. (1986b) *Female Migration and Peasant Livelihood Strategies in Highland Peru*, PhD dissertation, University of Liverpool.

Radcliffe, S.A. (1988) *'Así es una mujer del pueblo': low-income women's organizations under Apra, 1985–1987*. Working Paper no. 43, Centre of Latin American Studies, University of Cambridge.

Raffo, E. (1985) *Vivir en Huascar*. Lima: Fundación Friedrich Ebert.

Redclift, N. (1985) 'The contested domain: gender, accumulation and the labour process', in N. Redclift and E. Mingione (eds) *Beyond Employment*. Oxford: Basil Blackwell.

Reichmuth, M. (1978) *Dualism in Peru: an investigation into the interrelationships between Lima's informal clothing industry and the formal sector*, B.Litt. dissertation, University of Oxford.

Roberts, B. (1978) *Cities of Peasants*. London: Edward Arnold.

Roca, E. de Salonen, and Rodriguez, C. de Muñoz (1978) *Compilación y análisis de leyes sobre la condición jurídica y social de la mujer peruana*. Lima: Universidad Nacional Mayor de San Marcos.

Roldán, M. (1985) 'Industrial outworking, struggles for the reproduction of working-class families and gender subordination', in N. Redclift and E. Mingione (eds) *Beyond Employment*. Oxford: Basil Blackwell.

Roman de Silgado, M. (1981) *De campesino a obrero*. Lima: Universidad del Pacífico.

Roxborough, I. (1984) 'Unity and diversity in Latin American history', *Journal of Latin American Studies* 16 (1): 1–26.

Rubin, G. (1975) 'The traffic in women: notes on the "political economy" of sex' in R. R. Reiter (ed.) *Toward an Anthropology of Women*, NY: Monthly Review.

Rutté Garcia, A. (1973) *Simplemente explotados*. Lima: DESCO.

Sabot, R. and Berry, A. (1980) 'Unemployment and Economic Development', paper presented to the International Economic Association, Mexico City, August.

Safa, H.I. (1974) *The Urban Poor of Puerto Rico*. New York: Holt, Rinehart and Winston.

Sánchez, R. (1982) 'The Andean economic system and capitalism' in D. Lehmann (ed.) *Ecology and Economy in the Andes*. Cambridge: Cambridge University Press.

Sara-Lafosse, V. (1978) *La familia y la mujer en contextos sociales diferentes*. Mimeo. Lima: Pontíficia Universidad Católica del Peru, Departamento de Ciencias Sociales.

Sara-Lafosse, V. (1983) *La socialización de los hijos en contextos sociales diferentes*. Mimeo. Lima: Pontíficia Universidad Católica del Peru, Departamento de Ciencias Sociales.

Sarávia, P. (1982) *Las mujeres del campo y el trabajo de promoción social*. Paper presented to the Congreso de Investigación de la Mujer en la Region Andina, Lima, 7–10 June 1982.

Schminck, M. (1977) 'Dependent development and the division of labor by sex: Venezuela', *Latin American Perspectives* IV (12/13): 153–79.

Schminck, M. (1984) 'Household economic strategies: Review and Research Agenda', *Latin American Research Review* XIX(3): 87–101.

Schmitz, H. (1982) *Manufacturing in the Backyard*. London: Frances Pinter.

Schuurman, F.J. and Maerssen, A.L. (1988) *Urban Social Movements in the Third World*. London: Routledge.

Schurz, W.L. (1964) *This New World*. New York: Dutton.

Scott, A. MacEwen (1979) 'Who are the self-employed?', in R. Bromley and C. Gerry (eds) *Casual Work and Poverty in Third World Cities*. Chichester: John Wiley.

Scott, A. MacEwen (1986a) 'Economic development and urban women's work: the case of Lima, Peru', in R. Anker and C. Hein (eds) *Sex Inequalities in Urban Employment in the Third World*. Basingstoke and London: Macmillan for the ILO.

Scott, A. MacEwen (1986b) 'Industrialization, gender segregation and stratification theory', in R. Crompton and M. Mann (eds) *Gender and Stratification*. Cambridge: Polity Press.

Scott, A. MacEwen (1986c) 'Women and industrialisation: examining the "female marginalisation" thesis', *Journal of Development Studies* 22 (4): 649–80.

Scott, A. MacEwen (1986d) 'Introduction: why rethink petty commodity production?', in A.M. Scott (ed.) *Rethinking Petty Commodity Production*, special issue of *Social Analysis*, no. 20: 3–10. University of Adelaide.

Scott, A. MacEwen (1988) *Peruvian Employment Statistics since 1940: An Evaluation*, Working Paper no. 8. Institute of Latin American Studies, Liverpool University.

Scott, A. MacEwen (1991) 'Informal sector or female sector? Gender Bias in Labour Market Models', in D. Elson (ed.) *Male Bias in the Development Process*. Manchester: Manchester University Press.

Scott, C.D. (1979) *Machetes, Machines and Agrarian Reform: The Political Economy of Technical Choice in the Peruvian Sugar Industry, 1954–74*. Monographs in Development Studies no. 4, School of Development Studies, University of East Anglia.

Seminario, N. (1984) *La socialización de los hijos cuando la madre trabaja*. Mimeo. Department of Social Sciences, Pontíficia Universidad Católica del Peru.

SERH (1966) *Clasificación Nacional de Ocupaciones*. Lima: Servicio de Empleo y Recursos Humanos, Ministerio de Trabajo.

SERH (1970) *Empleo y Remuneraciones en la Industria Manufacturera*. Lima: Servicio de Empleo y Recursos Humanos, Ministerio de Trabajo.

SERH (1971a) *La pequeña industria y el empleo en el Peru*. Lima: Servicio de Empleo y Recursos Humanos, Ministerio de Trabajo.

SERH (1971b) 'Industria de la construcción, 1945–71', *Remuneraciones* no. 3, May.

Sethuraman, S.V. (1976) 'The urban informal sector: concept, measurement and policy', *International Labour Review* 114 (1): 69–81.

Sethuraman, S.V. (1981) *The Urban Informal Sector in Developing Countries*. Geneva: ILO.

Silverblatt, I. (1978) 'Andean women in the Inca Empire', *Feminist Studies* 4 (3): 37–61.

Silverblatt, I. (1980) 'Andean women under Spanish rule', in M. Etienne and E. Leacock (eds) *Women and Colonization*. New York: Praeger.

Sindicato de Trabajadores del Hogar (1982) *Basta: testimonios*. Cusco: Centro de Estudios Rurales Andinos.

Singer, H. (1970) 'Dualism revisited: a new approach to the problems of the dual society in developing countries', *Journal of Development Studies* 7 (1): 60–75.

Skar, S.L. (1979) 'The use of the public/private framework in the analysis of egalitarian societies: the case of a Quechua community in Highland Peru', *Women's Studies International Quarterly* 2 (4): 449–60.

Skar, S.L. (1981) 'Andean women and the concept of space/time', in S. Ardener (ed.) *Women and Space*. London: Croom Helm.

Skeldon, R. (1974) *Migration in a Peasant Society: The Example of Cuzco, Peru*. PhD dissertation, University of Toronto.

Skeldon, R. (1977a) 'The evolution of migration patterns during urbanization in Peru', *The Geographical Review* 67 (4): 394–411.

Skeldon, R. (1977b) 'Regional associations: a note on opposed interpretations', *Comparative Studies in Society and History* 19 (4): 506–10.

Skinner, R.J. (1981) *Community Organization, Collective Development and Politics in Self-Help Housing: Villa El Salvador, Lima (1971–76)*. PhD dissertation, University of Cambridge.

Slater, D. (1985) *New Social Movements and the State in Latin America*. Amsterdam: CEDLA.

Smith, C.A. (1986) 'Reconstructing the elements of petty commodity production', *Social Analysis* no. 20: 29–46.

Smith, G.A. (1975) *The Social Basis of Peasant Political Activity*. PhD dissertation, Sussex University.

Smith, G.A. (1979) 'Socio-economic differentiation and relations of production among rural-based petty producers in Central Peru, 1880 to 1970', *Journal of Peasant Studies* 6 (6): 286–310.

Smith, G.A. (1984) 'Confederations of households: extended domestic enterprises in city and country', in N. Long and B. Roberts (eds) *Miners, Peasants and Entrepreneurs*. Cambridge: Cambridge University Press.

Souza, P.R. and Tokman, K.E. (1976) 'The informal urban sector in Latin America', *International Labour Review*, 114 (3): 355–65.

Stanworth, M. (1984) 'Women and class analysis: a reply to Goldthorpe', *Sociology* 18 (2): 159–70.

Stein, S. (1980) *Populism in Peru*. Wisconsin: University of Wisconsin Press.

Stein, W.W. (1974) 'El peón que se negaba', *Allpanchis* vol. VI: 79–142.

Stepan, A. (1978) *The State and Society: Peru in Comparative Perspective*. Princeton, NJ: Princeton University Press.

Stevens, E.P. (1973) 'Marianismo: the other face of *Machismo* in Latin America', in

A. Pescatello (ed.) *Female and Male in Latin America*. Pittsburgh: University of Pittsburgh Press.

Stokes, S.C. (1991) 'Politics and Latin America's urban poor: reflections from a Lima shanty-town', *Latin American Research Report* 26 (2): 75–101.

Stycos, J. Mayone (1968) *Human Fertility in Latin America*. Ithaca, NY: Cornell University Press.

Suárez, F. (1975) *La movilidad ocupacional en Lima metropolitana*. Lima: Ministry of Labour.

Sulmont, D. (1974) *El desarrollo de la clase obrera en el Peru*. Lima: CISEPA.

Sulmont, D. (1977) *Historia del movimiento obrero peruano (1890–1977)*. Lima: Tarea.

Thorp, R. (1987) 'Trends and cycles in the Peruvian economy', *Journal of Development Economics* 27: 355–74.

Thorp, R. and Bertram, G. (1978) *Peru 1890–1977: Growth and Policy in an Open Economy*. London: Macmillan.

Touraine, A. (1981) *The Voice and the Eye: an Analysis of Social Movements*. Cambridge: Cambridge University Press.

Tueros, M. (1985) 'Barreras institucionales de entrada al sector informal en Lima Metropolitana' PREALC working paper no. 255, Santiago, Chile PREALC.

Turner, B.S. (1988) *Status*. Milton Keynes: Open University Press.

Turner, J. (1963) 'Lima barriadas today', *Architectural Design* 33 (8): 369–80, 389–93.

Turnham, D. (1971) *The Employment Problem in Less Developed Countries*. Paris: OECD.

US Department of Labor (1968) *Labor Law and Practice in Peru*. Report no. 338, Bureau of Labor Statistics.

Vega-Centeno, M. (1973) *El financiamiento de la pequeña industria*. Documento de Trabajo no. 9. Lima: CISEPA.

Villalobos, G. (1975) *Diagnóstico de la situación social y económica de la mujer peruana*. Lima: Centro de Estudios de Población y Desarrollo.

Villalobos, G. (1978) 'La mujer campesina: su aporte a la economia familiar y su participación social', *America Indígena* 38 (2): 405–46.

Warren, B. (1973) 'Imperialism and capitalist industrialization', *New Left Review* 81: 3–44.

Webb, R. (1976) *On the Statistical Mapping of Urban Poverty*. World Bank staff working paper no. 227. Washington, DC: World Bank.

Webb, R. (1977) *Government Policy and the Distribution of Income in Peru 1963–1973*. Cambridge, MA: Harvard University Press.

Weber, M. (1978) *Economy and Society*. Berkeley, CA: University of California Press.

Wilson, F. (1983) *The Representation of Gender in Current Indigenous Thought*. Mimeo. Project papers A.83.6. Copenhagen: Centre for Development Research.

Wilson, F. (1984) 'Marriage, property and the position of women in the Peruvian Central Andes', in R.T. Smith (ed.) *Kinship Ideology and Practice in Latin America*. Chapel Hill, NC: University of North Carolina Press.

Wilson, F. (1985) 'Women and agricultural change in Latin America: some concepts guiding research', *World Development* 13 (9): 1017–35.

Wilson, F. (1986) 'Urban craftsmen and their struggle against capitalism: a case study from Peru', *Social Analysis* no. 20: 69–78.

World Bank (1979a) *World Development Indicators*. Washington, DC: World Bank.

World Bank (1979b) *Peru: Long Term Development Issues*, Report no. 2204–PE, three vols. Washington, DC: The World Bank.

Young, K. and Moser, C.O.N. (eds) (1981) *Women and the Informal Sector*. Special Issue of *IDS Bulletin* 12 (3).

Youssef, N.H. (1974) *Women and Work in Developing Societies*. Westport: Greenwood Press.

PERUVIAN CENSUSES

Population Census 1940 Agricultural Census 1963
Population Census 1961 Economic Census 1963
Population Census 1972 Manufacturing Census 1974

Glossary of Spanish words

aprendiz	apprentice
ayuda	help, unpaid reciprocal labour
ayudante	assistant, mate, helper
barriada	shanty town
bazar	small shop selling variety goods
cachuelo	odd job, sideline
cholo	urbanized person of indian origin
clase alta	upper class
compadrazgo	godparenthood system
compadre	shared status of godparents and parents
colectivo	cars and small vehicles operating as buses
convivientes	cohabitees
decente	respectable (*decencia* = respectability)
diario	housekeeping money
dueños	owners
encomienda	royal grant of rights over Indian labour
encomendero	person holding such rights
enganche	debt bondage
guano	fertilizer made from pelican droppings
hacienda	large landed estate
humilde	meek, humble
latifundio/	landholding system of extremely large and
minifundio	small estates
machismo	gender ideology that stresses male virility (adj. *machista*)
maestro	master tradesman
mestizo	person of mixed race origin
mutual	savings fund
obrero	manual worker
oficio	trade
operario	journeyman
padres de familia	household heads
paisanos	persons having a common birthplace
palanca	substitute driver of a commercial vehicle
pantalonero	trouser-maker
patron	employer, boss
peon	unskilled labourer

propina	tip
provinciano	person from the provinces
prueba	trial, test
puesto	market or street stall
remodelación	street planning
saquero	jacket maker
sierra	mountainous area of the Andes
serrano	person from the *sierra*
tienda (-ita)	small retail store, often adjoining the home
trabajador	worker, labourer

Index